D0402618

URGE

WHY YOU REALLY WANT WHAT YOU WANT
(AND HOW TO MAKE EVERYONE WANT WHAT YOU'VE GOT)

JAMES A. MOUREY, Ph.D.

Copyright © 2014 James A. Mourey, Ph.D.

All rights reserved.

ISBN: 0615874622
ISBN-13: 978-0615874623

DEDICATION

To my amazing parents, James Mourey, Sr., and Sheryl Alvarez-Mourey.
I wouldn't have been able to do this without your love, sacrifices, and
support…also, I wouldn't even be alive if you guys didn't, you know, so…

CONTENTS

ACKNOWLEDGMENTS

Following the completion of my Ph.D. in early May of 2013, I had four months ahead of me in which very little (if anything) was expected of me for the first time since, well, ever. For whatever reason I thought this time would be a good opportunity to write a book because, you know, that sounds like more fun than backpacking through Europe or escaping to a beach in the South Pacific for a few months, right?

Now that the book is finished, however, I can imagine few things – actually nothing, really – that would have been more rewarding to do with my time except for maybe achieving world peace or fathering a child. Seeing as how I'm okay with not having done either of those two things, let it suffice to say that I am very proud of this accomplishment and, more important, the potential positive consequences this book will have for my students (and others who accidentally purchase it at the airport) as they embark on their careers and their futures.

This accomplishment is not my own, however. As such, there are several people I need to thank. First and foremost, I thank my parents for instilling in me at a young age this insane drive and passion for doing your very best, even if that means staying up all night or for days in a row to make sure something is done correctly. And thanks to my entire family – Chad, Heather, Kim, Declan, Kelly, Bill, my nephews, our dogs Mocha and Coco, and my extended family for keeping balance in my life – it is only because you keep me so entertained that I have the rich stories I have to tell. Also, thanks to my grandma, Shirley Alvarez, for being such a good sport and serving as an example throughout this book.

I also want to thank my colleagues at DePaul University for their guidance and support in this endeavor. Coming in as a new faculty member, my chair (Dr. Suzanne Fogel) certainly put a lot of faith in my ability to write this book. I thank her and the rest of the department for believing I could do it and that it would be an asset to our group, to our mission, and to our students. I thank Sue and Dr. Melissa Markley, specifically, for their role in recruiting me to the DePaul University team, a group of the kindest, brightest colleagues a guy could ever hope for. I also want to thank the broader Driehaus College of Business at DePaul for its commitment to pedagogy and service in a time when far too many business schools (and universities, in general) devalue teaching and service to the potential overemphasis of research. DePaul strikes a beautiful balance of world-class research, meaningful instruction, and service; our faculty and students are *very* lucky for this, as is the world these students go on to serve.

I want to thank Dr. Carolyn Yoon for being my amazing Ph.D. advisor, as well as her husband, Dr. Fred Feinberg, and Dr. Rick Bagozzi for teaching me so much about consumer behavior and marketing from an academic perspective. I also appreciate the many doctoral seminars with the faculty in the Marketing group at Michigan, as well as Dr. Amar Cheema for being such a great professor of Consumer Behavior when I was an eager undergraduate student at Washington University in St. Louis. And thanks to Dr. John Branch, whom I had the good fortune of studying under at WashU and then again at Michigan, for it his excellent teaching and life perspective that led me to this path in the first place. He also was the one who kept nudging me to write this book when academia sucked the life out of me, a time when I spent days, weeks, months, and years obsessing over research journal articles (that few people ever read anyway). Thanks to my WashU family – Residential Life, Student Involvement & Leadership, and the Olin Business School undergraduate advising team. Thanks to Bernie Milano and the Ph.D. Project community for unwavering support, as well as my cohort at the University of Michigan and my collaborators – Daphna, Andy, Lawrence, Jenny, Ryan, Ben. Thanks also to Kevin, Chris, Nathan, Veena, and Sam – my awesome Modern Marketing Lab students. Thanks to Kelsey for daily coffee and conversation and to Linda for our cruise conversations. And special thank you to Dr. Ryan Elder (BYU), Dr. Keisha Cutright (Wharton), Dr. Adriana Samper (ASU), Dr. Kelly Herd (Indiana), Dr. Stephen Spiller (UCLA), Dr. Eugenia Wu (University of Pittsburgh), and Dr. Lin Yang (UNC-Charlotte) for being my amazing academic family.

Thank you to my editors and fellow marketing gurus Jess Gilbertson, Jamee & Lynn Pearlstein, and Berenice Varela. Your comments and suggestions certainly improved the final product. Thanks to Jordan Roberts and Michael Frick for helping me improve the lives of others. And, finally, thank you, reader, for being curious to learn about the fascinating world of Consumer Behavior. I promise to make this experience as educational, entertaining, and fun as I can. After all, there may be a sequel someday.

Overview

I judge people.

I judge people a lot it turns out. Now, on one hand that's what I am paid to do: as a marketing guy it's essentially my job to get to the bottom of why people behave the way that they do, why they make the choices they make, why they buy what they buy. In fact, understanding why people are the way they are is so important to marketing that the majority of classes in a marketing Ph.D. program are in psychology. I guess you could say we marketers are *really* in your mind.

So it should come as no surprise, then, that when I see people reading SkyMall – that fascinating magazine featuring bizarre consumer products in the back seat pocket of just about every flight in the world (or really 88% of domestic American flights according to SkyMall itself) – I put on my social psychologist cap and ask the eloquent question, "Who buys this crap?" and, perhaps the more important question, "Why?" What sad thing happened in these people's childhoods that led them to this?

For example, did you know that you can buy fake clip-on hair bangs in SkyMall? You can. Looking for eyelashes for your car's headlights that are bedazzled with crystals? SkyMall has that, too. Need a portable hot tub for the many times you've been traveling and thought to yourself, "You know, I could really use a hot tub right now." Look no further.

Before studying marketing and, more specifically, consumer psychology, I used to just think that only ultra-wealthy morons (e.g., the Kardashians) or drunk people on planes (e.g., the Kardashians) actually purchased the stuff sold in SkyMall. One time, I saw an 80-something-year-old couple ordering Screwdrivers (the vodka and orange juice kind, not the tools) on a 7:00am flight. 7:00am! "Those people are going to buy a lot of junk for their grandchildren today," I thought as the wife pulled out the SkyMall magazine from the seat in front of her. Those poor grandchildren.

Now, I'm sure that a lot of well-meaning, educated, and sophisticated people purchase products from SkyMall. And, as it turns out, not *all* of the products are as ridiculous as the examples I mentioned. From Bluetooth speakers to pet gates, college memorabilia to espresso machines, hidden within SkyMall's pages are plenty of reasonable, useful consumer products that you or I would be likely to purchase. So why, then, has SkyMall become so associated with crazy, off-the-wall (or, in the case of the "World's Largest Write-On Map" – *on* the wall) products?

To answer that question, let's do a simple thought experiment. What sounds more enjoyable to peruse: a typical Sears catalog or a magazine featuring some really useful products and some zany, almost comical, conversation-worthy doodads? We hate being advertised to, in fact we actually automatically counterargue messages we hear in advertisements, so while a traditional catalog might have some appeal, a catalog that is an optimal blend of sales and sensationalism is probably a better sell for plane passengers. It certainly makes for good conversation or a useful introduction to a book about why consumers do weird things (...see how meta that was just then?).

Furthermore, from a company's point of view, there's a huge appeal to knowing you have a captive audience who, short of parachuting out of a plane, will be stuck in the same place for several hours eager for distractions. It's the same reason you find print ads above urinals and pre-movie advertisements on the screen at the theater. So if you're the producer of a crazy product that would have a difficult time gaining traction in a traditional retail setting – say a life-sized replica of Gandalf's staff from *The Lord of the Rings* (which, yes, SkyMall sells) – it makes sense to pay to have your product featured in SkyMall.

So SkyMall has successfully created a brand for itself that makes it both benignly silly and strangely useful while also solidifying its exclusive position as *the* magazine for the skies, the single publication to which nearly *every* airline passenger has access when flying in the United States. Thus, when it comes to the original question of *who* buys the products featured in SkyMall, we can imagine business travelers who love to golf, people who appreciate jokes and gag gifts, pet lovers (but the kind who treat their pets as children), hobbyists and die-hard collectors, kitchenistas looking for that perfect niche cooking accessory, and people who have really, really strange needs. Although you may not have the gall to be seen taking the magazine off the plane, there's no need to worry: SkyMall now has its own website.

The SkyMall example highlights an important point: it turns out that knowing who buys what or why people buy isn't nearly as straightforward as you would like to think. Some people buy products because they like them. Others buy products because *other people* like them. People often buy products they don't need (we're all guilty of that), and some even buy products they may not even want. On the surface, it's actually fairly difficult to know the motivation behind *why* consumers behave as they do, but if we dig a bit deeper we can start to uncover some systematic consistencies that help us make better predictions about why consumers do the weird things they do.

* * *

The purpose of this book is to provide you, the reader, with an introduction to Consumer Behavior – a collection of insights about how the thoughts and feelings of people, the features and characteristics of context, and various decision-making strategies influence purchasing, consumption, and markets. The book is divided into three sections: the Self (internal factors), the Situation (external factors), and the Solution (decision-making and outcome). And throughout the book I include as many real-world examples and application questions as I can to help you, my kind reader, make connections between concepts presented in the book and marketing in your day-to-day life both as a consumer and as a marketer.

I intend for this book to be a suitable (read: better) replacement for a typical course textbook for several reasons. First, college textbooks are ridiculously expensive; like "I may have to sell one of my kidneys on the black market" expensive. The reason for this, friends, is that the textbook market is a sort of monopoly: your professor requires you buy book X, only one publishing company sells book X, therefore said publishing company can charge whatever outrageous price they want. As such, this book is *much* cheaper than the books I could have made you read (…now you have money to take me out to dinner – hooray!). Second, college textbooks are *boring*, as in "punch me in the face to keep me awake" boring. My hope is that this first-person narrative, a wee bit o' humor, and a casual approach to discussing otherwise unnecessarily lofty topics will make learning about Consumer Behavior an enjoyable and, dare I say it, *fun* experience. If not, I'll do a magic trick for you…or something. Finally, one thing that always bothers me is that traditional textbooks always present definitions or concepts in a way that seems very far removed from the real world. So, in this book, I will do my very best to integrate key concepts in the context of real products, real companies, and real situations so that you live, eat, and breathe the concepts from this day forward. It is my hope that you'll never be able to go shopping in the same way ever again.

The breakdown of the book – into the Self, the Situation, and the Solution – is a handy way to keep the main concepts of the book organized and to help you have a structure when considering the various aspects of real-world marketing problems. That is, by the end of this book, you will be able to robustly analyze a marketing issue by thinking through these three broader areas and the more specific concepts that will be introduced under each. The Self and the Situation are pretty self-explanatory, but, to clarify, the Self concerns those biases that we, as human beings, bring to the table, as everything we experience is ultimately filtered through our brains (whether consciously or unconsciously). The Situation is everything *external* to us, the stimuli in our surroundings, our context, the situations in which we find ourselves (e.g., pressed for time, in freezing cold weather shopping at Christmas) that influence our thoughts and behaviors. Finally, the Solution is the culmination of all these influences into the valuation and decision-making process. The Solution section is named as such because much of consumer behavior involves addressing a problem or resolving an unmet need, scratching a proverbial itch so to speak. Sometimes the solution is to do absolutely nothing. Sometimes the solution is to purchase a product or service. Sometimes the solution is to save money until a product or service *can* be purchased. In any event, internal factors and external factors interact to produce some urge, an urge that then must be resolved via some solution.

I use the word "urge" for the title deliberately. I could have called it "need," "want," or the ever-so-sexy sounding, "desire." But wants, needs, and desires all imply emptiness, a void, or an unsatisfied longing for something. They represent states or static points in time whereas urge is dynamic and implies action. My goal here is not to leave you empty or focused on what is missing but, instead, to fill you with action.

As the subtitle of the book suggests, by the time you finish this book you will have a better understanding of why you want the things you want and how to use the ideas herein to make others want what you've got to sell, whether that be a consumer product or yourself (…not like that – I mean in the context of personal selling for a job position). Consumers can be tricky to understand because consumers do a *lot* of weird things. For example, shoppers may think a $30.00 t-shirt is too expensive but don't seem to mind when the same t-shirt is $29.99. Despite economics telling us that finding $20 or losing $20 should feel the same amount of good or bad, respectively, losing $20 feels like someone punched you in the gut, while finding $20 is nice but doesn't have the same visceral reaction in a positive direction that losing money has in the negative direction.

But consumption extends beyond shopping and so, too, do the weird behaviors of consumers. For example, some voters vehemently oppose abortion because they "value all life" but turn a blind eye to capital punishment and casualties stemming from lax gun control. Some people are okay consistently splurging on cigarettes and alcohol but try to spend as little money as possible on food and clothing for their children. Although some mindless consumption is benign, like impulsively buying a pack of gum at the checkout counter you didn't intend to purchase, other consumption isn't as safe: drug addiction, gambling problems, unsafe sex practices, gun ownership. We may not often think of these latter examples as "consumer behavior," but if you're *consuming* something – drugs, slots, sex, guns – it falls in the domain of consumer behavior, and the importance of understanding *why* people engage in such consumption becomes crystal clear.

The way you'll get the most out of this book is to engage <u>as much as possible</u>. This means not only reading the words but also thinking through the end-of-chapter application questions that highlight key concepts and facilitate real-world connections of the concepts. If you are reading the book as part of my class, a great way to earn participation points is to come prepared to class with other examples of a chapter's concepts playing out in the real world or examples where companies have defied the concepts (this happens all the time) and whether or not that strategy has helped or hurt the companies. Whenever possible, I want this book to be more of a conversation than a lecture. That's why I'm including an email address for you should you have any questions, thoughts, comments, good gossip, jokes, insider trading info, riddles, etc. – <u>Urge@JimMourey.com</u>. Other professors call me crazy for the amount of effort I put into my students, but this is what I was born to do – to teach – and specifically, to teach you. My goal is to change the way you see the world, to change the way you live, which is no small task. This will be quite the journey, I assure you, and I hope by the end of it you'll be forever changed for the better. So if you're ready, pack your bags, find your seat, put away your SkyMall, and let's get ready for takeoff.

A dog trampoline?! Genius! But sorry, Señor Chihuahua, this is actually just a raised bed because, you know, every dog needs a levitated bed. I liked it better when I thought it was a trampoline.

Apparently the lasers in this headset help rejuvenate hair growth; it also makes this guy look super cool.

*   *   *

Those aren't her real bangs.

*   *   *

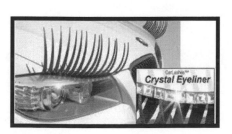

Why would you put eyelashes on your car? Worse, why would you put eyelashes on your BMW? Note how the light shines off the crystal. Classy.

This is simply not okay for anyone other than someone with the name Olivia Marie Griffin.

*   *   *

The Spa-N-A-Box. I wonder how many people order this product in haste, maybe even opting for "rush delivery," only to get it and realize it's kinda tough to find a water source in the middle of nowhere capable of filling the hot tub. Wah wahhh.

*   *   *

"Susie, now's the time to tell you that you're adopted, and this is where you came from." And why are her overalls enormous?! Seriously, look how long her pants are. Maybe it's all relative: the World's Largest Write-On Map requires one to wear the World's Largest Children's Overalls.

PREFACE:

THE FOUNDATION

Prior to diving into the intricacies and details of consumer behavior, it is first worthwhile to give an overview of Marketing more generally. In doing so it will be easier to understand why learning about consumer psychology matters and will give you, the eager pupil, a context in which to place the new information that is being presented throughout the rest of the book. As an example, in a few chapters I will discuss the human senses, including the sense of touch, which would seem like a totally random topic for a marketer to discuss if you didn't know that "packaging" is one of the fundamental Ps of Marketing, and that how a package "feels" can actually influence whether or not someone purchases your product. So, with that understanding, the following chapters provide a foundation of marketing principles: marketing as a science and art, components of marketing, segmenting, targeting, and positioning (STP), the 4Ps of Marketing, the 5Cs of Marketing, and more.

PREFACE I: What is Marketing?

Before we jump into the heart of consumer behavior, it is first important to place consumer behavior in the broader context of Marketing, and to do this it is worthwhile to get everyone up to speed on what exactly marketing is and what it is not. If you're a seasoned marketing practitioner or a recent student of an introductory marketing course, this should be a fun review. If you're new to Marketing as a discipline, welcome to the party – this introduction will provide you with so strong of a foundation in marketing that you'll be joining conversations at cocktail parties and selling popsicles to penguins in no time.

So, returning to the question at hand, if you had to answer the question, "What is Marketing?," what would you say? Go ahead. Think about it. Now answer the question in your head (or out loud if you're not in a public place sitting by yourself).

Every time I teach an introductory marketing course or consult for companies, I often begin by asking that simple question, "What is Marketing?" And almost *always* I get the exact same wrong answer...wait for it...wait for it...*advertising*. On occasion someone will shout out "sales" and/or "selling stuff," but more often than not, advertising and marketing are thought of as being synonyms. This, however, is incorrect.

Now, if you answered "advertising" a minute ago, please don't be sad. Just last year, a dear friend who graduated with his MBA from a top business school and now works as a consultant at one of the Big Three consulting firms (McKinsey, BCG, and Bain) asked if I would join him and his work team on a call. The team, which consisted of graduates from other top schools (HBS, Kellogg, Michigan, Chicago), was recently tapped to help with a marketing problem facing a client whose primary business involved inventory, storage, and shipping management. The team had prepared a few questions for yours truly pertaining to marketing, the first of which was, and I quote, "So...marketing and advertising are like...the same thing, right?" If MBAs from the nation's top business schools can get this wrong, then so can you.

To be clear, it's not that these answers–advertising, sales, selling stuff– are totally wrong; they are each *a part* of marketing, but marketing encompasses *so much more* than just advertising and sales. To think about it visually, picture marketing as an umbrella with advertising, sales, and many other components underneath.

Every now and then when the, "What is Marketing?" question is posed, some funny guy in the audience (usually a finance guy; I don't know why, but it's almost always a finance guy) will answer, "Uh, common sense," and then laugh at his own joke (because finance guys *always* laugh at their own jokes, you know, to fill the silent and lonely void of no one else finding them amusing). I then punch that guy in the face. Ok. I don't really punch him, but it is rather insulting when someone *assumes* your job essentially amounts to common sense. To illustrate with an example, here's a recent conversation that took place on a flight I took from Chicago to Ann Arbor when an older gentleman sitting in the seat next to me thought it would be a great idea to make small talk:

"I'm heading to Ann Arbor for my son's graduation from medical school," the man said.

"Ah, that's great!" I replied, "Congratulations to your son! I just graduated from Michigan in May myself."

"Oh, really? What did you study?" asked the man.

"I completed my doctorate in Marketing," I answered.

Awkward silence. Blank stare.

"...Yes, they have those," I tossed out into the silence, "And at great universities no less," I added, apparently in an attempt to compensate for some deeply-rooted insecurity stemming from when people assume I'm a medical doctor when they hear I did my "doctorate."

"Oh, well, congratulations!" said the man. After a brief pause he continued, "Marketing. Hmm. *Marketing...*" sounding skeptical.

"Yes, Marketing," I said. I wondered where he was going with this.

"Well, marketing has been around for, I don't know, over a hundred years," he said. I nodded, secretly thinking to myself that it has technically been around since, you know, forever – a peacock spreading his feathers certainly isn't doing it for *his* health. "Well, I mean, it's just selling things, which we all do, *so it's really just common sense then, isn't it?*"

There it was.

"Totally," I told the man, "Totally common sense."

I paused.

"Hey, what field is your son in again? Medicine, right?" I asked.

"That's right," he said.

"So he's in the business of keeping people alive, right?"

"Yes, that's right," he answered.

"And human beings have been trying to stay alive for, well, at least since the existence of homo sapiens, and certainly long before that if we accept the theory of evolution, so wouldn't you say that what he's doing is just, well, I don't know...common sense?"

At that very moment everyone on the plane around me started a slow clap, which turned into a standing ovation, and the man burst into tears before running off to hide in the bathroom for the remainder of the flight…

…okay, I'm totally joking. That conversation *did* actually happen, but instead of me saying, "Totally," and then going on my rant, I politely responded, "Well, you'd *think* it's common sense, but it turns out there are many components of marketing that most people don't think about, and we're always learning new things to make marketing more efficient." I then spent the next hour schooling him on the various components of marketing and what we, as marketing academics, do to expand the horizons of marketing knowledge in the world. My mom would be so proud.

Now, there are reasons why people equate marketing with advertising or think that marketing is just common sense. We're inundated with television commercials, print advertisements, and billboards (some estimate over 5,000 exposures *per day*), which explains the advertising connection. As the Real Daughters of Long Island who took marketing with me in undergrad liked to say, "I, like, really understand marketing because, like, I shop, like, all the time." I buy coffee every day, but I have no plans to run Starbucks anytime soon. Marketing is so much more than "We Buy Your Gold" commercials, smelly cologne insert advertisements in magazines, shopping a lot, and plain old common sense. In fact, when we get to later sections on decision-making heuristics and biases, you'll see that we often *defy* common sense when making consumer decisions.

So what is marketing then? When I teach my introductory marketing course, I tell my students to consider two groups: producers (people and companies who produce goods and/or services) and consumers (people who consume those goods and services). I draw circles on the left and right of the whiteboard representing these two groups. Then I tell them to think back to the old days of yore back to the great civilizations in which the "market" was *the* physical location where these producers and consumers came together. To help you imagine, think of the opening scene of the Disney movie *Aladdin* – THAT kind of market. It was there, at the market, that prices were negotiated, the benefits of products/services were communicated, deals were made, producers learned of consumer needs that existing products were unable to satisfy, and much, much more. I draw a circle in the center of the whiteboard and label that "The Market," and then proceed to draw a million arrows from the other two circles to the one in the middle. "This," I tell them, "is marketing." Quite literally, every single component necessary to bring producers and consumers together: pricing, promotions, advertising, competitive strategy, research, logistics, sourcing, production, supply chain/distribution management–any piece connecting "those who produce" with "those who need" is covered under the term "marketing." In short, marketing is a *lot* more than just advertising or common sense, and the rest of this chapter demonstrates this by presenting just a handful of the many *other* things marketing entails.

Marketing Research

To a marketing professor and a marketing practitioner, little else is more important than marketing research or, in other words, the data and statistics about potential consumers, suppliers, raw materials, and production. Marketing research, quite simply, refers to information about the various components within a market.

Say, for example, you own a high-end grocery that is considering opening a store in a new market. You'd probably be interested in knowing the population of the area, the number of potential consumers willing to pay a premium for their groceries, the average income of the neighborhood in which you are considering placing the story, the average rent cost of space in that neighborhood, the cost of shipping your products from your farm and factory sources to the prospective location, the performance of competing grocery stores in the area, among several other pieces of information. Sure, it's certainly possible to launch the new store without knowing any of this information, but chances are you won't stay in your position very long after the store fails miserably.

Collecting marketing research can be done in a variety of ways, whether from primary sources like surveys and interviews to secondary sources like financial reports and analyst predictions. The point of marketing research, in general, is that one goes from making uneducated guesses in the dark to making educated estimates based on real information. These estimates are rarely perfect but, more often than not, lead to better results than simply stabbing in the dark.

One fatal flaw in the real world is that practitioners don't always have a solid understanding of statistics, so when they see that consumers rated their product as a 9 on a scale while their competitor's product was rated a 7, on average, with no regard for sample sizes or standard deviations, this can be a problem. If that last sentence sounded like gibberish to you then I apologize on behalf of the paltry mathematics standards of the American education system and promise to do my best to make you a statistics wizard. Indeed, half the battle is collecting marketing research; the other half is analyzing and interpreting it correctly.

New Product Development

Consumer products and services are successful because consumers have a need for them (or *think* they have a need for them) and, as such, purchase products to fulfill those needs. If I tried to sell you a device you could hold in one hand to scratch an itch on your opposite arm, chances are you 1) wouldn't purchase it or, 2) if you purchased it, wouldn't pay very much money for the device. Why not? Well, because you already have a product that can scratch your other arm for you: the fingernails on your opposite hand. Now let's say that I tried to sell you a back scratching device that you could hold in your hand to scratch that hard-to-reach area of your back that always itches like crazy. Chances are that, in this case, you'd at least *consider* purchasing this device and might even be willing to pay a reasonable amount for a device that could satisfy your need to scratch your back. By purchasing this device you provide me with a few dollars for the product, I provide you with amazing relief…you scratch my back, I scratch yours…sorry, I couldn't resist.

The point is this: it is more difficult to sell consumers products for which they have no need than it is to sell them products that fulfill needs they have. But we are not psychics – we don't always know what consumers' needs are, and unlike the markets of hundreds of years ago, we live in a time when producers and consumers are not always interacting face-to-face in real time, so spontaneously conversing about a consumer's needs in real time doesn't happen the way it used to (the exception being real-time help service providers available on some websites).

Thus, one important part of marketing is developing products that will address the new and ever-changing needs of consumers. It is in this way that marketing and entrepreneurship are so finely intertwined – entire companies have sprung up based on the evolving needs identified via marketing. When this little thing known as the "Internet" started evolving to an enormous virtual world saturated with information that was difficult to find and to navigate, search engines like Google and Yahoo! were born. When the Earth's temperatures started rising consistently and glaciers started melting at a more rapid pace, consumers suddenly became more interested in purchasing cars that were more environmentally friendly. When consumers expressed an interest in traveling around the world but didn't want to have to do all the planning, Disney developed an entire business (Adventures by Disney) dedicated to planning global excursions by tapping into its expertise in high-quality travel planning and selling great trips to consumers who were all too eager to buy. A critical element of marketing is identifying and capitalizing upon new markets and opportunities within existing markets.

Advertising

This is the one most people know well, but advertising deserves its own discussion. Advertising can serve many purposes—to introduce a new product, to communicate the benefits of a product, to remind people that a product exists, to keep a product at the forefront of consumers' minds—but the gist of any advertisement is that it is a communication between the producer and the consumer.

For example, Coca-Cola is known for having some of the best advertisements; even our modern version of the red-robed, white-bearded Santa Claus is often attributed to a Christmas advertising campaign Coca-Cola ran in the 1930s (which, it turns out, was actually based on other representations of Santa Claus). Yet many people often wonder why Coca-Cola needs to advertise in the first place. The product is not new. Most people are already familiar with the soda. It has the most market share of its category. So why waste so much money to advertise a product with which people are already familiar? Well, the short story is that Coca-Cola wants to keep its product "top of mind" in the brains of consumers so that when a random person on the street is asked to name a kind of soda his/her first response will be "Coke" and not "Pepsi." Indeed, Coke is interested in maintaining its position as *the* prototype for soda in the U.S. and elsewhere.

Contrast this with advertisements serving a different purpose. In the 2000s, high-fructose corn syrup came under scrutiny as America's children (and population, in general) got fatter and fatter. Corn syrup, critics contended, was responsible for the surge in obesity, as corn syrup was often used as an artificial sweetener in beverages and food products in lieu of sugar, which some of these same critics argued was actually healthier than the manufactured corn syrup (or was, at least, not as *misleading* – consumers reading "corn syrup" instead of "sugar" might have erroneously thought the former was healthier than the latter). To combat this criticism, the proponents of corn syrup (the Corn Refiners Association) launched a series of advertisements discussing the merits of "corn sugar," as supported by "doctors, dieticians, and nutritionists," to communicate that "sugar is sugar," that the human body cannot tell the difference between corn sugar or cane sugar (you can see the commercial here: http://youtu.be/QWVFVNpEJFw). So, unlike Coca-Cola in the previous example, the purpose of this advertisement is not to maintain top-of-mind awareness in the minds of consumers but, instead, to communicate information in support of a food ingredient that received quite a bit of scrutiny in the media. Whether or not it was effective is anyone's guess, but people certainly still do eat food and drink beverages containing high-fructose corn syrup.

Yet another purpose of advertising is to create the image of what a brand represents. To see an example of this, one needs to look no further than Abercrombie & Fitch and/or Hollister (which are both owned by the same company). We can all agree that clothing is clothing: material made out of some fabric, natural or manufactured, for the purpose of covering up our nether regions and keeping us warm. Sure, different styles of clothing exist based on whatever trend happens to be in style at the moment, trends that disappear and return from time to time, but the purpose of clothing has not really changed since Adam and Eve were using conveniently-placed fig leaves oh so long ago. However, using advertising, clothing companies are able to communicate for whom, exactly, their clothes are intended and for whom they are not. Abercrombie's advertisements and packaging are known for featuring young, extremely attractive, and fit white models, suggesting that their "classic American clothing" is to be worn by young, extremely attractive, and fit white people. Unfortunately, this approach in its advertising carried over to the company's hiring practices, as well, and Abercrombie was sued in 2004 (González v. Abercrombie & Fitch) for discriminating in its hiring: young, attractive white people were hired to work in the front of the store while non-white individuals were relegated to support staff roles working behind the scenes (e.g., stocking inventory in the store room unseen). While the debate for whether or not Abercrombie should be allowed the artistic and creative freedom to communicate in its advertising what it means by "classic American clothing" is beyond the scope of this book, the example demonstrates how a company's advertising can shape its entire identity in the marketplace well beyond simply advertising something as simple as the products being sold (in this case clothing). If I say to "picture the typical person who wears Abercrombie or Hollister," we both know *exactly* the kind of person you'll think of.

Pricing

Economists like to pretend that they are the experts when it comes to pricing, but truth be told, we do not live in the perfectly rational world that economists pretend we do. Case in point, the famous researchers Danny Kahneman and Amos Tversky developed their famous "Prospect Theory" to explain why the pain of losing $20 is not equal and opposite to the joy of finding $20. Indeed, in an economist's perfectly-rational world, losing and finding $20 should feel equally painful and pleasurable, respectively, but one only needs to do a thought experiment to realize that losing $20 feels much worse than finding $20 feels great. Ever heard the phrase, "Losses loom larger than gains?" That's exactly the idea here.

Similarly, the concept of "sunk costs" in the economist's world suggests that once something is paid for and there's no way to recover your money, then you shouldn't let the expense from purchasing the item factor into your decision making. For example, say you purchased $150 non-refundable tickets to a concert taking place at a venue an hour from where you live. Now let's say that the weather the day of the concert has taken a turn for the worse; it's raining cats and dogs, and you're thinking about not going to the concert. Economists would tell you that the $150 has already been spent and, as such, should not factor into your decision to go or not to go. However, what we all would actually think is, "I am *not* going to throw away $150 for a few rain drops! I am going to that concert even if I have to build an ark or ride a tornado, Dorothy style."

Welcome to the world of pricing within marketing. As marketers, we can appreciate the brilliant insights from our economist friends, but we concern ourselves more with what people *actually* do in this very *real* world, not the fictitious, perfectly rational world of economists. Consider one of the most *irrational* behaviors of most consumers: assuming a high price signals high quality. Indeed, whether or not we like to admit it, we tend to treat higher-priced items as being of a higher quality without realizing that these higher-priced items are often made using the same production means and raw materials as their lower-priced counterparts, sometimes even at the same production facilities. Some of the clothing being sold at Saks and Neiman Marcus truly does not differ fundamentally from clothing sold at Target or Wal-Mart, but we fool ourselves into letting the higher prices of the apparel found at these former retailers signal something about the products' superior quality even though that may not be true at all.

We also let prices play games with our mind. For whatever reason, a price of $19.99 seems *so* much cheaper than $20.00, just as getting three $10 t-shirts in a "Buy two get a third for half off!" seems like the deal of the decade compared to a sign suggesting you could "Spend $25 instead of $30" or "Get $5 off your retail purchase" (which are the same as the original deal for those of you who may be math-challenged). Retailers realize this, of course, and use pricing tricks and promotions to increase foot traffic in stores and to move merchandise off shelves at record-setting speeds. Thus, a large part of marketing involves determining the value of products and services – both for the purpose of understanding what people are willing to pay and to make use of these heuristics and mind tricks we all fall for. Now is a good time to remind you about those folks who claim marketing is just common sense. I bet they fall for these tricks *all the time* and don't even realize it.

Logistics

One of the most overlooked components of marketing is logistics, which can cover everything from sourcing (i.e., obtaining the raw materials for production) to retail distribution (i.e., getting the products in stores), production processes to inventory management. Some universities have separate departments within their business schools dedicated to operations and logistics whereas others lump the operations and logistics professors in with the marketing department given the tight relationship between the two fields. The simple way of thinking about logistics is that it involves getting a product or raw materials from Point A to Point B, whether these points pertain to physical locations (e.g., from South Africa to the United States) or to the physical condition of the materials (e.g., from a raw diamond in a diamond mine to a polished ring in a jewelry store). An introductory course in operations and logistics typically teaches a new way of thinking about *efficiency*, how to do a job effectively and accurately for the lowest possible cost, both financially and with respect to time.

An example of how logistics relates to marketing comes in the form of Amazon.com. Amazon is known for being an online retailer whose products range from books and movies to household appliances and electronics. Perhaps even more impressive than Amazon's wide array of goods, however, is its ability to deliver many of its popular products within 24 hours. To do this, Amazon relies on a carefully constructed logistics network that is able to retrieve products from its many warehouses scattered throughout the U.S. and to ship those products right to the doorstep of its consumers, no matter how urban or rural. As you can imagine, this system also involves a very careful understanding of inventory—storing too much of the wrong product in all its warehouses is expensive, while storing too little of the popular products would prove equally catastrophic. Indeed, much of the success of Amazon as a company rests not within its product and service offering but, instead, within its carefully crafted logistics scheme that competitors simply cannot match.

Another company often noted for its superior logistics is probably one you would never guess: Southwest Airlines. Since its inception, Southwest Airlines is the *only* airline that has consistently turned a profit in a rather unprofitable industry. Why? Well, the folks at Southwest realized early on that the only way an airline can make more money without raising fares astronomically is by having more flights (from the company's website: "Planes make money in the air, not on the ground."). Thus, in the early days of Southwest it was decided that turning planes around at the gate should be a top priority, so high a priority that even the pilots of the plane should leave the cockpit to help the cabin crew clean the plane so that the plane could take off again more quickly than its competitors' planes. Even the open seating plan of Southwest is designed to simply get more people on the plane as quickly as possible. While Southwest now flies to most major airports, part of its strategy is to fly to lesser-traffic (a.k.a. cheaper) gates and to focus its planes on smaller or separate terminals at major airports so it can manage itself more efficiently and/or pay cheaper gate fares. It is believed that Southwest offers its employees bonuses for turning planes around on-time (and early), an approach United Airlines used to reward its employees with an "on-time" bonus in late 2012, as well. By providing its employees with stock options, Southwest ensures that every employee shares the same incentive as the company does to keep its logistical plans as efficient and running as smoothly as possible, as each on-time flight is more money in the company's (and the employees') coffers.

*   *   *

The list above is not meant to be exhaustive as there are other marketing components not captured above–identity and branding, market and growth strategies, promotions, customer relationship management, and more. But the point should be very clear: marketing is *much, much* more than just advertising.

The concepts you will learn in this book about consumer psychology should be considered not only in the domain of advertising but also in the other marketing domains like pricing, logistics and operations, promotions, and new product development. Developing this robust understanding of marketing and being able to apply ideas from consumer psychology across these many components is *critical* to mastering marketing; the most brilliant, valuable minds in marketing do precisely that.

But marketing isn't *all* science. That is, unlike the comparably "less exciting" fields of finance and accounting whose equations are exact, unchanging, and programmable (unless you, dear reader, happen to work in finance and/or accounting, in which case I assure you that you are irreplaceable and that your work is action-movie-level exciting – picture it: *The Fast and the Furious 17: CPAs in Tax Season*, coming soon to a theatre near you!), marketing rarely follows an exact formula. Although some strategies may be widely applicable, it is sometimes the case that what works in one industry, for one product or service, or at a particular point in time may not work in other instances. This, friends, is where the artistic, creative side of marketing comes into play. Often using what logic, research, and the more formulaic approach would suggest as a starting point, the savvy marketer knows how to tweak a marketing execution in *just* the right way to give it that little something extra. For some people, this is the most frustrating part of marketing, particularly people with a no-nonsense rule-based training in mathematics or engineering (a.k.a. Germans). For others, myself included, this is the *best part of marketing*. Why? Well, we can all learn the fundamental principles of marketing and then, when faced with the same marketing challenge, generate dozens to hundreds to thousands of different solutions to the same problem. That is art. It's also the same reason marketing, unlike finance and accounting, is difficult to outsource–there's a certain *je ne sais quoi* about marketing–something you can't quite put your finger on that is specific to the culture, the context, to the specific point in time. Why is this the case? Well, at its heart marketing is about people, and if there's one thing consistent about people it's that they're always changing. The more tapped into this human heartbeat a marketer is, the better. Consider this book your stethoscope.

APPLICATION QUESTIONS

1) If someone told you marketing and advertising were synonymous, what would you say?

2) What are some of the components of marketing? Why is it important for a business to consider these components in order to be successful?

3) It is often said that Marketing is both a science and an art. Give a specific example of how marketing could be thought of as a *science*. Give a different specific example of how marketing could be thought of as an *art*.

4) To the people who claim that marketing is just common sense, give an example of a pricing-related issue that would suggest otherwise? What about in the context of advertising – can you think of an advertisement that *seems* to be communicating one message (common sense) but is actually communicating something else?

5) Why does it make sense that logistics and operations are included under the "marketing umbrella?"

6) Coca-Cola, a well-established brand, uses advertising as a means to keep the product and brand "top of mind" for consumers. Can you think of a specific example of a *new* company/brand and how it used various components of marketing – e.g., advertising, promotions, logistics, pricing, etc. – to "make a noticeable splash" in the market?

7) Given marketing's broad reach, how would you delineate marketing from other typical business divisions like finance, management/human resources, accounting, etc.? Does "marketing" take place within these divisions? If yes, how?

8) New products can be risky, as many startups fail shortly after launch. Think of a recent company or product that failed after launch and has since been discontinued. Knowing what you know about marketing up to this point, why do you think the product/service failed? What do you think could have been done differently that may have improved the product/service's likelihood for success?

9) I'm sure you've heard the phrase, "The customer is always right." In marketing, we tend to obsess about the consumer, particularly with respect to marketing research. Why might this obsession be warranted? On the other hand, why might focusing only on the consumer be unwise?

10) Marketing research is not without its limitations. Indeed, many companies have done their due diligence with respect to capturing data regarding consumers and their respective preferences yet ultimately failed to survive in the market. What are some mistakes companies might make when collecting and analyzing/interpreting marketing research that could lead to failure?

PREFACE II: STP, 4Ps, 5Cs

When I was studying French in college, one of my professors, a lovely, blonde-pigtailed, smokes-like-a-chimney lass whom we shall call "Anne" always wore all-black outfits and, no joke, little black berets.   Her appearance was so stereotypically French and her personality so cynical that sometimes it felt like you were watching this amazing "film noir" movie, but no, it was just "Anne."   One day Anne decided to open up to all of us and to reveal why it was she *always* wore black (despite no one asking). "Maybe she's in mourning?" I thought, "Maybe she's color blind and has trouble matching colors?" ..."Zie reason I only wear zie black clothes is because it is, how do you say, cheaper and easier to do zie laundry when you have only one color," Anne said, completely debunking my well thought out theories. Oh, and she also said it in French, but I like to think she would have said it like how I wrote it if she had said it in English.

Imagine it: a world where *every* article of clothing is black.   Every hat. Every shoe.   Every shirt.   Well, hold on to your little black beret: this seemingly post-apocalyptic, *Hunger Games*-esque world once existed.   In the early days of the auto industry, when the Model T was all the rage, Henry Ford famously quipped that, "*Any* customer can have a car painted *any* color that he wants...so long as it is black."   The reasoning for this limitation, much like my French professor's logic, came down to two things: simplicity and cost savings.   It was simply cheaper for Ford to buy only one color of paint in bulk, to have the same color always available for touchups, and to paint cars more efficiently compared to switching colors. Coincidentally, the Model T's nickname, the Tin Lizzy, is also my grandma's rapper nickname.

This era of marketing is referred to as **mass marketing**, a.k.a. **undifferentiated marketing** in which just about every part of the marketing process (from production to promotion) is identical for every product and every consumer.   Mass production refers to producing the same product, with little to no variation, in large quantities to capitalize on economies of scale (i.e., the savings and efficiencies that come with producing a lot of the same thing in the same way).   Ford is often credited with the ushering in of the mass production era thanks to his assembly line and the machinery that made quick production of identical products very easy, but this approach was quickly copied in a variety of industries by entrepreneurs who saw the benefits this undifferentiated approach brought. Mass production certainly had its perks: cheaper costs, lower prices (more sales), higher profit margins. Along with mass production comes mass distribution (distributing to everyone in the same way), mass promotion (promoting to everyone in the same way), etc. Even today some companies (usually utility monopolies like electric companies) are able to get away with offering *one* product to *everyone* in the *exact same way*. But with these advantages come great disadvantages: differences in personal preferences went unaccounted for. That is, if I wanted a red Model T and you wanted a blue one, we would be out of luck. Similarly, if I want the majority of my electricity to come from renewable resources and you prefer coal-generated energy, we both have to accept that we only have one electricity option, an option that satisfies neither you nor me completely.

Fortunately, marketing evolved as business owners began to realize that customers not only had different preferences (which they probably already knew) but also that customers would be willing to pay *more* for products that better addressed their needs than the generic, one-size-fits-all version. As technology and other means of production improved, businesses were able to spice up their product offerings and to offer a variety of options, limited at first but, later, a more diverse array of goods and services.

Fast forward to modern times in which most products—from automobiles to apartments, clothing to coffee drinks—are customizable. Consumers are able to design the *exact* product they want in a variety of product categories and industries in a way that our ancestors would have never dreamed of as they drove by in the boring, conformist black Model T cars. This era, in which products are customized and differentiated in order to meet the specific needs of individual consumers, is referred to as **mass customization.** Not only do we have vast arrays of products to choose from within product categories, we also have the ability to *create* our own products – like M&Ms in the color we want with personalized messages and pictures (www.MyMMs.com) or canvas wall hangings that feature images from your own personal photography collection (www.costcophotocenter.com). With this benefit comes a problem: entitlement. Anyone who has ever worked retail or in the restaurant industry knows what it's like when consumers cannot get *exactly* what they want. Rather than appreciate the options they *do* have, customers sometimes focus on what's missing because they are so used to getting everything their way. I bet you and I are *never* like that, though…never.

So if mass customization is the era in which we currently live, it is only reasonable to consider what the next stage in the marketing era evolution might be. A fair bit of my research explores what some of us believe is the "next step" in the evolution of marketing, what I refer to as **momentary marketing** or **momentary customization**, which involves exactly what the title suggests: customizing a product or service offering to meet the specific needs of an individual *in the moment.* Sounds crazy, right? Impossible? Surprisingly, it's already happening. Thanks to the adoption of smart phones, the use of GPS technology, and an ability for consumers to update their thoughts, feelings, and preferences in real time on a variety of websites and applications, companies know now, more than ever, what needs consumers have in the very moment they need them. If I set up an algorithm that picks up keywords from your status updates talking about being hungry or thirsty, then I can shoot you a coupon for a restaurant or convenience store just steps away from you thanks to the GPS. Part of this sounds creepy, I know, but part of it is just pure and simple marketing: helping consumers fulfill their needs. Momentary marketing is mass customization to the nth degree, and you may wonder how marketing could evolve any further short of companies knowing what consumers want *before* consumers even know themselves…

I hate to freak you out any further, but research conducted by Stanford-based researcher Dr. Brian Knutson and his colleagues showed that an fMRI brain scan is capable of predicating an individual's intentions to purchase a product better than the individual's own self-reported intentions to purchase an item. Specifically, the team showed that distinct neural circuits associated with gains and losses were activated by preferences (positive, gain) and extreme prices (pain, loss), and that, together, this information could predict purchase intentions. Now this is where consumer advocacy groups totally flip out, but there's no need to panic unless you have figured out away to strap extremely heavy, multi-million dollar fMRI machines on the heads of consumers as they go about their day.

Under the current era of marketing – the mass customization approach – marketing as a science and discipline has developed some rather useful tools to make the systematic study and application of key concepts possible. The remainder of this chapter covers what I consider to be *marketing essentials* – that is, the concepts that anyone who has anything to do with marketing *must* know. From STP to the 4Ps to the 5Cs, this section will teach you quite a bit of marketing language – it's like Rosetta Stone: Marketing – in a way that will make you sound super smart and informed when you're talking in large groups about marketing. You can throw out words like, "Positioning," and "Target market," and people will immediately bow in your presence. These terms are so important that if you meet someone who claims to work in marketing and they *don't* know these concepts, get out of there as fast as possible. They're dangerous impostors! They could be a spy or an alien or something.

STP: Segmenting, Targeting, and Positioning

When I first start talking about STP in large groups, people grow visibly uncomfortable in their seats because many people mistakenly think I'm going to talk about herpes and Chlamydia. I supposed one *could* talk about that in the context of consumer behavior, but ST*P* stands for Segmenting, Targeting, and Positioning and represents one of the most basic, fundamental ideas of marketing: rare is it that our product can be *all things* to *all people*, so customizing products to meet the needs of homogeneous target segments of consumers is a smarter, better way to market.

To introduce you to the STP concept, I am going to take you through a specific example that, while completely fictitious, takes place in the context of a real-world product. Let's pretend you work for PepsiCo, the parent company of Gatorade, and that the company is thinking about launching a new beverage whose ingredients promote "extreme mental focus" in one flavor based on marketing research suggesting a need for this kind of product in the market. Where do we start? As of this book's writing there are just over 7 billion people on the planet. So we should just produce 7 billion bottles of this new beverage, right?

Hardly. Why not? Well, for starters, you realize that not everyone in the world shares the same taste…literally. If you're reading this book in a public place right now, chances are you would find several different opinions regarding the tastes of Gatorade's current lineup of drinks, and this new beverage is likely to be no exception. And even if everyone *did* share the same taste for this new beverage, the cost of producing over 7 billion bottles of this new beverage to sell to everyone in the world is simply impossible, no matter how efficient the company might be.

People are different and, as such, people have different needs. Marketers understand this fact and, as a result, a lot of a marketing department's time is spent figuring out what kinds of people exist in a particular market. To introduce this idea to my students, I take them back to a painful time in their lives: high school. Remember the high school cafeteria? It seems that in every American high school teenagers engage in the same cafeteria shenanigans. If I asked you to visualize your high school cafeteria, you'd likely have a very clear memory of the physical space, the setup of the tables, and, most importantly, *who* sat *where*…unless, of course, you were home-schooled in which case you probably sat at your family's kitchen table next to Jethro, your loyal dog, and Miss Skittles, your independent and sassy cat (for an example of what a public high school cafeteria is like, go watch *Mean Girls*). Just kidding – home school is great: those kids always win spelling bees.

At the average American high school, the cool kids sit at a particular table, the nerds at a different table, the jocks/athletes at a table, the theatre kids at a different table, and so on. So if we return to our Gatorade example, chances are you would pitch this new "extreme mental focus" beverage very differently if you went after the jocks/athletes than if you went after the theatre kids. The foolish marketer is the one who develops a single campaign in an attempt to capture every kid in the cafeteria in the exact same way. This is the point of segmentation: breaking down a larger heterogeneous market into smaller homogenous segments whose needs can be better identified, better addressed, and better communicated. Now, this isn't to say that overlap doesn't take place: there's no reason that a cheerleader can't be a "mathlete" or a theatre kid, but generally speaking, segmentation is about creating efficiency wherever possible so that marketers don't waste money attempting to be everything to everyone when certainly not everyone is interested in purchasing your product/service.

Segmenting. So how do marketers break the entire market into more manageable segments? There are several ways ranging from the super simple use of demographic information (e.g., age, gender, location, socioeconomic status) to the far more sophisticated psychographic information (e.g., attitudes, values, beliefs). It turns out that most segmentation exercises involve a mix of these methods, as well as behavioral information on consumers' past purchases, shopping habits, and other observable characteristics. The typical belief is that psychographic and behavioral information are more useful when it comes to truly identifying a segment, which is probably true; however, demographic information should not be discounted. Consider, for example, that marketing a feminine hygiene product is likely unnecessary for most men – demographics rule the day! However, from there, knowing what kind of woman wants a relaxed fit and comfort versus a woman who wants super absorbency regardless of fit comes down to non-demographic factors. How did we wind up talking about feminine hygiene products? Ugh, this conversation is SO high school.

Let's return to our Gatorade example. If we pretend that our market (i.e., the world) is the entire cafeteria, then we can break down the cafeteria into smaller, homogeneous segments by simply looking at the tables where the students sit. If we focus on basic demographic variables (e.g., location, age, gender), we could break down the cafeteria by class – freshmen, sophomores, juniors, and seniors. Simple enough. If we focused on the freshmen, maybe we could position the mental focus drink as the "Perfect beverage for acclimating to the demands of high school!" If we focused on the juniors or seniors, perhaps we could position the mental focus drink as the "Perfect beverage for acing the standardized tests that will get you into college!" But it is probably evident to you that this sort of generic approach, although better than trying to target the *entire* market, still lacks teeth – it's pretty generic.

AN ASIDE ON SEGMENTATION

There are many different ways to segment a market. Here are a few different approaches and a brief explanation of how each works:

- **Geographic:** Involves segmenting a market based on physical location alone, like country, state, zip code, neighborhood, region – e.g., Asian segment, European segment, South American segment

- **Demographic:** Involves segmenting based on measurable characteristics about the people within a market such as income level, ethnicity, age, gender, and other observable characteristics – e.g., women 18-25, women 25-35, women 35-45, women 45-55, women 55+

- **Psychological:** Involves segmenting based on psychological variables – beliefs, morals, values, interests, opinions – with no regard for other information about the individuals – e.g., environmentally-conscious segment, environmentally-apathetic segment

- **Psychographic:** A combination of demographic and psychological segmentation, psychographic segmentation incorporates general measurable characteristics about individuals with psychological differences – e.g., religious African-American mothers, non-religious Caucasian mothers.

- **Socio-cultural:** Involves segmenting based on group membership and the shared values of that particular group; in other words, the group already exists in society and the group has particular needs – e.g., members of a **private social club, health care professionals.**

- **Use-related:** Involves segmenting based on the frequency of use of a particular product or service – e.g., segmenting frequent users, rare users, and non-users

- **Benefit:** Involves segmenting a market based on knowledge about how consumers use a product or service and what benefits they extract from a product or service – an example would be segmenting coffee drinkers based on whether they drink the beverage because they like the taste, like the caffeine/energy benefits provided, like the low-calorie status of the beverage, etc.

- **Hybrid:** Using any of the above approaches together to develop segments

And don't forget: ideal segments are homogeneous within segment and heterogeneous between segments. In other words, you want members of a specific segment to be as much like other members of that segment as possible but different from people not included in that segment. Segments should also be stable and sizable otherwise they are probably not worth targeting.

So let's go one step further and consider psychographic variables (e.g., counter-culture, artistic, fashion forward). What is it about these students, more deeply, that they self-select to sit at the tables they do? If we focus on the jock/athlete table, we may get students of a variety of ages who share a common goal: excellent performance on the playing field, regardless of their sport. So if we pitched our new beverage to this group we might call it "Gatorade: Sport Focus" and describe it as "The tasty, thirst-quenching drink that keeps your head in the game!" That's one option. But now let's consider a very different segment: the Mathletes. These mathematical whiz kids solve complex equations for fun and represent their school proudly at math team competitions. If we were to pitch the new product to this segment, we might call the new product something like "Gatorade: Brain Boost" and describe it as "The tasty, thirst-quenching drink that super strengthens your smarts." See how that worked? A slight change in the product's name and positioning helped us to customize *the exact same product* to two different segments. We could continue playing this game for other possible segments—the theatre kids, the stoners, the preppy kids, etc.—but the main idea stays the same: it's extremely difficult to be *everything* to *everyone*, so it's usually better to narrow your scope and target particular segments.

Targeting. This brings us to the "targeting" component of STP. Once you have broken a market down into potential segments you essentially have a big pie that has been cut into pieces. Now we have to select which piece of the pie to eat, so to speak. The decision for which segment(s) to target depends on a variety of potential factors: how lucrative is the segment; how easy is it to reach the members of the segment; are competitors also attempting to lure members of the segment? Marketing research provides this kind of information, which then helps us make an informed decision. Say, in our example, that the marketing research tells us that the jocks/athletes get most of their beverages provided for them and that the school has an exclusive contract with a competing beverage company. Suddenly, the jock/athlete segment seems a lot less attractive for targeting compared to the Mathlete target. Perhaps the marketing research shows that Mathletes are also significantly more likely to have part-time jobs than the jock/athletes, whose demanding practice schedules prevent them from holding similar positions. This may mean that Mathletes have more of their own disposable income to spend on our new beverage than the jock/athletes. Thus, when it comes time to pick a target, it seems that Mathletes would be the appropriate segment to target.

Now a question that often comes up with respect to targeting is whether or not it's okay to choose *more* than one segment to target. This is where marketing as an art, and not as an exact science, comes into play. Say we could also make the argument that the marching band segment could benefit from the new drink. The marching band kids are actually a nice hybrid of our jock/athlete segment–given the former group's long parades, halftime shows, and scorching summer band camps in the blazing sun–and the Mathlete group–the band kids are super into music, theory, and their unique skill set. If we find out that this group also has disposable income and would be likely to purchase our product, should we include them as a potential target? The rule of thumb is essentially this: if it is possible to target more than one segment efficiently, such that economies of scale can be achieved or that the costs of targeting an additional segment do not outweigh the benefits likely to be accrued for doing so, then do it. If we can market the product to another segment or two without incurring significant costs and achieve considerable returns, then we most definitely should include them in our marketing strategy.

Positioning. This brings us to the final letter of STP – the P, or *positioning*. We've already touched on this a bit in the example above, but positioning is essentially everything that goes into communicating your product to your intended target(s). This includes everything from what you call the product to the packaging in which you sell your product, the phrasing you use to describe your product, the places you sell your product, the price you charge for your product, and the point of differentiation (POD) that sets your product apart from any other comparable product in the market. In short, positioning involves every element of introducing your product to your end consumer and will influence, from that point on, how consumers mentalize and think about your product. So you can think of "positioning" as the main, overall theme of what and how you want your intended audience to think of your product. This is no small task.

Now, we know that trying to say the *same* thing to *everyone* is a terrible idea. Mathletes have different needs/interests than band kids who, in turn, have different needs than jocks/athletes who, in turn, have different needs from theatre kids, etc. So if we decide to target only Mathletes, we could stick with the name "Gatorade: Brain Boost" and the tagline "The tasty, thirst-quenching drink that super strengthens your smarts." If we decide to go after both Mathletes and band kids, maybe we could call the beverage "Gatorade: Refreshing Focus" and include the tagline "The focus your brain needs to perform and compete." Bam. Just like that we have a product name and tagline that covers our target markets in a way that will allow us to customize specific marketing executions (advertisements, promotions, etc.) to these similar-but-different targets effectively and efficiently.

The 4 Ps of Marketing

Positioning is more than just a clever name and a catchy tagline. Indeed, as mentioned above, positioning is literally *every* aspect of how consumers learn about, come into contact with, and experience your product or service. Usually, marketers will write a "positioning statement" as the sort of gold standard to which every subsequent marketing execution is compared to make sure each tactic is "on message." Thus, if we positioned our Gatorade beverage as a drink designed to improve mental focus, an advertisement talking about physical strength with no mention of mental acuity is not "on message" and, as such, probably should not be pursued.

When it comes time to begin thinking about designing a marketing strategy, folks in marketing have developed an easy-to-remember set of important considerations referred to as the 4Ps of marketing. The 4Ps, in no particular order, include: product, price, placement, and promotion.

Product. The first P in the 4Ps has to do with the very product (or service) we are selling. To carry on with our Gatorade beverage example, the "product" would be the beverage itself. We already discussed that the beverage is formulated to improve one's mental focus perhaps by the inclusion of some herbal ingredient like ginkgo biloba. But what about the product's flavoring? Its color? Its taste texture (i.e., is it a smooth, water-like beverage or more of a grainy, smoothie-like beverage)? What about its aftertaste? What size should the product come in and in what kind of product packaging? Bottles? Glass? Plastic? In short, the "product" P has everything to do with the characteristics of the product. Creative types love discussing the many possibilities in which a product can be presented to potential consumers, but even the most creative product pitch would fail if it did not have research supporting the decisions.

Say, for example, that we find out that samples of our intended targets – Mathletes and band kids – tasted a variety of flavors, colors, and textures of the proposed product. Research may show that the targets preferred a refreshing, lightly-flavored beverage that had a smooth, water-like texture, as the smoothie-like, heavier beverage did not taste refreshing in the heat of the sun. Furthermore, when testing color profiles, research may show that the sample tested preferred light colors that appeared more like tinted water than extremely saturated, artificial-looking colors. So instead of a deep, dark red beverage for Strawberry flavoring, the sample tested preferred a very clear, pink-tinted beverage. And when testing flavor profiles, the Mathletes and band kids were more likely than other groups tested to prefer hybrid flavors – strawberry-kiwi, cherry-lime, blueberry-pomegranate. The preferred packaging consisted of stylish twisting of the colors associated with the flavors (e.g., red and green for strawberry-kiwi), in a sleek plastic bottle (as participants felt glass was too heavy-feeling and too easily broken while boxed drinks felt cheap and childish). Regarding the copy or text on the bottle, participants preferred a minimalist design and the name: "Gatorade: Brain Power" with the words "Refreshing focus." underneath the name of the product. Health facts about the beverage also scored highly among the sample tested, so the ideal packaging would include pull out statistics and factoids about how the ingredients of the product aid the mental focus and health of the beverages' consumers. So thanks to a bit of marketing research and the creative minds of a few marketers, a new beverage is born!

Price. This new beverage isn't free, of course, which brings us to our next P in the 4Ps. Every product/service has costs associated with creating it, so at the very minimum whatever price we charge for our product needs to be higher than the costs involved in making the product (Side note: this isn't actually *always* true – there's a strategy known as "loss-leader pricing" in which a product is sold at a price *lower* than its cost in an attempt to stimulate demand for a pricier related product that will compensate for this strategy; examples include razors, which are super cheap, and razor blades, which are super expensive or video game consoles, often sold at a loss, and video games, often sold at a premium). But, for the most part, the price of products typically includes a fraction dedicated to covering the cost of producing the product and a fraction that serves as the "premium," or the amount of a price that comes back to a company as profit. You may remember from a prior business class that "Profit" (symbolized by the Greek symbol pi - π) is simply equal to the total amount of Revenue a company brings in minus the total Costs involved of doing business. So, on the individual product level, the "per unit" profit is simply the price charged for the product minus the total costs involved in making that particular unit.

So if profit is simply the total price minus the total costs, why not charge an insanely high price and capture as much profit as possible? Well, that's not a terrible idea, but there's one important complication: we simply cannot charge whatever we want. For you see consumers are fairly good at determining how valuable something is in their mind and, even if they weren't, our competitors do a fairly good job at setting reference prices in the minds of consumers. So if other comparable beverages were priced between $1.50 and $3.00, then charging $10 would be outrageous while charging even $5.00 would seem pricey to consumers. Again, we can turn to research and testing to determine the ideal price point for the new beverage. Let's say that our intended targets are willing to pay, at most, $2.00 for a beverage, then we'll want to keep the price right around $2.00 or less to make sure they'll still consider buying the product when it launches. From a cost perspective, knowing that we cannot charge much more than $2.00 might inform how lavish we make the packaging design, how much of the beverage we include in each serving, and how many varieties of flavors we are able to offer. The point is that we want to keep our costs manageable and low so that we can make sure the per-unit profit we make on each bottle sold is as high as it can be. That's business.

There are four primary pricing strategies to which marketers often refer:

- **Premium Pricing:** This strategy involves setting relatively higher prices because you offer a product perceived to be of substantially better quality than your competition.

- **Economy Pricing:** This strategy involves setting relatively lower prices because you deliberately offer a product that offers fewer frills compared to your competition.

- **Penetration Pricing:** This strategy involves purposefully offering a lower price than you normally would to increase your share of the market. Companies will often do this in competitive markets to get their foot in the door and gradually increase price over time closer to the industry average.

- **Skimming Pricing:** Perhaps the most confusing of the four strategies, skimming involves charging a higher price *not* because you offer a superior product but because there is little competition in the market. The reason this is called "skimming" is that, as more competitors enter the market, you have to adjust your price downward as product supply increases. Thus, you are "skimming" at the top and continue to do so as you work your way down.

Certainly other pricing strategies exist, and the right strategy to use depends on the market situation and a company's goals (e.g., acquiring new users, increasing usage from current users, etc.), but these examples nicely illustrate how something as simple as price can be used to influence a consumer's thoughts and behaviors.

Placement. So now that we have our product designed and have a price to charge, we need to know where we are going to sell our product. That's what placement is all about: specifically, placement refers to any *place* that consumers will be able to purchase our product. In this case, because we are working with a beverage, we may already have in mind some typical places that beverages are routinely purchased: grocery stores, convenience stores, concession stands, vending machines, etc. Because Gatorade does not sell directly to its end users (i.e., the people drinking the beverage), placement introduces another idea in the marketing process – retailing. Part of our job, then, is to convince the middlemen – grocers, convenience store owners, schools deciding which drinks to stock in its vending machines – why purchasing our Gatorade: Brain Power drink would be in their best interest. Again, we can turn to marketing research, which may reveal that our Mathletes and band kids tend to purchase the majority of their beverages at the school's vending machines or at a particular nearby convenience store across the street from their respective schools throughout the country. Thus, our placement strategy would involve negotiating contracts with various schools, perhaps some of which already have exclusive deals with our parent company Pepsi, to include Gatorade: Brain Power as one of the options in their vending machines. Similarly, we may look and see which convenience stores are located within one mile of most American high schools and focus our efforts on negotiating deals with those stores to stock our Gatorade: Brain Power product. Now, it could have also been the case that these students bring beverages from home for their afterschool practices, in which case our attention would instead be focused on the primary purchaser for their household – say moms – and the grocery stores at which they make their purchases. In short, we want to know *where* our target is seeking and obtaining its refreshment beverages so that we can be sure to *place* our products in these locations.

Promotion. The final P of the 4Ps of marketing is quite comprehensive, as it pertains to literally every single communication a company has regarding its product to the market at large. The more traditional examples of this include things like television commercials and print advertisements, but more modern examples include social media sites and elaborate word-of-mouth campaigns. It is important to note that half the battle of executing great promotional pieces involves coming up with attention-grabbing, effective communications, while the other half of the battle is *placing* those creative executions effectively. It's not enough to create a brilliant ad; you have to make sure the target audience is going to *see* it and, perhaps even more important, *pay attention to it.*

In the case of our Gatorade: Brain Power product, we may know from research that our target segments – the Mathletes and the band kids – like witty humor, don't care much for celebrities relative to other segments, and appreciate factual information more than flashy fluff. Knowing this, a proposed ad featuring a celebrity endorsement by Kim Kardashian driving around Miami drinking a bottle of Gatorade: Brain Power while heavy-bass dance music is playing *probably* isn't going to perform very well with our intended target. Instead, picture a graphic of a brain engaging in physical activities – like running on a treadmill, doing jumping jacks, bench pressing heavy weights – and then a camera scrolling out to see a regular high school kid working on a math problem, or playing in a marching band routine, or conducting a science experiment with safety goggles, a mysterious chemical, and a Bunsen burner. The narration may say something like, "Your brain burns 15% more energy than your body; you feed your body, but have you fed your brain today? Gatorade: Brain Power – Refreshing focus." See how that works? The accompanying print ads of the campaign would reflect a similar design: a thought cloud showing the brain engaged in physical activity, the student the brain belongs to engaging in a mental-yet-physical activity, and a picture of the product with some scientific facts regarding the beverage contained within the print ad's copy.

But remember what I said earlier? Half the battle of a solid promotional campaign rests in the media placement of the creative executions. Even the best designed advertisements will be ineffective if the intended target audience never sees them. Say our marketing research suggests that Mathletes and band kids are much more likely than other segments to watch television shows like "The Big Bang Theory," to surf the web using Yahoo! instead of Google, to listen to Pandora while doing homework, and to play brainy application games on their mobile phones (compared to fighting games or massively multiplayer online games – MMOGs). Well, then we should be purchasing media slots during "The Big Bang Theory," ad space on Yahoo!, commercial time for the relevant Pandora stations, and ad placements for brainy app games.

For the most part, companies are fairly smart about their media buying (well, the media buying firms they hire are smart anyway). However, you will certainly see some creative executions in rather unexpected places sometimes. One of two things is likely: someone isn't very good at his/her job or, more interesting, the people *you'd never think* are likely to buy a particular product or service actually do and a company realizes this. If I were to ask you on whom casual gaming companies (e.g., mobile app games, video games) should focus their efforts, you might be tempted to say teenage boys or young adult men. But did you know that about 70% of moms are casual gamers? So instead of purchasing expensive ad space in *Wired* or *Maxim*, gaming companies might be just as smart to purchase ad space in *Good Housekeeping* or *Cosmopolitan* for games like Candy Crush or Wedding Dash.

Promotion includes more than just traditional advertising, however, and one way to keep track of the many things included in the term "promotion" is to make use of a term known as **Integrated Marketing Communication (IMC)**. IMC refers to a variety of tools at a company's disposal to promote its message, product, service, brands, and/or company. The "integrated" part of the term is a nod to the idea that the executions should be consistent in tone, look, and feel across the various approaches. Here's a list of IMC tools:

- **Television.** Television includes our familiar television advertisements that typically come in :30 and :60 timeslots. However, another common use of television involves the use of product placement; that is, subtle placement of a company's branded product or service during a television show. Under Armour placed its products on the contestants in *The Amazing Race* whereas Coca-Cola placed large cups on the judging desk of the *American Idol* judges for years.

- **Print.** Print includes the advertisements you see in magazines as well as the paid advertisements you see in newspapers and other forms of print media.

- **Outdoor.** Outdoor includes billboards, larger posters at bus terminals and metro stops, posters plastered on construction site walls in large cities, and things like blimps and banners trailing planes at large events. Basically just about anything outdoors.

- **Promotions.** Promotions refers to discounts, sales, rebates, contests, samples, and special events – basically short term events designed to increase sales, engagement, and/or awareness. It can get a bit confusing because one of our 4Ps is "Promotion," more generally, and one specific kind of promotion is "promotions." Be sure to recognize the difference.

- **Direct.** Direct marketing refers to reaching out to consumers as *directly* as possible – via mail that is delivered to their home (e.g., promotional cards, catalogs), "personalized" emails, calling them on the phone (e.g., telemarketing), or even paying them an at-home visit (e.g., door-to-door selling).

- **Trade Shows.** Trade shows are events in which vendors can purchase space, usually at a convention center or a hotel, and buyers can come, interact with products, and ultimately decide to purchase products to sell in their stores. Some industries are based primarily on this model, such as the graphic tees market, which consists of a few trade shows like the annual PROJECT show in Vegas.

- **Sponsorship.** Sponsorship refers to the situations in which a company will pay a good amount of money to support an event in return for inclusion in the event itself, either with its products, its branding, or some other engagement. Most NASCARs have sponsors and, as such, each car is painted with company logos. The Discovery Channel famously sponsored Nik Wallenda's tightrope walk (without a net) over the Grand Canyon in summer 2013, and Red

Bull sponsored Felix Baumgartner's free fall from the edge of space in October 2012, both likely to appeal to thrill-seekers and thrill-watchers likely to watch the network's thrilling shows and to drink the energizing Red Bull.

- **Sales/Customer Service.** An often forgotten part of marketing, sales and customer service involve your in-store sales interaction, as well as your in-store, on the phone, or online customer service experiences. These should follow a theme consistent with the overall IMC theme, as they also represent important consumer touch points. Note: any collateral (i.e., the tangible brochures, pamphlets, etc.) involved with these services should also be consistent with the broader campaign.

- **Web.** Web refers *specifically* to a company's website and the websites for its various brands and product/service offerings (if there are several). This includes managing a company's reputation and the reputations of its brands and products on other sites, even those not owned by the company, in which customers can purchase the products/services.

- **SEO/SEM.** A different form of online marketing, SEO refers to search engine optimization and SEM to search engine marketing. SEO/SEM involve coordinating a company's position within search results and designing particular keywords and search engine phrases that increase the likelihood of being found on the web.

- **Social Media.** Social media marketing involves sites like Facebook, Instagram, Twitter, and other online companies through which it is possible to connect with large groups of potential customers and current users in meaningful ways.

- **Mobile.** An emerging medium in the past decade or so, mobile refers to the marketing efforts placed on reaching consumers through their mobile phones *and* their mobile handheld devices (e.g., iPads, Kindles, etc.). This can come in the form of text message advertising, notifications via apps, and ad placement in mobile applications.

- **Public Relations.** PR involves the clever use of news media, publicity stunts, and other "news-making" activities that garner a lot of consumer and media attention without requiring the company to pay for "traditional" forms of advertising. Note, however, that some PR stories are "placed" – companies will pay PR firms to write "press releases," which newspapers and magazines pick up as "news stories" despite the fact that they are not *really* news but really advertisements in disguise. Consider, for example, the 2005 publicity event in which Snapple produced the world's largest frozen popsicle (25 ft. tall, 17 tons) to introduce its new line of frozen treats. What's the silly thing about introducing a popsicle outside at Union Square in late June? The sun. The popsicle melted almost immediately, leading to a huge sticky flood that took over the park. An accident? Maybe. Or a deliberately-planned publicity stunt that garnered the company *much* more free media attention than it would have received otherwise? I guess we'll never know!

- **Word-of-Mouth.** Somewhat similar to PR is word-of-mouth, which is anything that deliberately encourages consumers to talk about your company, products, and/or services. Both PR and word-of-mouth are considered valuable to companies because the sources are people *other than* the company, so what they say feels more objective than when a company is trying to persuade consumers. The recent trend of including links to tweet, share on Facebook, and pin to Pinterest are all in the spirit of encouraging word-of-mouth engagement.

- **Non-Traditional.** The non-traditional category is a "catch all" for the other kinds of engagement that cannot be easily assigned to one of the aforementioned categories. Often "guerilla marketing" campaigns fall into this category. Guerilla marketing refers to creative, staged events that draw attention to a company or brand such as Oscar Mayer's "Weinermobile" – a sizable hot dog car that travels all over the United States and gets customers engaging with the company's products. Who wouldn't want their picture in front of that iconic ride? If Chiquita, the famous banana company, were to have a man in a gorilla costume scale the Empire State Building carrying a Chiquita banana, this would likely garner a lot of media buzz. I guess you could call that example gorilla guerilla marketing.

Again, it is worth mentioning that the various pieces of an Integrated Marketing Communications campaign should all share a similar theme and reinforce one another. Each campaign is not required to include all the components listed above, but be sure that if your company decides to include any one of these tools that it *does* fit within the context of the overall IMC campaign.

The 5 Cs of Marketing

Marketers really like catchy, mnemonic devices, so in addition to the 4Ps of marketing, which pertain to issues more closely related to the product, service, or company themselves, the 5Cs of marketing cover considerations marketers should make that are really *external* to the product, service, or company but that may influence them. The 5Cs include Customers, the Company, Competitors, Collaborators, and Climate (or Context depending on whom you ask). More generally, these Cs can be thought of as the "other stuff" happening in and around a market that could influence the marketing plan for your product or service. Here's a brief description of each of the 5Cs:

Customers. This relates back to our STP discussion. Essentially, you want to always be "in the know" with respect to both your current consumers and their preferences, wants, needs, etc., as well as those folks who are not your current consumers but whose needs you might be able to address somehow. In short, you need to know your customers well and your non-customers just as well.

Company. This is like therapy for yourself. You want to know what your company is doing well, what it's doing poorly (and can improve upon), what it *could* be doing, and what who/what might be coming after it. There's a tool we often use for this called a SWOT analysis. SWOT refers to Strengths, Weaknesses, Opportunities, and Threats. Strengths and Weaknesses are internal to the company, whereas Opportunities and Threats are more external.

Competitors. A company cannot be successful unless it knows against whom it is competing. Some competitors are easy to identify because they are offering products/services directly comparable to the products/services you are selling. Other competitors aren't as straightforward. Consider, for example, how automakers can easily identify other automakers as competitors (e.g., Ford v. GM v. Audi v. BMW). However, these companies must also compete against alternative forms of transportation like motorcycles (e.g., Harley-Davidson) and even public transportation (i.e., government organizations).

Collaborators. Collaborators include partners in the business world with whom collaborating might lead to the mutual benefit of all parties involved. Common collaborators include suppliers and retail partners. Consider, for example, how Apple entered an exclusive partnership with

Best Buy temporarily to sell Apple-branded products in Best Buy stores. This increased store visits to Best Buy, which had been struggling to get shoppers in stores now that people purchase so many tech products online, helped Apple extend its physical reach beyond Apple Stores, and benefitted consumers who could engage with Apple's products in person even when the closest Apple store was hundreds of miles away.

Climate (aka Context). Climate or Context refers to all the external conditions that may help or hinder your company's business. The easy way to think of the attributes associated with climate comes from a dear professor of mine and now colleague, Dr. John Branch. Dr. Branch makes use of the SLEPTIC model, which refers to Social, Legal, Economic, Political, Technological, Industrial, and Cultural attributes. Various social trends, cultural practices, economic market situations, legal decisions, emerging technology, and industrial regulations are *always* changing. So an important part of doing business is being aware of the latest changes and, whenever possible, the impending changes that are soon to occur. A good example of this is the BluRay v. HD-DVD war that raged around 2008. Toshiba pushed for HD-DVD as the "next generation" of high definition optical discs for films (i.e, the successor to DVDs, which were not HD) while other companies were pushing for BluRay discs. Consumers, of course, were not about to have two different devices, one for playing HD-DVDs and another for playing BluRay discs, so it became clear that one would have to win out. Companies around that time were producing *both* HD-DVDs and BluRay, and any company not paying attention to the fact that BluRay was gaining traction as the clear frontrunner in the war likely found themselves stuck with an inventory of useless HD-DVDs when Toshiba finally threw in the towel.

So there you have it. We have just covered STP, the 4Ps, and the 5Cs – the foundational concepts within this modern era of mass customization – and the pillars of any modern marketing education. Nice, right? Hopefully it wasn't too painful. Maybe you even enjoyed it a little bit? Maybe?

Going forward, the best way to apply these concepts is to think of each marketing challenge you face by considering STP, the 4Ps, and the 5Cs. Ask yourself, "Are we targeting the right segment in the right way? Are all of our marketing executions consistent? Is there something external to our company that we're not taking advantage of or that is preventing our success?" A quick run down of these 12 concepts (3 STP + 4Ps + 5Cs = 12, the Dirty Dozen) will cover a lot of ground.

And one final point, please don't forget that a bulk of "business" isn't actually B2C (business to consumer) but rather B2B (business to business). Companies don't often make television commercials to advertise to other companies; instead, these companies rely more on interpersonal interactions, sales meetings, trade shows, and other face-to-face communication to do business, communication in which understanding how people think is just as important, which means we're now ready to talk about consumer behavior. So grab a bottle of Gatorade: Brain Power, and let's get this party started...

APPLICATION QUESTIONS

1) What does STP stand for and why is this a useful concept in Marketing?

2) Few people realize that the same company, Gap, Inc., owns Old Navy, Gap, Banana Republic, Piperlime, and Athleta. How does the parent company Gap, Inc., make use of the STP concept with respect to its various store brands?

3) Markets are rather efficient at developing new niche products that serve the needs of very specific consumer targets – it's why there are hundreds of kinds of toothpaste in the grocery store's dental aisle. Think of a product category that might be missing out on a new or adapted product that could serve the needs of a specific target. What would the product be and whom would it target? Why?

4) Consistency is important in the marketing world, in general, and in the 4P Marketing Mix, specifically. This is why we are skeptical when a luxury product is offered for a surprisingly low price – instead of thinking we're getting a good deal, we often assume something shady is going on. Give an example of a consumer product whose 4Ps are consistent with one another and another consumer product whose 4Ps are inconsistent (e.g., Starbucks-branded premium iced coffee drinks being sold at a boutique grocery store v. a discount grocery store like Aldi)

5) Carrying on with our consistency theme, promotional campaigns spanning several different media tend to perform better when similar themes are used throughout. Think of a current marketing campaign that relies on a variety of media (e.g., TV ads, print ads, sponsorship, product placement, etc.) whose executions reflect a common positioning statement and creative theme. Now think of a different current marketing campaign whose executions are highly inconsistent from

medium to medium. How would you go about redesigning this latter campaign to make the executions consistent?

6) From a marketing perspective, why is it important to know about the Climate of the 5Cs (i.e., social, legal, economic, political, technical, industrial, and cultural factors)? Give a specific example of how one of these factors helped a consumer product/service and an example of how one of these factors hurt a consumer product/service in the market.

7) Most people realize that thinking about the competition is an important part of doing business, but identifying those competitors isn't always so straightforward. Consider, for example, how Starbucks must concern itself with other coffee retailers (e.g., Dunkin Donuts, Tim Horton's), other quick service companies who also provide coffee in their long list of products (e.g., McDonald's, Jack in the Box), at-home coffee sellers (e.g., Maxwell House, Folgers), and, one you may not have guessed, caffeine drinks in general (e.g., Red Bull, Coca-Cola). Think of another product or service and come up with a list of its competitors, both obvious and non-obvious.

8) Positioning a product well is an art that integrates marketing data, consumer preferences, competitor activity, and other factors. Think of the last purchase you just made. How does that product differentiate itself from other options you *could* have purchased? Do you think that this positioning is very effective? Why or why not? How could you make the positioning *better* for this product? Why do you think your new positioning would be an improvement (and don't just say it's because you did it ☺)?

PART I:

THE SELF

People are self-centered. This isn't so much a statement of judgment as it is a statement of fact: we interpret our world, our surroundings, and our experiences through this filter known as the "self." We can't help it – that's just how we're made. Two people can see the exact same event unfold but perceive the event in very different ways. So that we can better understand the role the "self" plays in interpreting the world, the next few chapters are dedicated to characteristics pertaining to the self: needs, wants, motivation, perception, attention, learning, memory, affect, emotion, mood, personality, attitude, and persuasion.

Chapter 1 | Studying Consumer Behavior

Urges.

We have a *lot* of them. And you better thank your lucky stars above that we do, too, otherwise, we wouldn't even be around to have urges.

Now, regardless of your personal beliefs about God and evolution and what not, let's suspend said beliefs just for a second and acknowledge that survival is critical for any species to exist...I mean, that's kind of the definition of survival, right? An animal needs to do *whatever* in can to keep itself around for *as long as possible* and to engage in *whatever behaviors* that will result in a *future generation* of that critter. An alternative way of thinking about it is that certain creatures do things – think, behave, etc. – either by chance or deliberately that keep them alive and, as a result of being the last ones left standing, they can reproduce with one another and pass those abilities on to a new generation...and so on, and so on. Ah, the circle of life [cue "The Lion King" music here].

If we travel back in time some *billions* of years (yes, *billions* – roughly 3.5 billion years to be more precise), we arrive to the first single-celled creatures that, in theory, represent our common ancestor. Some of these single-celled prokaryotes lived in the most extreme environments (e.g., volcanic vents), while others opted for more serene habitats (e.g., gentle ocean waters). Although it's fun to picture a single-celled prokaryote leisurely bathing in the gentle waves of the ocean doing absolutely nothing but, you know, just sort of floating, it turns out that some of these prokaryotes did something quite extraordinary: they *moved*. A simple, single-celled organism moving? Impossible. These prokaryotes are brainless, uneducated, limbless, and *single-celled* – how could they possibly move?! And why?!

Well, it turns out that 3.5 billion years ago, there were no food delivery services. In the prokaryote's world this meant that if food didn't happen to come to the prokaryote, the prokaryote needed to find its way to the food, in this case the food being the ever-amazing, all-inclusive, all-you-can-eat, energy-providing nourishment known as the sun and its light. Comparable to how plants rely on the sun for photosynthesis, prokaryotes needed the sun for energy and, as such, sought out the sun. Now, before you start picturing a snazzy, smart little cell swimming its way to sunlight, you should know that the movement was more akin to a drunk cell wandering out of light, realizing the light disappeared, and then doing an about-face to get back into the sunlight, as if the cell were afraid of the dark. However, some cells did exhibit true phototaxis (i.e., the fancy name for this phenomenon of moving toward a light source), using more directed, deliberate movement to get to a source of light (as opposed to leaving things to chance as in the prior example). With this movement toward the sun, it seems our little ocean-floating ancestor decided that tanning sounded nice, too. We should really throw a family reunion...I'll make t-shirts.

You might be wondering what a single-celled prokaryote moving toward the sun has to do with anything consumer related? "Who cares?" you're thinking, or, "I think I bought the wrong book?" as you frantically search for your receipt so you can return this book and buy the latest Nicholas Sparks tearjerker. Well, the reason I begin with this example of one of *the most basic* forms of life demonstrating phototaxis is to provide evidence that even at this *extremely simple level* organisms seem to have urges and motivations. In short, it's in our DNA to consume.

But while prokaryotes spend their days inching toward sources of light, we spend our days inching toward McDonald's or Hollister Co. We scurry to Major League Baseball games and Beyoncé concerts. The way I think about consumption involves thinking of what motivates that microscopic protokaryote to move in the first place: if you're hungry or need energy, you need to find food. You see, we all strive to maintain some steady state, and when that status deviates – we feel hungry, tired, sad – we seek out food, rest, and happiness. Some of these needs are purely biological, innate and built-in from birth, while other needs are learned over time through culture and experience. But what motivates us seems to be *any* deviation from a desired steady state that allows us to go about our day.

Once our internal milieu (that ever-present internal feeling we have), is no longer operating at a steady state, we are motivated to think, to behave, to do whatever we can to restore that balance. Just as the prokaryote needs sunlight for energy, so, too, does a high school kid *believe* he needs name brand clothing to resolve that internal discomfort he feels from being excluded from a particular social group. Just as a plant needs water to survive, so, too, does a couple *believe* they need to purchase the safest car on the road to protect their family and to be responsible parents.

Although consumer examples sometimes sound trivial or superficial, particularly when compared to needs like eating or breathing, fulfilling consumer needs often make us *feel* better or at least *stable* (...whether they actually make us better off or not is a subject for debate). Imagine the opposite: imagine always wanting that name brand clothing in high school but never getting it and, as such, living in a self-imagined agony the rest of your high school existence, never socializing with anyone; imagine wanting that safe car for your children but not purchasing it and all the worrying that ensues every time you get behind the wheel of the unsafe care you purchased instead. Life could be miserable. So really fulfilling consumer needs, on some higher level, is as helpful to survival as the single-celled organism finding its way to light. Basically anything we think or do that helps us achieve some desired end state is likely to keep us around longer. In some strange, convoluted way, consumption of products and services is comparable to the consumption of food, air, water, rest, and the things that are essential to our survival.

This isn't an endorsement of rampant consumerism. The fact of the matter is, no matter how much you consume or how little you consume of anything, you still consume *something*. We all do. What motivates that consumption can be something as fundamental as hunger or something as lofty as the symbolism we associate with a particular product, service, or brand. The key is that, by consuming whatever "it" is, we are fulfilled – at least temporarily – and the urge subsides.

So now when people ask you what you're studying in consumer behavior and if it's common sense you can look them in the eyes and very solemnly say, "I'm studying life. Nay, I'm studying *survival*," ...then stare them in the eyes dramatically for like 5 more seconds without saying anything and slowly walk away...and then, when you've taken a few steps, dramatically turn your head back around to look them in the eyes while still walking away...then turn forward...and never look back.

Chapter 2 | Needs, Wants, and Motivation

San Francisco is a charming city.

From the bright orange pillars of the famous Golden Gate Bridge, to the mysterious, fog enshrouded wonder that is Alcatraz, San Francisco is full of memorable sights, tastes, and even sounds, as the "ding-ding" of famous trolley cars ring throughout the city's hilly terrain.

So imagine the scene on a beautiful day in 2006 when San Franciscans, waiting for a public bus, smelled an unexpected odor that seemed to be coming from nowhere in particular.

The odor? Freshly baked chocolate chip cookies.

That's right – the delicious smell of warm, sweet cookie dough, complete with the scent of fresh, melt-in-your-mouth chocolate morsels, baking right at the perfect temperature for the warm cookie to touch your tongue and then melt ever so softly.

Close your eyes and imagine the smell of chocolate chip cookies baking in the oven. No, seriously – do it! Close your eyes and try to recreate the experience of smelling fresh chocolate chip cookies baking in an oven nearby. If you try hard enough not only will you capture the odors and flavor of the chocolate chip pieces and the cookie dough, you may even be able to sense the *warmth* of the cookies baking. You may even begin to believe that your nostrils are actually sniffing the delicious scent right over a pan of warm cookies. Are you doing it? For real, I can't be sitting next to you to make sure you're actually trying, so do me a solid and actually *attempt* it – you won't regret it. I'll be here waiting when you're finished.

[This is when you take one minute to imagine warm, delicious chocolate chip cookies baking nearby.]

Welcome back, and thanks for playing along. You'll find this book has a lot of audience participation, so thanks for indulging my weirdness.

So let's go back to San Francisco where the passengers waiting for the bus are still standing, waiting, and smelling the exact same smell you just imagined with your sensory system. However, the chocolate chip cookie smell at the bus terminal was not the result of very vivid imaginations. No, instead chocolate chip cookie-scented oils were concealed within the bus terminals and wafted out into the crowd of unsuspecting bystanders. Hundreds to thousands of commuters throughout the city were greeted with the sweet, delicious smells of fresh cookies and, strategically placed nearby on the print advertisement areas of the bus stops were advertisements for…wait for it…*wait for it*…milk. You thought I was going to say cookies, didn't you?

Indeed, the entire campaign was actually coordinated by the California Milk Processor Board in an attempt to sell more milk. By relying on the learned cultural association of cookies and milk and, in particular, chocolate chip cookies and milk, the organization and its advertising partner devised a plan to stoke the hunger (and thirst) pangs of commuters to encourage them to buy milk. I don't know about you, but there are few experiences worse in life than eating a warm, melt-in-your-mouth chocolate chip cookie only to find that there is no more milk left in the refrigerator. In fact, if you're smart, you'll always check to make sure that there is milk before you eat chocolate chip cookies (…unless you're lactose intolerant, in which case, I can sympathize and will gladly join you for a round of soy or almond milk).

What's interesting is that the pairing of chocolate chip cookies, particularly warm, freshly-baked chocolate chip cookies with ice-cold milk is *so* well engrained in our culture that the presence of one often stimulates our desire for the other. Interestingly, the effect seems unidirectional – i.e., if you give someone a glass of milk first it is unlikely that they would have a hankering for chocolate chip cookies as opposed to say Pop Tarts or cereal or any other food item if any at all. This urge to drink milk after eating chocolate chip cookies or, in your case, dear reader, mentally *smelling* chocolate chip cookies (side note: I'd totally bake you cookies if I could – maybe we'll have the technology to do that someday) is so strong that advertisers realized the potential for a campaign that relied on this learned association.

Unfortunately, as with anything fun, the Man shut it down. Within 36 hours of placing the clever advertisements, the Municipal Transportation Agency of San Francisco forced the oils to be removed for reasons that are still debated. Some claim that the scented oils could have been a health hazard for people with allergies. Others claim that the campaign was unfair to homeless people who couldn't afford milk, cookies, or any combination thereof (…which I think is offensive and presumptuous: for all we know several of those homeless people could be super wealthy and just not wanting to deal with the annoyances of modern home ownership). In any event, the campaign itself was brilliant – relying on a very powerful urge to sell an otherwise arguably unsexy product. Despite being cancelled prematurely, you would be hard pressed to find a marketer who would not appreciate the simplicity and effectiveness of such a sweet marketing campaign.

*　　*　　*

Although the association between cookies and milk is an extremely strong bond that many of us share, this pairing is an example of a learned, cultural association and, as such, is probably not *universal*. That is, I imagine that somewhere in some remote village of an undiscovered tropical island there is a tribesperson who, when given a chocolate chip cookie, would not immediately make a mad dash to milk the utters of an unsuspecting goat nearby to quench an evoked thirst for milk.

However, there are some deeply-rooted needs that *are* more universal in that across cultures and over time these same needs appear to be evident in otherwise very different populations of people. A fellow by the name of Abraham Maslow so nicely summarized some of these needs in a very stylish pyramid. Actually, I have no idea if *he* created this triangle or if someone else did it later on, but the story still applies: basically Maslow's point is that we, as human beings, all share innate needs that primarily stem from biological, survival motivations (kind of like our prokaryotic ancestor from the previous chapter).

The triangular/pyramid shape is meant to serve as a subtle reminder that we must start by fulfilling those foundational needs at the bottom and that only upon doing so can we scale up to the more sophisticated needs at higher levels of the triangle. Now, there's quite a bit of debate in the modern psychology research world about whether this "hierarchy of needs" is actually a "hierarchy" at all – i.e., isn't it possible for me to fulfill my sexual needs on the third level even if I haven't fulfilled my sleep needs on the first level (…not mine personally, per se, because that makes it awkward for you, the reader…but generally speaking).

The gist of Maslow's work, and the work of others using his work as a starting point, is that human beings operate with a very robust set of needs that motivate our thinking and behavior. I should point out that this is not an idea to be taken lightly, particularly in the context of this book, because that's precisely the point of what I'm trying to teach you: if we know humans are motivated by underlying needs then identifying, understanding, and even creating those needs is critical.

Physiological Needs. We will avoid the debate about the hierarchy of Maslow's needs in this book and, instead, we'll just start at the bottom and work our way up. The "foundational needs" involve very basic physiological needs required for, well, existing in the first place: breathing, eating, drinking, sleeping, this idea called "homeostasis," and…wait for it…excreting. What I love about the foundational needs is that most people, when asked to name things humans can't live without, are quick to say air, food, water, and *sometimes* rest. Almost no one says pooping even though we all (hopefully) do it a few times a day and the idea of not doing when we *really* have to go is agonizing. And most people don't even know what homeostasis is, so someone spontaneously tossing that answer out there would be weird…unless that person is you, in which case you're awesome and a genius. For those of you who may not know, homeostasis refers to the delicate balance of the human body and all its many pieces working in concert so that we can go about our day normally. The thing about homeostasis is that it's remarkably unnoticeable by definition – it's when something knocks that balance out of place and the body cannot restore itself that the importance of homeostasis is revealed.

Given their universal application, these foundational needs are frequently used in marketing. I dare you to pick up the next magazine you come across and try to go from front cover to back cover without finding an ad for food, using food, or referencing food (e.g., friends eating at restaurant). Sometimes you'll see sex included in the foundational needs with people making a distinction between "sex" in a primal, propagate-the-species survival sense and "sexual intimacy" in a "let's cuddle and talk about our feelings" or "let's set the mood with candles and Michael Bublé" sense, the latter which is considered a "more advanced" need by the hierarchy proponents. In any event, we have all heard about the prevalence of sex, sexual imagery, and the notion that "sex sells" in advertising. Thus, another dare is to pick up the next magazine and try to make it cover to cover without finding a super hot person.

These kinds of basic or crude exploitations of foundational human needs are fine and dandy, and they seem to be working or else we wouldn't use them, but my favorite marketing executions are the ones that are a bit cleverer. Consider, for example, the case of NyQuil. You may be familiar with NyQuil (and its daytime partner DayQuil) as the drinkable or pill-form medicine perfect for your colds and pain relief. You may also be familiar with NyQuil as a sleeping aid that many people use to help knock them out at the end of a long day. Well, not surprisingly, Procter & Gamble, the maker of NyQuil, wasn't exactly comfortable with people associating the medicine with casual use as a sleeping aid for people looking for something to knock them out, particularly in an era in which so many people abuse prescription and non-prescription drugs. Yet, from a business perspective, the company likely didn't want to miss out on sales from consumers using the product as a sleeping supplement. The solution? Create a third product – ZzzQuil – explicitly marketed as a non-medicinal sleeping aid with the phrase "Non-habit forming" prominently displayed on the packaging. In doing so Vicks, the parent brand of the products, was able to capitalize on this very fundamental need – sleep – in a way that did not put the standing of its other consumer products at risk.

Safety Needs. Moving up the Maslow needs triangle we have those needs associated with safety. One way to think about this is that once human beings have mastered the art of simply existing they must do their best to keep themselves and their offspring safe…or else they aren't going to last very long. Playing with the idea that everything someone has could disappear in an instant is another pervasive marketing tactic. In fact, that fear is essentially what drives the entire insurance industry. This is what sells home alarm systems, anti-aging body creams, UV-blocking sunscreen, visits to the doctor, and more. It's also a reason people work: jobs provide security in that they provide resources one can dedicate to food, water, shelter, etc., for oneself and one's family. And, like anything else, the job market is a *market* – people who want jobs, people who provide jobs, and the delicate dance between the two that takes place in the market. Indeed, few things are as motivating (and as frightening) as a boss threatening an employee with unemployment.

In advertising, it sometimes simply takes bringing to attention safety risks people may not even realize they have in order to sell a product. In the past decade, the threat of identity theft increased exponentially as more consumers began shopping online. The term "identity theft" may have elicited blank stares in 1990, but now, most everyone is familiar with the term. Realizing a market opportunity, Postal Vault Secure Mailboxes jumped on the identity theft craze to point out to consumers that their identities are vulnerable if thieves steal their snail mail from their actual mailboxes as opposed to phishing for internet passwords and hacking into email accounts. The company is in the business of selling mailboxes designed so that when a mailman inserts mail the mail drops into a lower compartment in the mailbox that can only be accessed from the rear of the mailbox with a key. Simple enough. However, now is when I sarcastically remind everyone that postal mail service in the U.S. goes as far back as the Pony Express. Somehow identity theft was never problematic enough to warrant crazy new mailboxes, even when the only security for mail was a tired, tired horse who probably hated his life, but to each his own. Still, by preying on the worried and tapping into the topical identity theft trend, Postal Vault simply needed to remind people about this security risk to motivate their behavior…otherwise people might get a hold of your credit card numbers and your dirty magazines.

Love/Belonging Needs. Taking another step up the Maslow triangle we come to needs associated with love and belonging. From a hierarchical perspective, it makes sense that once we have our own fundamental affairs in order, we are in a place to reach out to and to connect with other people. Now, the anti-hierarchical folks would say, "But wait! Don't we rely on others to achieve our foundational needs?" Indeed, we do, but in those instances other people are a means to an end and not the end goal itself. On this love/belonging level, the end goal consists of the relationships with family, friends, and intimacy partners. A better argument for the anti-hierarchical camp would be a consideration of just how fundamental the desire to connect with others is. Physiologically, chemicals like oxytocin (not to be confused with oxycontin) and vasopressin (which are both technically neurohypophysial hormones) are automatically released within the body during events like childbirth, to promote the bonding between a mother and child, and during and immediately following orgasm, to promote the connection between sexual partners. So the next time someone tells you about how their one-night stand didn't mean anything to them, you can explain to them how, physiologically, that's actually not true.

Companies are so well aware of the importance of social needs that even the notion of a "family-owned" company is thought to create value in the minds of consumers. It's as if Jan in rural Oklahoma thinks, "Oh, how nice! Walmart is family-owned. Had it not been family-owned, I don't think I'd have shopped there." Silly Jan. Also consider how the tourism industry highlights how a vacation getaway helps bring the family closer together. Disney's marketing for its theme parks, cruises, and global tours relies heavily on the idea that families will "make memories" together. It's often surprising that moms across the United States aren't collapsing under the pressure some advertisers place on them with respect to making good decisions for their family given the amount of purchasing moms do for the household. "Are your kids getting enough Vitamin C? Drink our orange juice! Are the colors in your family's clothes as bright as they can be? Buy our detergent!" That's a lot of pressure. But perhaps the best recent examples of rapidly growing markets based on needs associated with love/belonging are online dating sites. Whether Match.com or eHarmony, OkCupid or Zoosk (…and my personal favorite: FarmersOnly.com, which, at the time of this book's printing, is a dating site designed for lonely farmers…no joke), online dating has evolved from being taboo in the late 90s and early 2000s when people like Oprah used to warn that they were death traps for creepy serial killers just waiting to lure in unsuspecting victims, to one of the primary methods for dating. And it's not just dating: consider the website AshleyMadison.com, a site designed to help married people have affairs with one another…and, despite sounding totally crazy, that's mild in comparison to some other sites. In short, companies realize the needs people have to connect with others and are certainly exploiting those needs. Of course, this shouldn't be surprising at all: this need for social connection is at the very heart of the "oldest profession in the world." Even OkCupid, Match, and eHarmony are informally categorized as hook-up site, dating site, and marriage site (in that order…unless you are on OkCupid, reader, in which case I *know* you're genuinely looking for the "love of your life" and not just your "love for tonight").

The next two steps on the Maslow triangle are a bit different from the prior three in that they are a bit more abstract and, therefore, can be a bit more difficult to grasp. The basic idea is this: once the *basic* foundational needs have been met as well as needs for affiliation and bonding, we can begin addressing needs for *validation* (both for the self and with respect to our relationships with others) and then *enhancement/creation*, moving beyond. Let's discuss each of them next...

Esteem Needs. The esteem-related needs involve a motivation to validate or come to a conscious understanding, both your own personal understanding (e.g., self-esteem, confidence, achievement) and the acknowledgement from others (e.g., respect from others), that you are a fulfilled person who has met his/her fundamental needs and then some; that you're not simply scraping to get by or flying by the seat of your pants. You've made it. Others wouldn't feel embarrassed inviting you to a party.

Examples from various markets that cater to esteem needs range from the status programs resulting from customer loyalty (think airline status from frequent flyer miles) or purchasing (think buying into a membership) to the various ways companies acknowledge the status of their customers. Consider, for example, American Express and its famous "Centurion Card" (a.k.a. "The Black Card" and "The World's Most Exclusive Charge Card"). The card, which is super exclusive and only offered to a small number of high-earning, influential folks, is essentially a signal that says, "Hey, you. You made it. Here's our exclusive card that validates your worth."

Self-Actualization Needs. The self-actualization needs are even headier than the esteem needs, but think of them as being akin to "enlightenment" or reaching nirvana: you've accomplished all that mere mortals need to do to get by, everyone agrees, and now you're free to create, to make new ideas, new beliefs, new solutions. Marketing examples catering to self-actualization needs include anything that allows consumers to be creative, to extend beyond the basic needs a product or service provides and into this realm of novelty, augmentation, and "extra." Consider the NIKEiD page at Nike.com. Nike, the world-famous shoe company, allows online shoppers to pick a base shoe and then to customize the shoe's upper styling and the midsole styling, as well as the colors for the upper design, the overlay, the famous swoosh, the shoe's lining, the laces, the midsole, the midsole topline, and even the print and color appearing on the tongues of the shoes. If we think about the needs a nice pair of Nike running shoes addresses, we can come up with a story for how the well-crafted shoes provide safety for the body and/or the self-esteem fulfillment given the social currency owning a pair of highly-coveted Nike shoes is likely to provide. So even if we stopped there, the shoes have addressed very important consumer needs. But no, Nike had to take it one step further and allow customers to customize their shoes, to add their own unique flair – this extra step moves us into the realm of self-actualization.

Another famous example of self-actualization in action is Build-a-Bear. If you are unfamiliar, Build-a-Bear is a store in which kids of all ages can build their own bear (or other stuffed animals) using the raw materials needed to make a stuffed animal. That is, the store provides the fabric of a stuffed animal, as well as the stuffing, a heart to record an audio message on and place inside, customized clothing for the animals, and even a station where you can name and register your stuffed animal into a database. It's pretty intense. Build-a-Bear is always a fun example to use with marketing students because essentially it is a company that charges its customers a premium *for the customers to make their own product!* Now, one could argue that the premium is paying for the experience of creating Theodore J. Teddy Bear III or Mittens the Kitten, but the cynic sees otherwise. In any case, it is this sort of higher involvement with a consumer product – addressing this self-actualization need – that Build-a-Bear does *so* well. A teddy bear from Build-a-Bear that *I* created is much more valuable to me than *the same exact teddy bear* that was pre-made; the former bear addressed my self-actualization needs while the latter bear did not.

Trio of Needs. Our friend Abraham Maslow was not the only scientist concerning himself with the study of human needs. Psychologist David McClelland proposed his own theory of needs, a theory that is now often referred to as **Need Theory** or the **Trio of Needs** given that there are three core needs postulated: 1) the Need for Achievement, 2) the Need for Affiliation, and 3) the Need for Power. McClelland's research was most often applied to organizational contexts, with McClelland philosophizing on how effective various leaders would be depending on which need(s) were driving their behavior. Rather self-explanatory, the Need for Achievement-oriented folks tend to enjoy succeeding at jobs and tasks, the Need for Affiliation-oriented folks enjoy social engagement and group interaction, while the Need for Power-oriented folks are motivated by positions of leadership and giving directions to others.

To reconcile this with Maslow's work, it is not difficult to see overlap between Love/Belonging Needs and Need for Affiliation, Esteem Needs and Need for Achievement, and Self-Actualization Needs and Need for Power. Just as Maslow's Needs can be directly applied to consumer products and services, so, too, can those of McClelland. Consider, for example, loyalty and reward programs like Panera's in which after so many purchases you get a free pastry item or specialty beverage. As silly as it may sound, there's a certain satisfaction of achieving this accomplishment, which is one reason why loyalty programs are so effective. As for affiliation, one of the primary motivations for purchasing particular brand names is to essentially buy our way into the network of people we perceive as fellow purchasers of that brand. Whether Louis Vuitton bags or Hollister clothing, BMWs or Harvard Business School (yep, I said it), sometimes we are more concerned with purchasing opportunities to affiliate with a particular network than with the product or service we are actually buying. As for power, essentially any product with "perks" caters to our needs for control. From the exclusive status programs of an airline or credit card company to the top-of-the-line Crest tooth whitener that whitens teeth in hours as opposed to days like the regular option, products and services that make us feel empowered help us satiate this need we have to be, quite bluntly, power mongers.

Whether we follow Maslow or McClelland or any of the other great scientists researching needs, a key takeaway is that human beings operate with these underlying needs that must be addressed, and that products/services that address those needs can be very valuable…and, therefore, sold for the right price.

Needs v. Goals. Psychologists often make a distinction between needs and goals with the understanding that while both are motivational, the latter tends to refer more to a desired end-state while the former can refer to both an end-state and the means to arrive at the desired end-state. Consider, for example, the need for Love/Belonging or, in McClelland's terminology, Affiliation. A goal we may have is to have a significant other or a close network of friends upon moving to a new city. Thus, we set a goal to engage with others more in social settings thereby fulfilling our need for affiliation/belonging. In laboratory settings, psychologists will often use a technique to motivate behavior that involves having participants compare their *current* or *actual* self to their *ideal* self. In the context of weight, for example, a participant may think of his current weight (actual self) and then his ideal weight (20 pounds lighter). Discrepancies between the actual and the ideal self tend to be motivating for individuals, so researchers often find that having participants simply imagine these preferred end states can lead them to work harder on tasks or otherwise take action they would not normally take. Thus, although goals and needs are *related*, they are not synonymous. Goals often tend to be more consciously considered, as the infamous SMART (specific, measurable, accurate, realistic and timely) goals approach suggests, but recent research on automaticity suggests they need not be consciously thought out (e.g., exposing people to party favors evokes an automatic goal to be more sociable).

Biological v. Learned Needs. One important distinction worth making on the subject of needs is that some needs tend to be rooted in our basic biology whereas others are learned via experience and/or culture. As previously mentioned, our needs for belonging, love, and affiliation are rooted in chemical reactions that occur naturally. Whether post-orgasm or post-birth, chemicals that promote bonding between sexual partners or between a mother and a child are released *automatically*. That's a biological process. The chocolate chip cookie and milk example, on the other hand, is an example of a learned need: the only reason you want milk after eating a chocolate chip cookie is that you have learned an association between the two such that you know milk tastes great with a warm chocolate chip cookie. Had you been born in a culture, like the one on our fictitious, undiscovered tropical island, in which the locals have never heard of chocolate chip cookies, it is highly unlikely that you would feel a *need* for milk upon eating a chocolate chip cookie. Some needs are so deeply engrained in our brain that they *feel* biological – it's difficult to imagine cookies without milk, and the fact that our mouth salivates and our brain so strongly wants milk after biting into a warm cookie makes it *seem* biological – but the fact of the matter is that this is a *learned* relationship.

Positive and Negative Motivation. So now that we understand a bit more about how needs and goals motivate our behavior, it's worth pointing out that not all motivation works in a *positive* direction. Put differently, our motivation for engaging in certain behaviors can be for positive reasons – e.g., I will work out every day so I can get ripped and star in a P90X infomercial – while the same behavior could be the result of motivation from a negative perspective – e.g., I will work out every day so I can avoid becoming morbidly obese and having health problems. The difference often comes down to how we frame a situation; just about any motivation can be positioned as positive *or* negative. One may get a job to earn money for a nice car (positive) or to avoid living on the street (negative). One may brush his/her teeth to have nice and shiny pearly whites (positive) or to prevent cavities (negative). To put these concepts in the language of academics, some of our motivation involves an **approach orientation** in which we engage in behavior to deliberately obtain certain stimuli, products, services, etc. (positive), while some of our motivation involves an **avoidance orientation** in which we engage in behavior to deliberately avoid certain stimuli, products, services, outcomes, etc. (negative). Although the behaviors in which we engage (e.g., working a job, brushing our teeth) and the event outcomes (e.g., earning a wage, having healthy teeth) may be the same regardless of the motivation's valence, some research suggests that the valence of how we frame our motivation can have short- and long-term effects on choice and behavior. For example, too many fear-based, negative motivations in the workplace could lead to lower workplace satisfaction and higher levels of stress than a more balanced or positive framing of work motivation.

Liking v. Wanting. Although it seems painfully obvious when I write it out, *liking* and *wanting* are not one and the same. For example, I may like tigers, but I don't want to own one. On the contrary, I may want a six pack so defined I can wash my clothes on them, but I may not like the work involved in maintaining abs of steel. To demonstrate this neurobiologically, researchers conducted a study with mice in which they examined the neural pathways associated with "liking" and "wanting" food. The researchers found that there are relatively few pathways associated with "liking" but several associated with "wanting," suggesting that it is much easier to get people to *want* your product but relatively more difficult to get them to *like* your product. As the researchers put it, "It's relatively hard for the brain to generate pleasure…it's easier to activate desire because the brain has several pathways available for the task." (Berridge 1996). This may be good news for us marketers: sometimes people will want a product without even knowing whether or not they like it. Yet this finding also represents a challenge: getting consumers to *like* your product is no small task.

Arousal of Motives. So now that you have learned a great deal about the innate needs that we, as humans, possess, and how those needs differ from and/or relate to "goals" and "liking," you might be wondering *when* those needs compel us to take action. That is, when do needs translate to the urges that direct and guide our decision-making and behavior? What I call an urge is also referred to as **arousal of motives**, which is essentially the point in time a need or needs trigger a motivation to behave.

The arousal of motives tends to come from one or more of several sources: cognitive arousal, emotional arousal, physiological arousal, and environmental arousal. **Cognitive arousal** refers to thinking; that is, if you are actively pondering about your health or your weight this may lead you to decide that now would be a good time for a jog outdoors. **Emotional arousal** refers to feeling; say you are feeling sad or lonely, well, this may trigger a trip to the nearest frozen yogurt stand to fill that void with the sweet taste of loving fro-yo. **Physiological arousal** refers to the internal states previously described, such as the feeling of hunger, that motivates behavior. **Environmental arousal**, on the other hand, refers to an external source of motivation – say the smell of freshly baking cookies – that triggers a motivation (e.g., tracking down a cold glass of milk). While some of these urges can be very explicit, such as the mental cognition of needing to purchase soap because you ran out, it is often the case that our urges emerge subconsciously, like scratching an itch or deciding to go to splurge on a gift because you're in a good mood.

*　　*　　*

By now, I hope you have managed to find some warm cookies and some cold milk to enjoy while reading this book. Maybe even some freshly-popped popcorn and a nice, thirst-quenching beverage to complement the salty, warm, buttery goodness would be a good snack? Or, if you are sophisticated and of age, a fine wine and cheese pairing?

So strong are some associations in our minds that thinking about or having one item creates a want or need for another. All this talk of needs, wants, likes, and motivation is fine and dandy, but how can a product or service trigger these urges in the first place? How do we even notice or pay attention to a stimulus enough for it to act as a trigger? Do we pay attention to every stimulus? How do we sense the stimuli in our environment, and why might we pay attention to some stimuli but not others? The next chapter addresses these questions and more.

APPLICATION QUESTIONS

1) What was the most recent purchase you made? Got it? Think deeply about *why* you purchased the product/service. What is the reason that comes to mind? Can you tie this easily back to one of the needs proposed by Maslow?

2) Some products can serve several needs. Consider hailing a cab from Point A to Point B. See if you can figure out how to tie a cab ride to each level of Maslow's Needs? Which are easy to relate? Which are not? What does that tell you about the service?

3) Some products, like greeting cards, exist solely to reinforce the social connections we have with others. What are other obvious examples of products/services that fulfill social needs? What are some non-obvious examples?

4) You are working on a service project for children in which you are trying to motivate the kids to engage in more physical activity to help them keep fit. Using concepts from this chapter regarding *goals* and motivation, give a specific example of something you could have the kids do to get motivated.

5) A quack on some talk show is talking about how babies *learn* to connect with their mothers. He contends that the urge to connect with others is a learned behavior, not a biological behavior, and goes on to say most if not all needs are learned. You are an audience member of the show. What might you say in the Q&A segment of the show that would put his theory into question?

6) Of the following examples, identify which ones are examples of approach orientation and which ones are examples of avoidance orientation:
  -Going to the gym to get ripped
  -Stockpiling household products because they're on sale now
  -Practicing cooking to impress your date
  -Working longer hours so you don't have to work the weekend
  -Taking your puppy out before heading out for a few hours
  -Automatically depositing a percentage of your income for retirement
  -Going to the gym to prevent gaining holiday weight

7) Drug addiction is a consumer behavior problem. Using the concepts of "liking" and wanting," discuss how drug users may like but not want, want but not like, want and like, or neither want nor like the substances that bring them harm.

8) Because we like more positive contexts than drugs, do the same exercise in question #7, but this time talk about liking and wanting in the context of dating and relationships (e.g., liking but not wanting, wanting but not liking, wanting and liking, neither wanting or liking). Should be interesting to hear your answers ☺

9) Casinos are arousing by design. Using the Arousal of Motives approach, give specific examples of how a consumer could experience each type of arousal in the context of a casino.

10) Think of your favorite retail store. What, if anything, happens in the store that triggers arousal in you? If the store currently isn't relying on one of the four arousal motives mentioned in the chapter, come up with a creative new in-store experience that could exploit this arousal motive.

Chapter 3 | Perception and Attention

Meet Mike…and Ike.

Now you may recognize this famous duo from vending machines, concession stands, and convenience stores, as Mike and Ike have been around since the 1940s, when the Just Born, Inc., candy company first hatched these fruit-flavored chewable candies. Just Born, Inc., is the same company responsible for the Easter season marshmallow favorites Peeps, as well, along with the mouth-scorching Hot Tamales chewable candy.

Mike and Ikes, the pluralized moniker by which the candy is often referred, come in five fruit flavors: cherry, lime, orange, lemon, and strawberry. Over the years there have been various extensions of the brand including Cherri and Bubb (cherry and bubble gum flavors), Lem and Mel (lemon and watermelon flavors), and some less-creatively-named extensions like Mike and Ike: Strawberries 'n Cream, Mike and Ike: Oranges 'n Cream, Mike and Ike: Tropical Typhoon, and others. In short, the Mike and Ike family has a long, varied, and rich history…kind of like the Kennedys.

But like any brand that has been around for a while, the Just Born, Inc., company decided that Mike and Ike could use a bit of an update (read: something probably needed to be done to jumpstart sales of an aging brand). Now, Just Born., Inc., could have simply updated the flavors of the candy and tweaked the design of the candy's iconic green box, but do you think you would have been able to taste the difference in the candy? Would you have even known that the packaging had changed?

These were probably the questions running through the brains of the Mike and Ike brand managers at Just Born., Inc., in early 2012. Shortly thereafter, in April 2012, Just Born, Inc., announced that Mike and Ike would be "splitting up" over "creative differences." The marketing campaign that ensued consisted of squiggly lines crossing through the name of either Mike or Ike in the familiar Mike and Ike titles on product packaging and on billboards around the country. So "Mike and Ike" became "~~Mike~~ and Ike" or "Mike and ~~Ike~~," apparently in an attempt to conjure up intrigue and suspicion with the hope that customers would perceive and pay attention to the changes.

I remember the first time I saw a box of Mike and ~~Ike~~ candy, squiggly line included. At first I thought, "Hmm, maybe a product defect?" and then went about my business. It was only after the second or third time upon seeing the squiggly-line product packaging that I thought something might be going on. Now, as a marketing guy, I decided to look into the situation, but I remember thinking at the time, "Would anyone else actually care about this as much as someone who lives for marketing?" It seemed unlikely.

It was then that I discovered that Mike and Ike were undergoing a revamp. It was unclear *why* the two had broken up, where the transition was going, or when (or if) it would ever end. "Maybe," I thought, "They're going to launch two separate candies – Mikes…and…Ikes?" I really had no clue, but worse, I realized that I just *didn't care*.

Now fast forward to summer 2013 when I just so happened to see a television commercial for, of all things, Mike and Ike. First, I was surprised to see a commercial for Mike and Ike, as I never recalled seeing a television commercial for the candy. The ad was presented as a trailer for a new action, thriller, spy-like movie in which two men–yes, actual human beings– played the roles of Mike and Ike. These two characters, apparently a onetime successful detective-like duo, had broken up and need to reunite to solve…something. What that is, well, we don't actually know. They are told to return to their roots while suspenseful music plays and shaky camera angles add to the excitement just like a real action movie trailer. Oh, yeah, and people are running and throwing candy around. I never recalled anything spy-like, action-movie-ish, or thriller-themed about the Mike and Ike campaign up to this point, so seeing this kind of commercial, which clearly seems to have a young, male target demographic in mind, seemed…strange (perhaps the most blatantly obvious example of their intended target was having Nelly, the one-time rap megastar, announce the reunion of Mike and Ike, but even that seemed off, as Nelly is "old school" for today's youth). Here's the commercial: http://youtu.be/7bHxN4G6Rus.

It's worth noting that, as this book's writing, the YouTube video of the commercial has only received 840,000 views despite being posted in March of 2013 and, of those views, only 550 likes, or roughly .06% – not exactly a smashing social media success. Compare that to some of the commercials made by friends of mine at the novelty company Vat19. Their latest video, "The Log Jam," a slow and steady love jam about fireplace candles featuring singing lumberjacks, was released less than 24 hours ago and has already amassed 42,000 views (5.82% like rate). If we assume a constant viewership rate for the next four months, the sultry jam will have been seen by over 5,040,000 people. Seem unreasonable? Two of Vat19's other videos have received 7.5 million (.68% like rate - http://youtu.be/zuDtACzKGRs) and 5 million (.34% like rate - http://youtu.be/kRcCWIuvDis) with far smaller budgets compared to Just Born, Inc.'s campaign. I belabor this point to remind you that marketing is also an art, and solid creativity can go a long, long way.

Back to the point…apparently there was a lot more to the Mike and Ike breakup saga, details I never came across. First, there was somewhere online where you could read about the "creative differences" of the two characters that led to the break up: Mike wanted to explore his art projects and Ike got into hip-hop. This seemed a bit disconnected from the spy-like thriller movie trailer, but then again the entire campaign seemed a bit disjointed. Second, there was some public confusion about a romantic relationship between the two, à la Bert and Ernie, which drew the ire of the Family Research Council who claimed, "It's just another subtle example of society chipping away at the value of marriage." That's a bit of a stretch, but the fact that the campaign was executed during 2012-2013, when the gay marriage debate was in the spotlight thanks to California's Prop 8 and the landmark Supreme Court case regarding the Defense of Marriage Act, it's only reasonable that *someone* would make the connection. This also made the campaign seem a bit difficult to understand.

Despite the seemingly pieced-together, hodged-podgedness of the "breaking up" campaign, the marketing folks at Just Born, Inc., are quick to point out how successful the campaign has been: according to the company, sales were up 7% in 2012 and the number of Facebook fans tripled to just under one million. What they fail to mention is that some of those "fans" on the Facebook site publicly lament about how the company, "Took one of the best candies that have been around since forever and ruined it," or that the new flavors are, "Too sour," (a comment that received 113 likes) or how, "The new flavor sucks…bring back the original" (which received 240 likes). In the comments regarding a promotion for the "Mike and Ike Movie Mania Sweepstakes," one commenter says he won't participate, "Unless the prize is a case of old Mike and Ikes." Clever. The skeptic in me also wonders whether the increased sales and social media growth were due to the "breaking up" campaign specifically or rather due to the fact that Just Born, Inc., was doing *something* instead of nothing.

In any event, one cannot dispute increased sales or increased Facebook fans, and naysayers are always going to be along for the ride. In spite of this, however, what is clear is that the "breaking up" campaign could have been carried out much better, with greater consistency throughout its various media executions and less confusion about what, exactly, was going on throughout the campaign.

Furthermore, although sales increased overall, the goal (as stated by senior marketing manager Donald Houston) was to make the brand "current and relevant with teens." I can't help but wonder how many of those new sales and Facebook likes came from teens v. adults.

Now before you think I'm totally poo-pooing on Just Born, Inc.'s Mike and Ike campaign, you should know that it's not that I *didn't* like or appreciate the campaign–it was different, for sure–there just seems to be so many missed opportunities that could have made the campaign *better*.

For the purpose of comparison, let's contrast the Mike and Ike revamp with a product revamp in the same candy category from a few years ago. Shortly after New Years in 2004, M&M's announced that the color had "gone missing" from its melt-in-your-mouth-not-in-your-hands candy-coated chocolate confection. For several months, *every* bag of M&Ms, from plain to peanut, consisted of only black and white M&Ms and black and white packaging. Literally *every* consumer touch point reinforced the campaign theme: the television commercials were in black and white (including this gem: http://youtu.be/FRHJzNNu0MA), the colorful M&M's NASCAR car was redesigned to be black and white, and print ads were absent of any color. Why? Well, Mars, the company that owns the M&M brand was planning to change the famous M&Ms colors and faced a choice: it could either change the colors in the regular bags overnight or, alternatively, could make the color change a spectacle, an opportunity to engage consumers.

The company opted for the latter, turning the black and white campaign in the "Great Color Quest," including a Willy Wonka-esque promotion in which somewhere in the world there would be six bags of colored M&Ms, each full of M&Ms of the same updated color (red, orange, yellow, green, blue, or brown). The finders of these bags would each win a new car painted the same color as the M&Ms they found along with $20,000. Not too shabby. Plus, from a PR angle, each time a new color was found, M&Ms was immediately catapulted back into the evening news; great, cheap coverage for the world-famous brand.

Unlike the Mike and Ike campaign, which, for the longest time, went unnoticed or noticed-but-uncared-about by most consumers, the M&Ms campaign was noticed immediately *and* cared about. Why? What's the difference? Well, first, it's difficult *not* to notice when a company known for colorful candy and packaging removes *every trace of color*. But second, and perhaps even more interesting from a psychological perspective, there was a very profound consumer insight at play in the M&Ms campaign: *everyone* has a favorite M&Ms color. Despite the fact that every M&M of the same variety (i.e., plain, peanut, peanut butter) tastes the same as any other M&M in that package, we often find ourselves saving a certain color for last or delighted when we pull a particular color out of the bag. Weird, right? The folks at Mars probably know this, though, so taking away *all* the color at once hit all of us where it hurt. Whether or not we would admit it, there's something *painful* about our favorite colors being taken away from us, and, dare we admit, a certain *longing* we have to get those colors back. *That* was the beauty behind the Great Color Quest campaign. So the Mike and Ike breakup campaign, although admirable, just wasn't as well thought through or executed as the M&Ms campaign.

So why, then, do I go on at length about these two candy campaigns? The answer is straightforward: by making a big deal out of their product reformulations, Just Born, Inc., and Mars *forced* consumers to pay attention to the changes in the products' taste, look, and experience, changes that were otherwise so subtle that consumers may never have noticed them. Is the cherry flavor of a new Mike and Ike drastically different from the cherry flavor of an older Mike and Ike? Was the red color after M&Ms Great Color Quest campaign noticeably different from the red color before the campaign? Perhaps. Perhaps not. However, with such elaborate marketing campaigns accompanying the changes, consumers would certainly be more likely to *perceive* these differences as being significant and substantial, and, at the end of the day, *perception* is all that matters.

Not surprisingly, companies don't always bring these kinds of product changes out into the open. In fact, sometimes companies do their very best to make sure consumers don't notice the changes they're making to a product or service. Consider, for example, how Dial once very quietly shrank its bar soap size by 10%, from 4.5 ounces to 4.0 ounces, while keeping the price the same. Or, staying within the candy industry, consider how Cadbury decreased its Dairy Milk chocolate bars in 2012 from 49 grams to 45 grams (roughly an 8% decrease) while still charging the same price. This happens every day, of course, and companies bet on the likelihood that we, the consumers, won't notice any difference. And why shouldn't they? Most of the time we have no idea that the products we know and love are changing right before our very eyes.

Other times, companies highlight changes only to evoke anger and protests from consumers. Consider Coca-Cola's attempt to steal back market share from Pepsi in the 1980s with the introduction of "New Coke." Meant as a new beverage to replace the original Coca-Cola, New Coke was despised by Coca-Cola loyalists who broke out their pitchforks and torches and demanded a return to the original Coca-Cola flavor, which the company swiftly did. Ever wonder where the name "Coca-Cola Classic" comes from? But what if Coke had quietly changed the formula of its beverage slowly or gradually over time? Would consumers have ever noticed?

From candy to colas, soap to cereals, consumer products shift and change with consumer tastes and sentiments all the time. But how do we perceive these changes? Do we even notice? Should we notice? Does a candy called by any other name taste as sweet?

*   *   *

Perception and reality are two, *very different* things. From a consumer behavior perspective it doesn't matter so much what *reality* is but rather what consumers *perceive reality to be*. When McDonald's added salads to its menu in an attempt to portray itself as a provider of wholesome, healthy choices, many consumers eagerly snatched up the leafy greens despite the fact that some salads, like the Premium Bacon Ranch salad with Crispy Chicken, contain more calories (390) than a cheeseburger (300), an Egg McMuffin (300), or even medium French Fries (380) according to McDonald's own nutrition information chart (as of July 2013). In fact, some recent academic research has shown that the inclusion of healthy options on a menu actually increases the purchases of *unhealthy* menu options, presumably because consumers "satisfy" health goals simply by *seeing* the healthier menu items.

In a different consumer example, consider Trop50 – the "healthier" version of Tropicana orange juice that has since spawned other juice-based beverages. Allegedly, Trop50 is simply the tasty Tropicana orange juice we all know and love…with more water. So, in theory, you could probably buy a full bottle of Tropicana orange juice, add your own water, and get a lot more orange juice for your buck, but thanks to a clever marketing campaign capitalizing on the health craze sweeping over middle-aged American women, Trop50 is perceived to be a novel, healthy, refreshing beverage as opposed to some watered-down Tropicana. Perception matters.

The purpose of this chapter is to discuss perception, attention, and the relationship between the two. **Perception** can be thought of us the way we, as humans, sense and interpret bits of incoming information via one of our many senses: sight, smell, taste, touch, sound…and ESP if you believe in that sort of thing (just kidding). The five senses may seem basic or even trivial; I mean we learn about them in kindergarten, right? But if you think about it, the five senses are critical to our survival. To tie into our prior discussion on fundamental needs, our senses allow us to recognize that we have these needs and, just as important, how to seek out ways to address those needs. When we're hungry, our sight helps us seek out a potential food source. Our sense of smell lets us know if that food source is rotten or not. Our sense of taste encourages us to eat things that taste good and to shirk revolting flavors. Our ears allow us to hear whether someone else is coming to potentially run off with our food. Our sense of touch allows us to beat away that would-be food thief in a way that his/her sense of touch teaches them never to mess with our food ever again. In sum, our senses are *adaptive*; the reason we are able to feel pain and to see so that we can move in a three-dimensional world is because these abilities aided our ancestors in survival and, as such, were passed on to us like hand-me-down clothes.

Psychologists contend that "perception" is a process involving three key stages. First, a **distal stimulus** is something present in one's environment – a bell ringing, light hitting an object. From there, the distal stimulus information is sent via sound waves, light waves, etc., to one of our sensory receptors (aka our eyes, ears, nose, mouth, nerve endings). When this information is conveyed to one (or more) of our sensory receptors, we call this the **proximal stimulus**. This makes sense, of course, as "distal" is a fancy word for "further away" while "proximal" is a fancy word for "nearby." This incoming information is then sent to the brain, our body's headquarters, where it is interpreted and made sense of. The brain's interpretation at this point is called a **percept**, and voilà, just like that, we have perception.

Here's a concrete example: A cute, adorable puppy runs into a room and starts barking. The dog barking would be a distal stimulus. From there, the sound waves travel from the dog to your eardrums while light bounces off the dog and travels to your eyes. This stimulation of your sensory system by sound waves and light waves would be considered proximal stimuli. Then, the nerves connecting your eardrum and eyes to your brain will trigger the lightning-fast neural activity that leads the brain to interpret the idea, "Dog barking." Congratulations! You have just perceived a dog barking!

Some additional terminology is often incorporated into perception language involving the distal stimulus, the proximal stimulus, and the percept. Specifically, researchers refer to **exposure, sensation**, and **attention**. Exposure involves the initial exposure to stimuli in one's environment (distal stimuli). Sensation involves the process by which information from the distal stimulus reaches one or more of the body's senses (proximal stimuli). And finally, attention refers to the point when the brain attempts to make sense of the information coming from the proximal stimulus (i.e., the percept). In a few moments I'll argue that the brain need not always pay *conscious* attention to incoming information, an idea fairly well supported by psychologists and neuroscientists who study attention and consciousness, but for now, it's useful to know the common language of perception.

It is worth pointing out *why* perception is in the "Self" section of this book. Although the majority of stimuli may start in our surroundings, it turns out that this last step (i.e., making sense of the world in our brain) is very important because the brain often does some pretty weird things that affect how we experience the world around us. Consider, for example, the following image:

There are no lines drawn defining the edges of the triangle you see; in fact, who's to say there's even a triangle to begin with? In reality, there is no triangle, just three Pac-Man shaped circles. However, our brain perceives there to be a triangle. Similarly, look at the picture of the letter C covered by a box. Is it a letter C? Or is it just two separate arcs with a conveniently placed rectangle? We have no way of knowing, but our brains can't help but see the letter C. Weird, isn't it?

Furthermore, no two people will perceive every stimulus in the *exact* same way. Because we all filter incoming information through our sensory experiences and our brain, there are plenty of opportunities for that original stimulus to be altered in processing. For example, if I were from a culture that did not use the standard Latin alphabet – say a Chinese or Arab culture – I may not see the "C" in the example above. So we could both be looking at the same stimulus but interpreting it quite differently.

So if we can accept that our brains don't always interpret the world as it *actually* is (i.e., reality) but, instead, experiences the world as we *perceive* it to be, then we can begin to understand how to apply perception in the domain of consumer behavior. Perception is the reason people see the green, flower-like logo of BP and believe that it is an environmentally friendly company despite the catastrophic BP oil spill (Deepwater Horizon spill) in 2010 that devastated areas along the Gulf coast and is considered the largest marine oil accident to date. Perception is the reason generic soda manufacturers use a very familiar red color in the packaging of their cans and boxes, along with a script typeface, with the hope that consumers will perceive the generic soda's taste to be more like the Coca-Cola its trying to emulate. Perception is the reason that reading "Made in Germany" on a product assures excellent quality while reading "Made in China" makes us worry about shoddy manufacturing or unsafe chemicals, even without any knowledge or evidence regarding the specific products in question. To reiterate an important point: what matters is *not* what "actually is," but rather "what consumers believe it to be."

The Five Senses. In kindergarten you spend a lot of time doing fairly basic things – learning the alphabet, counting to 100, making pasta jewelry, and talking about the five senses. Below is a primer on the five senses with just enough detail to make you smarter on the subject so that you can be the envy of strangers at the next cocktail party you attend:

Sight. Vision is often considered to be the sense responsible for taking in the majority of information our brain processes. The area of the brain responsible for processing visual information, the visual cortex, is located at the very back of our brain in an area known as the occipital lobe. Some of the most fascinating brain research in recent years involves patients with damage to their visual cortex who possess a scotoma, or a hole in their visual field as a result of the brain damage. Researchers have found that patients are able to respond to visual stimuli that they do not consciously see (e.g., correctly identifying whether or not people were smiling or frowning in images shown in their blindspot – called "blindsight"), contributing to the important idea that perception *need not be consciously attended to* to affect our choices and behaviors. This idea, seemingly minor, is actually the foundation for priming research and theories regarding how subtle exposure to a stimulus can have significant consequences for downstream choices and behavior. The human eye can "see" wavelengths between 390 and 700 nm, and the photoreceptors of the eye – rods and cones – are specialized such that cones are great processors of color while rods are better adapted for detecting movement. That's why any deficiency of cone photoreceptors tends to result in colorblindness. Also, rods outnumber cones by 20:1.

Smell. Smelling, also known by the fancier term olfaction, is the sense by which sensory receptors in the nose combine with chemical compounds floating in the air that represent an "odor." The chemical information stimulates the olfactory receptors, which, in turn, send signals to the olfactory bulb of the brain, which is located not too far behind the nose in one's head. The identification of an odor's chemical structure and its classification/categorization actually take place in separate brain areas. Furthermore, there seems to be a connection between the olfactory areas of the brain and the hippocampus, a part of the brain implicated in memory, and the limbic system, which is implicated in emotion and memory. This may explain why certain odors evoke very strong memories and feelings. In fact, some researchers contend that if people encode information when a certain smell is present, say freshly-baked popcorn, then those same people would have an easier time recalling information if the smell of freshly-baked popcorn is present during the recall. Fascinating. Other research shows that wafting in smells of citrus leads people to subconsciously leave their workspace cleaner than other people who did not have citrus smells present. Later, in the chapter on Context, Environment, and Situation, I'll discuss in detail how companies use odor to their advantage without you even realizing it! One final interesting point: the concept of a 'flavor' relies equally on both taste *and* smell, which is probably why your mom told you to hold your nose when eating yucky-tasting vegetables as a kid so you wouldn't taste it. However, quite different from taste (which involves only five possible variations), the human nose can smell *hundreds* of different smells. That may sound impressive, but consider this: a human nose has about 5 million receptors while a Bloodhound has over 300 million receptors. Indeed, when it comes to a sense that dominates information retrieval, smelling is to a dog as vision is to a human.

Taste. I was surprised to learn that taste (fancy name: gustation) boils down to just five "basic tastes." I honestly had no idea how I made it into my twenties without knowing the five basic tastes: sweetness, sourness, saltiness, bitterness, and umami. The first four tastes are fairly well known. Even right now, you can probably imagine the sweetness of cotton candy, the sourness of a lemon, the saltiness of butter popcorn, the bitterness of an orange peel (...yep, that's bitter – next time you eat an orange, taste the peel...you'll probably never do it again). What is less well known, at least to Western palates, is umami. Deriving from a Japanese word for "good taste," it is unsurprising that the taste is often found in Eastern cuisine. The best way I can help you mentalize the taste is to have you imagine tasting soy sauce. The taste isn't exactly bitter and it's certainly not sweet or sour – so by process of elimination, whatever taste you're left with when you're eating soy sauce, that's umami. In much the same manner that the nose is able to smell the chemical compounds that wind up in our nasal passages, our tongue is equipped with thousands of taste buds that are each, in turn, equipped with dozens of taste receptors. As with smelling, the chemical compounds in food are detected by the taste receptors, which is what then produces the taste sensation. Chemically speaking, it is no surprise that sugars contribute to sweetness, acidity to sourness, and sodium ions to saltiness. Bitterness and umami are a bit more complicated in their chemical composition, but rest assured that every taste you have your mouth is the result of a chemical reaction party. Because of this chemical connection, food scientists and others who research taste often compare food items to standard representations of the basic tastes, like sucrose for sweetness, using an index (e.g., fructose, a common food sugar, is almost 50% sweeter than sucrose). You may also wonder why you love cherry-flavored candy but hate cherries or love tomato-based ketchup but can't stand eating tomatoes. Well, part of the reason for this is that *taste* and *flavor* are actually two very different ideas. Taste is the actual chemical connection between a food item and your taste buds whereas flavor incorporates not just the taste chemical reaction but also the texture, aroma or odor (olfactory/smelling sense), and things like the warmth/coolness and the actual temperature of the food. So while I love cherry cough drops (seriously, I eat them like candy in winter), I would never, ever, ever eat a fresh cherry. Oh, and I have bad news. It turns out that we lose nearly half of our taste receptor cells by the time we graduate high school. This explains why my grandma only ever eats sweets…she can't taste anything else. Oh, grandma!

Sound. As a musician, I know that not all sound is created equal and not everyone hears sound in quite the same way. Take my father, for example, whom I love dearly but who sings like the Bee Gees, in a high falsetto voice all the time, sometimes on key, sometimes off. He likes to claim that when he was in 6th grade he received a standing ovation after performing the song "Monday, Monday" (by the band The Mamas and the Papas) for a school talent show, but my mom likes to say the audience was standing up because they were getting up to walk out. At the end of the day, some people can recognize musical pitches, others cannot. Some can distinguish musical pitches so well that they can identify a note just by hearing it. The human ear is capable of hearing a range of frequencies between 20 to 20,000 Hz, but this, of course, varies as a function of many things – physical conditions, age, wear and tear for those people who enjoy attending death metal concerts. One interesting consumer phenomenon that emerged in the past few years was the creation of ring tones of such a high frequency that only young people could hear them. Thus, junior high kids and high schoolers would set their ringtones and text message alert sounds to this high frequency so that they could communicate with friends during class without their teachers (whose ears were older and poorer in comparison) knowing. Of course, there are other examples of how sound is incorporated in consumer contexts. Just yesterday at Bed, Bath, and Beyond, I saw a dog-training device that relied on high-pitch frequencies to help Fido or Fluffy learn where it's okay to potty and where it's not. But beyond using hard-to-hear pitches for consumer purposes, there are other subtle ways in which sound affects consumer behavior. One oft-quoted use in the context of casinos is the familiar dinging sound emitted from the machines, a.k.a. the sound of "winning." If you want people to keep feeding the machines money, you want them to think people are winning all around them. Translating this to a non-gambling domain, makers of popular online and mobile games often use sounds increasing in pitch per each accomplishment in a game (e.g., clearing a row of colored jewels, candy, etc.), which subconsciously leads users to wonder, "Just how high can this sound go?!" Anything to keep you playing longer and, consequently, viewing the advertisements embedded within the game. Later, in the chapter on Context, Environment, and Situation, I will discuss how stores use music to influence your shopping without your conscious realization…if that's not music to your ears, I don't know what is.

Touch. Touching is such a common sense that we often take it for granted. Whereas we know when we are putting something in our mouth or when a new odor has found its way to our nose, we're *always* touching something, whether it's our feet on the ground, our rears in our seat, or even our skin in water, it's almost impossible not to touch something. This sense of touch works via a variety of receptors – chemoreceptors (chemicals), mechanoreceptors (mechanical pressure), nociceptors (pain or "noxious" stimuli), thermoreceptors (relative temperature change) – which convert the incoming information into neural signals that travel up the spine to the brain where they are processed in what is probably one of the most fascinating ways. Within the brain is an area referred to as the primary somatosensory cortex, which is the area of brain implicated in sensory processing. And located within this primary somatosensory cortex is what is referred to as the cortical homunculus, which can be thought of as a mini-representation of the entire human body – no joke – it's like a little area of the brain that is a miniature model of you. Now, it's not that there is a tiny Barbie or Ken version of you in your brain; no, instead there exist "neuron concepts," areas of the brain that activate and correspond to particular areas of the actual physical body. This is part of the reason why people who lose limbs often feel the presence of a "ghost limb," as although they may have lost the actual physical limb, the collection of neurons associated with that area of the body are still intact. Touch influences consumer behavior in weird ways, too. Consider, for example, the research that shows how people will say that the *same* water tastes better when drinking it from a sturdy plastic cup instead of a flimsy plastic cup or how the *same* wine tastes better when drinking it from a glass instead of a plastic cup. However, this effect *only* works for people who later report not being "touch snobs," i.e., people who pay attention to touch. So, without even realizing it, what we touch actually can affect our perceptions.

It is only fitting that we use our five "senses" to make *sense* of the world around us. These physiological, chemical, and neuroelectrical processes are carrying on, with great coordination, automatically this very second and every second of our long lives. Most of the time, we don't even notice or pay explicit, conscious attention to what these remarkable senses are doing. Other times, we *do* notice…we pay "attention."

Attention. We live in a world where it's very difficult to pay attention. Most people now walk around with their heads down staring at some smartphone and checking text messages, emails, and Facebook among other things. Thus, understanding the definition of attention is relatively easy because we live it every single day. **Attention** can be thought of as the cognitive process by which we deliberately focus on a particular stimulus in our context or mind while simultaneously blocking out other stimuli. The word "attention" derives from Latin where it meant "to pay heed to," and is the basis for words in other, related languages like French in which the word "attendre" means "to wait for," "to expect," and "to pay attention." Just like an *attend*ant *attends* to the needs of a king or queen, when we "pay attention," we *attend* to a particular stimulus.

However, you may notice that it is quite difficult for our brains to attend to *every* stimulus in our context simultaneously. Right now you may be sitting somewhere where there is music playing. The chair you are in is either very comfortable and padded or very painful and wooden. Perhaps there is a smell of something fresh baking nearby or a smelly person who clearly forgot to put on deodorant today (or ever). Maybe you have minty gum in your mouth or maybe you have that kind of breath you get when you sit somewhere for a long time with your mouth closed. Your eyes are affixed to the words on these pages, but I bet that just beyond the book something is moving around – people, children, flowers blowing in the wind. When I list each of these separately and you go through each one in your head you are able to think of and pay attention to each. But try paying attention to all these stimuli simultaneously. How does that work out for you?

Although our bodies are amazing perceivers of information, if we attempted to process *all* the incoming information consciously, our brains would explode. There's simply way too much information in our context, not to mention all the crazy thoughts going on in our mind already, that paying attention to everything would be debilitating.

Fortunately, we have evolved to process a lot of information automatically and to attend to only those stimuli that demand or require our attention. Often times we won't even notice incoming information unless that information meets or exceeds a particular threshold. To understand this, I introduce the concept of the Just Noticeable Difference (JND). A **Just Noticeable Difference (JND)** (a.k.a. **Weber's Law** and **differential threshold**) refers to the *smallest* change possible in a stimulus from a starting point to an end point that is *detectable*. For example, say you and I are in a room with the lights dimmed (ooh là là!) and I ask you to turn up the lights ever so slowly. The light switch is a dial that, when you turn clockwise, increases the strength of the lights. You may have to turn the dial a good deal before I am convinced that the lights have become stronger. Similarly, we have all been in the backseat of a car and asked someone up front to turn the music up or down only to yell at them minutes later because we didn't notice a change even thought he/she swore they turned the dial. Stimuli are changing around us all the time – noise levels, temperatures, odors, seat textures, etc. – but unless those changes are large enough we may not pay any attention to them.

The concept of Just Noticeable Difference is summarized by the equation below (a.k.a. the **Weber Fraction**):

$$\frac{\varDelta I}{I} = k$$

This is about when my non-math folks freak out. Don't worry. I'll explain what this equation represents. I represents the original intensity of the stimulus. So let's say that on a 20-level radio dial, our radio was initially set to 6. $\varDelta I$ represents the unit change needed to detect a difference (i.e., *this* is the JND at a particular level of intensity I). So let's say that the dial has to be turned up 2 notches or down 2 notches before we even notice that the radio is louder or quieter, respectively. This means $\varDelta I$ would be equal to 2. k, then, represents the constant in the domain of this radio that tells us the % change that needs to happen in order for us to notice a change in the volume of the radio *regardless of the dial's starting point*. In this example k = .33 (2 / 6 = .33). So if, at a different time, the initial setting on the radio was 12, and someone says to turn up the radio, we would need to turn the dial up 4 notches to 16 to notice a difference (12 * .33 = 4, and 12 + 4 = 16). Weber's Law doesn't work *all* of the time, but it does explain why we only have to whisper in a library to get someone's attention but need to yell at a rock concert to do the same. The point at which we will notice a difference in a stimulus (i.e., the just noticeable difference) is relative to the initial intensity I of the stimulus.

When M&Ms decided to change the colors of its M&Ms in 2004 it could have very easily changed the dyes overnight without telling anyone, but the changes were so tiny that it seems unlikely that anyone would have noticed. However, Mars could have engaged in JND testing, altering the intensity of the hues used for the candy to levels that focus groups may have said they noticed. Instead of drastically altering M&Ms colors in this way, Mars opted to go with the Great Color Quest campaign – taking color away (talk about a noticeable difference) and reintroducing newer, brighter colors just months later.

A concept related to the Just Noticeable Difference is that of the absolute threshold. The **absolute threshold** simply refers to the absolute minimum amount of stimulation that must be present for a stimulus to be sensed in the first place. For example, when you cook dinner and add a particular spice you may find that one shake of the bottle produces no noticeable difference in the taste of your dish. You add another shake. Nothing. Three shakes. Nada. Finally, 20 shakes later you can taste the faintest trace of the spice. You've just surpassed the absolute threshold. Now, from this point on, any *noticeable* difference in the intensity of the spice's taste corresponds to a just noticeable difference (differential threshold).

Common Methods for Getting Attention. When we are babies, all we had to do to get our parents' attention was cry. If I were trying to sell you something, I imagine crying in front of you would be an effective way to get your attention. It would also be really, really weird. Thankfully, there are other ways by which marketers can capture the attention of consumers. Here are a few:

- **Intensity of stimuli.** As addressed above, increasing or decreasing the intensity of a stimulus beyond a differential threshold is likely to capture the attention of an individual.

- **Contrast.** Related to the intensity of a stimulus, contrast is less about gradual change and everything about drastic change. Clashing colors, super loud commercials during quiet television shows (the worst), and tart, palate-cleansing sorbets between appetizers and your main course are all examples of using contrast to capture attention.

- **Movement.** Remember earlier when I said that the human eye has about 20 times more rod cells than cone cells and that rod cells are more concerned with detecting movement while cone cells are optimized for color processing? Well, it turns out that the human eye is well adapted to detect movement. This helps us see the boogeyman in the dark (hope you're not reading this at night) and is why companies incorporate dynamic billboards and pay people to stand on street corners twirling signs bearing their name. It is also the reason that a spider scurrying across our wall immediately captures our attention (I am really on a roll with these creepy examples right now – sorry, reader!).

- **Surprise.** I remember the first time I saw a talking trash can at McDonald's. It was in the mid-1990s in rural Illinois. The reason I remember is because I almost had a heart attack thinking that some crazy person had climbed into the trash can and was going to pull me in, too. When events occur that we do not expect or that violate our scripts/schemas of the way things *should* be, we tend to pay attention to them. In a way, Google's surprising simplicity was a pleasant surprise when it came onto the web search scene following years of Yahoo!'s cluttered web experience. Surprise is also the unfortunate tool terrorists use to get attention, striking when and where people are not expecting an attack. You should know that one of my bucket goals in life is to get a large group of people together, fly to a nation known for harboring terrorists, go to a crowded marketplace and conduct the largest flash mob dance ever to a medley of ABBA songs to demonstrate to these morons that there are far better ways to get people's attention than killing innocent people. I'm smelling a Fulbright idea in case anyone is interested.

- **Size.** Despite what people say, sometimes size *does* matter. Whether extremely large – like 7-11's Double Big Gulp (which allegedly holds 200% more than what an average adult's stomach is capable of holding) or Starbucks' Trenta size (31 oz.) – or extremely small – like Mac's extremely light MacBook Air or Dairy Queen's "mini" size – companies often tout the size of their products to capture our attention. A friend in San Francisco, when describing a man she was dating, once described him as "Starbucks tall," because even though he thought he was tall, he was objectively short. Let's all try to work "Starbucks tall" into day-to-day conversation, okay?

- **Involvement.** Creating opportunities for customers to engage in some meaningful way with a product or service is, almost by definition, likely to get them to pay attention. A tactic often used at theme parks to shift people's attention away from the miserably long lines, often in the blazing sun, are interactive games the guests can play as they proceed through the queue. For example, Disney offers a game called "Scuttle's Scavenger Hunt," in which everyone's favorite (and possibly intoxicated) seagull needs help finding his beloved doodads and thingamabobs from the human world on interactive television screens that the people will pass by while they are in line for The Little Mermaid: Ariel's Undersea Adventure. My wish in life is that the Transportation Security Administration (TSA) would copy this strategy and create an interactive game for the security line at the airport. Maybe the game could even teach people the rules of what is and isn't allowed so by the time we all get to the scanners everyone will have already thrown out their liquids exceeding 3 oz. instead of holding up the line. A man can dream, I guess.

The relationship between perception and attention is a tricky one. Sometimes we perceive things we don't pay attention to. In rare instances, such as those times we *think* we heard our name or *think* we saw a dark shadow walking down our hall at night we may pay attention to things we did not *actually* perceive. But typically, in consumer contexts, perception and attention work together to help us to understand what various products and services have to offer and, consequently, our preferences for these products and services.

Perceptual Maps. Savvy marketers know very well that perception matters more than reality, so it is not uncommon for companies to use perceptual mapping as a way to visualize how consumers perceive their particular products, services, and/or brands. A **perceptual map** can be thought of as a visual tool that portrays products, services, or brands, and their relative position to competing products, services, or brands, as measured on key attributes that are important or valuable to consumers. Each attribute represents one dimension, with the simplest maps being unidimensional (rare), the most-frequently used maps being two-dimensional, and complex maps incorporating three or more dimensions. An example perceptual map of the candy industry is included here for your reference.

Creating the map. Before interpreting the map we need to first consider the inputs and how the map is created. First, a marketer may have asked consumers to identify "Which attributes or characteristics are most important to you when you think about candy?" and subsequently "How important is [attribute] to you when considering a candy to eat?" From there, the researchers would have looked at the data in terms of frequency and importance to determine which two attributes seem to be the most important to consumers – in this case, the sourness/sweetness of the candy and the texture (soft v. hard/crunchy) – and then designated the former as the X-axis (horizontal) and the latter as the Y-axis (vertical). Then, the

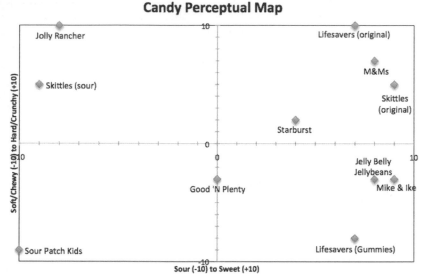

researcher would have generated a list of candy on the market and asked consumers to identify how the candies rate on a list of attributes, including our two key attributes of interest, on a scale. These measures represent how consumers *perceive* the candy on the respective attributes. Using this data for each candy, the researchers could then plot a perceptual map for the candy industry like the one above. Hooray for marketing research!

Interpreting the map. This is the fun part. The perceptual map gives us a visual representation of the candy industry insofar as sweetness and texture are concerned. It should be no surprise that in the *candy* industry most of our candy winds up on the "sweet" side of the map. One way of thinking about this as a marketing strategist is that there seems to be a *lot* of competition in the sweet candy space. You'll notice there are really only three candy options on the sour side of the map with the not-really-sweet, not-really-sour, gross-black-licorice tasting (unless, like my mom, you think this tastes good) Good 'N Plenty candy falling in no-man's-land. Within that sour space, it seems like candy is either really hard and crunchy, like the teeth-breaking Jolly Ranchers and the slightly-crunchy-then-chewy Skittles Sour, or soft and gummy, like Sour Patch Kids. Thus, if you wanted to enter the candy market, this map suggests that it might be wise to create a new candy with the consistency of say Starbursts or Mike & Ikes but with a super sour flavor.

Mapping ideal points and Consumer Clusters. In addition to creating a perceptual map, marketing can also create a **preference map** in which consumers are asked to identify their *ideal points* – in this case their ideal level of sour/sweet and their idea level of soft/chewy and hard/crunchy.

We can then map an x-y coordinate that represents each of our consumers and his/her ideal point. The preference map below represents the ideal sour/sweet and soft/hard levels of our 50-person sample:

Candy Preference Map

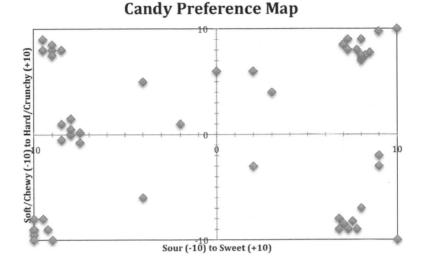

There are a few things to notice about the preference map above. First, we can see that there are several "consumer clusters," that is, areas where the ideal points of many consumers are similar. There appear to be five clusters – one in the lower-left hand corner (super sour, super soft/chewy), one in the left center (super sour but neither too soft/chewy nor too hard/crunchy), one in the top-left corner (super sour and super hard/crunchy), one in the top-right (super sweet, more hard/crunchy), and one in the bottom-right (super sweet, super soft/chewy).

Here's where things get interesting. If we superimpose or layer the two maps on top of each other, we get an even better understanding of the candy market. Of the five clusters, four of them seem to be served quite well by existing candies (e.g., Jolly Ranchers and sour Skittles likely meet the needs of the top-left cluster; original Lifesavers, M&Ms, and original Skittles are all duking it out for the top-right cluster). But look at the cluster in the left center of the preference map. If we refer back to our perceptual map we see that no company has a candy playing in this area. This cluster's preferred super sour but not-too-soft/chewy, not-too-hard-crunchy preference is not addressed! Thus, it might be smart for someone to launch a candy like this. Notice hard Jolly Ranchers have the right amount of sourness to them but are far too hard/crunchy. Maybe Hershey's, Jolly Rancher's parent company, should consider developing a new product extension with the consistency of Starburst but the same sour, tart flavors for which it is already known? [No joke. I just Googled and found that Hershey's just launched a brand new product, Jolly Rancher Bites: Sour, in March of 2013 that fits this exact proposed product – I told you I know a thing or two about marketing!]

Perceptual and preference mapping's advantages and disadvantages. The major upside of the mapping techniques should be clear: the maps allow marketers to visualize a market or industry with great ease and to gain insight on potential competition, market opportunities, and current positioning effectiveness. The downside to the mapping approach is that the process doesn't really shed any light on *why* consumers perceive the products, services, or brands the way that they do. To understand those reasons we would have to dig a bit deeper. Another slight problem is that perceptual and preference maps, unlike real perceptions and preferences, are static. Consumers are bound to change their thoughts and feelings about products, and competitors are equally likely to change up their positioning plans for their respective products. So the maps really just give us a snapshot of the market at a given point in time. In spite of these limitations, perceptual and preference maps are simple, useful, and…dare I say…*fun* tools for marketers to use.

The subjectivity of perceptions. Perceptual maps are based on averages across groups of consumers or particular consumer segments, as perceptions of the same stimuli vary from person to person. Some common subjective perceptions in consumer behavior involve perceived quality, perceived price, and perceived risk. **Perceived quality** refers to the subjective belief that a product will be able to deliver on its promises regardless of its *actual* ability to do so. Perceived quality is the reason that we prefer purchasing name-brand paper towels, like Bounty, instead of the generic store brand. We *perceive* Bounty paper towels to be of a superior quality – more absorbent, stronger – than the store brand. In reality, it could be the case that both paper towel varieties are manufactured at the same plant using the same materials or even that the generic brand is better in market testing of the paper towels than the branded paper towels. Reality doesn't matter, however, because we buy based on our perceptions.

A related concept, the **perceived price/quality relationship** explains the phenomenon in which we, as consumers, tend to link higher prices with greater quality despite this not always actually being the case. Indeed, part of the reason we think Bounty's paper towels are better than the generic brand is because the branded towels cost more. "Certainly they must be charging me more for *something*," we think. This quirk exists in just about every product/service category you can imagine. You see a chicken breast at the deli that costs $5 and another that costs $10 – they look identical in that they are the same size and appear to have very little fat – yet something inside of you says that the $10 *must* be better. T-shirts selling for $80-$100 apiece at stores like Saks and Neimans are probably the greatest farce of all – they are made from the same materials using the same printing processes as shirts at Target or Walmart yet cost over 10 times as much – someone, somewhere is getting a nice premium. This doesn't mean you shouldn't buy nice things from time to time to show off that you can afford it (or whatever self or social goal that might be underlying the purchase), but just because something costs 10 times as much does *not* mean that its quality is 10 times better.

Finally, **perceived risk** refers to the cost-benefit analysis that we conduct in our heads in which we compare the resources that we must expend to the gain(s) that we believe we are likely to receive for doing so and the likelihood or uncertainty of those outcomes. For example, despite knowing that the odds are never in their favor, millions of people participate in lotteries each day. In this case, the perceived risk is fairly low because the cost of a lottery ticket is cheap – typically $1 or so. Say a lottery increased the price of its ticket to $50 or $500. The chance of winning $425 million (which, incidentally, is the value of the PowerBall lottery as of this chapter's writing) is certainly appealing, even if a ticket costs $500, but your odds of winning are *so* small that the perceived risk is just far too much. Mind you, your *actual* odds of winning the game haven't changed from when the ticket only cost $1, but your *perceived* risk is much greater in the $500 instance compared to the $50. Perceived risk also changes as a function of expertise or experience. I love traveling to Europe, and I speak enough French and Spanish that I can get by in Western Europe without any problems. I do not speak Mandarin, however, so if I am considering two vacations, one to Western Europe and one to China, both priced around the same amount, I may perceive the Chinese trip to be a much riskier purchase than the trip to Europe because of my lack of knowledge. Chances are my trip to China would be a great time, yet my perceived risk leads me to go on the Western European trip.

In sum, our perceptions dictate our choices and behaviors even when those perceptions are not accurately reflections of reality. Thus, as marketers and as consumers, it is worthwhile to pause from time to time, to take a step back, and to ask ourselves the question, "Are we seeing the world the way that it really is or as we perceive it to be?" Most of the time, the answer is obvious.

*   *   *

M&Ms and Mike & Ike were able to take considerable changes to their core product and make them the centerpiece of rather extensive marketing campaigns, one (M&Ms) better integrated throughout its various executions than the other (Mike & Ike). However, in both examples, the companies were successful at making consumers perceive and pay attention to the deliberate product changes: brighter colors, better flavors, new packaging. Although there will always be some naysayers, some consumers who prefer hanging on to the past, Mars and Just Born, Inc., managed to successfully transition their brands without too much flak (à la New Coke).

Just Born, Inc., could have really played up its Mike and Ike breakup campaign to garner more attention for the candy. For example, why not sponsor an arm-wrestling competition to air on Esquire or ESPN? If the target demographic were young men then staging this kind of Mike v. Ike competition on the same networks that run sports and shows like American Ninja Warrior would have been a cheap, easy, effective way to reach the intended target. Now that I write it out, why not have designed the new boxes to read "Mike **VS.** Ike" to encourage the competitive element instead of the confusing scribble-through? People could decide which camp they supported, which would have given the company greater opportunities to come up creative back-stories for the two characters and what they were up to. An interactive quiz could ask the question, "Mike vs. Ike: Which one are you?" – kind of like those personality quizzes in magazines you can't help but do. Sports-related tie-ins could have seen Mike and Ike taking different sides in major athletic showdowns like the World Series, the Super Bowl, etc. Ultimately, the two could have decided they were better together, which could have been a campaign unto itself, just as M&Ms turned its return to color period into the "Chocolate is Better in Color" campaign (see a great commercial from that campaign here: http://youtu.be/4puQAC2UAY4).

Coincidentally, as I write this book, Yahoo! is currently executing a marketing campaign that will result in a brand new logo for the internet company for the first time since the company started 18 years ago. Could Yahoo! have simply updated its logo overnight? Sure. Instead, the company's site is featuring a new logo every day for a month until the new logo is revealed at the end of the campaign. In doing so, Yahoo! hopes more people will not only perceive a change but also *pay attention* to it and, if they are lucky, tell their friends and engage in online discussions, too.

Understanding how consumers perceive products and services is an important first step, and capturing attention in an increasingly complex and busy world is a logical second step. But beyond mere perception and attention, how do we *teach* consumers about our products and services? And, just as important, how do we make them *remember* this information? To address these questions, the next chapter is dedicated to consumer learning and memory.

APPLICATION QUESTIONS

1) How would you make a distinction between perception and reality? Why should marketers concern themselves more with the former v. the latter?

2) Sony Music assembles its many music producers to discuss album development. Most albums have about 12 tracks but some vary from as few as 7 to as many as 20 on a single album. The boss man/lady proposes going with the smallest number of tracks possible to save money for the company, while one of the producers disagrees and says more songs should be included to make consumers happier and, therefore, increase sales. Using a concept from this chapter, explain what you might contribute to the conversation so that everyone thinks you're a genius.

3) You work as a marketing manager at Lululemon, the fitness company specializing in yoga gear and attire. Your research and development (R&D) team comes to you and says it has figured out a way to manufacture your best-selling premium yoga mat at nearly half the cost. "Now we can cut the price in half," the team suggests. Although you agree that price may be able to come down slightly, explain why consumers may not see decreasing price too much as a good thing.

4) Think of the last consumer product you just purchased (e.g., for me that would be an iced coffee). Now, using each of the six "common methods of getting attention" listed in the chapter, say what you would do as a marketing manager for that product to capture the attention of consumers (e.g., size: making a jumbo coffee cup, contrast: introducing non-coffee, caffeine-free, calming products to the menu, etc.).

5) A friend approaches you about becoming a partner in a new restaurant venture. He has already done some research that results in a perceptual map and a preference map of consumer tastes and local competitor restaurants. There is a clear market cluster whose needs are unaddressed for spicy/ethnic food in the target neighborhood, and your friend anticipates raising enough capital and building so that the restaurant opens two summers from now. What, pray tell, is the problem with your friend's grand plan?

6) You and a group of friends are planning to throw a fancy party because, well, why not? Everyone has to dress up and fancy food will be served. Then, that one friend in your group (we all have one) buys fancy paper plates, fancy plastic cups, and fancy plastic eating utensils for the event. Using a concept from this chapter explain why you might disown the friend and disinvite him/her from the party.

7) How might taking a class on Finance change your willingness to invest in the stock market despite the risks associated with investing not improving or, in some instances, even getting worse?

8) Your local community government is considering changing its annual chili cook-off competition from July, when it typically takes place, to February. "No," yells a passionate citizen, "People are more likely to have nasal congestion in February!" The other citizens look at this woman like she's crazy, but you speak up for her point. What do you say?

9) Many retail stores have bells that ding each time a customer enters its doors. Using the concepts of "distal stimulus," "proximal stimulus," and "percept," explain what is happening from a perception perspective when you walk into a store and a bell rings.

10) Say you are interning at a major credit card company and you notice that there exists a sizable consumer cluster whose ideal points on two critical attributes – fair interest rate and diversity of rewards – are both just slightly above what your card is currently perceived as offering. What would you suggest to your internship director: changing the features of the card to offer exactly what the cluster wants, creating an entirely new card that caters to exactly what the cluster wants, attempting to change the clusters' beliefs about what they want/need, or designing an ad campaign that changes the perceptions about what the current card is capable of offering? Explain why your chosen proposal is better than the non-chosen options.

Mike & Ike Varieties. The product packaging for Mike & Ike: Orange 'n Cream and Mike and Ike: Strawberries 'n Cream. I think my sister and I should start our own candy line: Jim and Kim.

*   *   *

Candy Crush. Here we see Mike and Ike (presumably) as they used to appear before they turned into the white guy and the black guy from the commercial. It remains to be seen how Mike and Ike will be personified going forward, but you can see how this might be problematic.

Out of the Box: The first box is the packaging Just Born, Inc., used to draw attention to their campaign while the second box is the revamped Mike and Ike box. You can see that the design is certainly sleeker and decidedly masculine. The use of gradients and hard curved lines to create distinct sections also elicits more eye movement than the older box.

*   *   *

Outdoor Media. The Mike and Ike breakup included billboards in which a painter appeared to be putting green paint over the name Mike or Ike. I think it would have been funnier to have an anthropomorphized cartoon lemon Ike painting over Mike's name and a cartoon cherry Mike mischievously painting over Ike's name, with the tagline, "Fruit so bad they're good."

Chapter 4 | Learning and Memory

April 8, 2013 was not a great morning for Ron Johnson.

Johnson, a Stanford- and Harvard Business School-educated businessman, had earned a reputation for taking consumer brands and typical shopping experiences and turning them on their head...in a good way. While the VP of Merchandising at Target, Johnson was responsible for bringing in designer clothing brands and creating specialty areas within the store, changing the consumer perception of Target to that of a retailer with both stylish clothing *and* decent prices. Yep, Ron Johnson is the guy who made Target cool again.

Shortly thereafter, Johnson changed technology shopping forever by leading the team responsible for developing the famous Apple store experience. With their clean design, interactive product samples, and friendly geniuses roaming around to demonstrate cool products, Apple stores became a destination for people of all ages, so popular that Microsoft created its own Windows stores that look strikingly similar to Apple's stores, and Samsung has emulated Apple's store-within-a-store concept at partner retailers like Best Buy. Yep, Ron Johnson is the guy responsible for you spending all your money on Apple products.

After such remarkable successes at Target and Apple, Johnson was tapped to become CEO of struggling retailer J.C. Penney in November 2011 with the thought being that Johnson could employ his turnaround tactics at the classic department store, which was struggling with its archaic image and lack of a strong foothold in online sales. Just 17 months later, on April 8, 2013, Johnson was ousted.

What went wrong?

Johnson's plan for J.C. Penney included several drastic changes to company's usual ways of operating. Central to Johnson's strategy was eliminating all "sales" at the retail giant. In lieu of sales, Johnson indicated that J.C. Penney would provide a simple pricing structure reflecting the lowest possible prices in a plan called "Fair and Square" pricing, the "square" theme playing off J.C. Penney's updated square logo. Beyond the removal of sales, the design of the stores themselves was to change to reflect a "town square" theme in which a central meeting area would provide seating, snacks, beverages, and even entertainment to shoppers who, in turn, would hopefully spend more time in the stores, which would translate to more sales revenue in much the same way the increased foot traffic in Apple's stores led to increased revenues. And, one final change, Johnson would lure higher-end, luxury designers to J.C. Penney and create unique mini-stores-within-the-store along the perimeter of each J.C. Penney store, a page out of his Target playbook. What could go wrong?

A lot, it turns out. First and foremost, the new pricing scheme turned out to be *extremely* confusing to consumers. Shoppers had a very difficult time understanding the tiered pricing structure and, more importantly, missed the special sales they had grown to love and expect over time. Getting rid of all sales also led to a logistical problem for the company: shopper traffic. J.C. Penney, like most companies, often relied on sales to increase customer traffic at particular times – holiday weekends, particular seasons, downtimes, clearing inventory. No longer offering sales meant that stores could no longer strategically control customer traffic using sales as a tool. The redesign of the store also proved to be confusing for consumers. Instead of being able to shop for jeans in one place, for example, clothing was separated by brand, so Levi's clothing might found in one area while Wrangler clothing would be found in a separate area. For consumers who shop within the same brand, that's amazing. For everyone else, it's terrible – imagine having to walk to different areas of a huge department store just to compare jean sizes, styles, and prices. The addition of higher-end designer brands while simultaneously offering the "fair and square" lowest prices led to an identity crisis for J.C. Penney: how can a store be both posh and exclusive while also claiming to have the lowest prices? It tarnishes the image of the top designers and their respective products to be associated with extremely low prices, and it confuses customers who may worry that the *low* prices cannot be the lowest if such fancy brands are in store.

Johnson's strategy included other changes, as well. For example, employees were told to dress casually and were given handheld checkout devices (à la Apple stores) so they could freely roam about the store as opposed to standing behind a check-out kiosk typical of a department store. The problem, as you can imagine, is that customers had *no idea* where to go to check out or even if the person helping them was actually an employee of J.C. Penney. In hindsight, changes like those proposed by Johnson seem like terrible, terrible ideas, yet many of these same ideas proved to be extremely successful at other retailers. But the result at J.C. Penney was a stock valuation that just kept plummeting and a posting of the lowest sales in *decades* of the 100-year old company, earning the company the distinction of being the *worst* performer in Standard and Poor's 500 index.

In just seventeen months, Ron Johnson went from being one of the retail industry's most beloved darlings to being considered one of the *worst* executives in the history of companies and executives. I guess sometimes life just isn't fair…or square.

*　　*　　*

In the previous chapter, we covered how information gets from the outside world into the Self. The senses take in loads of information, some of that information is actively attended to, and most of it is not. We stopped there. But if all we did was make snap judgments on the fly each time a situation arose, our lives would consist of millions of in-the-moment snap judgments, many of them repeats of situations we've seen before. Fortunately, we are able to *remember* and to *learn* so that we're not constantly reinventing the wheel each time we face a familiar situation. But how do we learn? And how do we remember? The purpose of this chapter is to give an overview of learning and memory, both of which are critical components of consumer behavior. We did have to *learn* how to order and to purchase consumer products at some point, after all.

Case in point, just yesterday a friend posted a picture of his son (on Facebook) ordering a meal for the first time ever at McDonald's. His son is 20…just kidding, his son just turned four. Seeing the image reminded me that, at one point in time, we are all apprehensive about doing something as simple as placing an order at McDonald's. Even to this day my father, a fairly intelligent and outgoing man, gets a bit nervous at restaurants with complicated menus or ethnic dishes bearing their native names (my mom and I enjoy teasing him about this). At some point, though, the consumption process becomes so routine that you would never think you *didn't* know how to do it. That was *exactly* the problem facing Ron Johnson at J.C. Penney.

To be clear, Johnson's core ideas were not bad ideas, objectively speaking. Increasing the time shoppers spend in the store? Good idea. Simplifying a complex pricing system? Not bad. Making salespeople more mobile and personable? Why not? The problem with Johnson's plans was not that the ideas were bad. The problem was that the ideas were *so different* from what J.C. Penney shoppers were used to and had been used to for over 100 years. Forgetting these habits and routines and learning new pricing schemes, shopping behavior, checkout processes, etc., doesn't happen overnight.

In psychology we have a fun technique that we like to use called the "white bear" effect. In studies on thought suppression researchers will ask participants to do everything in their power *not* to think of a white bear for five minutes. So, I'm going to ask you, dear reader, to do that right now. Whatever you do, for the next five minutes, DO NOT THINK OF A

WHITE BEAR. No white bear, got it? Your five minutes starts… NOW!

…

…

…

Make it? Chances are you did not, but don't feel bad: most people are unable to do this. In fact, the way our brain tends to attempt this feat is by thinking, "Okay, Jim, do X to avoid thinking about that white bear" (…in which we inherently think about the white bear). I bring up the white bear example to make the following point: if I can introduce a brand new idea to you (i.e., a white bear) and make it impossible for you to suppress it, imagine how hard it is to suppress *years* of learned behavior. Pretty darn difficult. Side note: the white bear effect works with anything, really, not just white bears. Purple penguins, orange octopi – you name it. Have fun doing this one with your friends.

So if Johnson's core ideas weren't terrible but, instead, his disregard for consumer learning and memory is what drove the nail in his retail career's coffin, what could he have done differently? Well, for starters, *any* of the proposed changes should have been tested first. At that, any change should have been introduced gradually and accompanied with very clear instructions and information about the change. Any pushback in the early stages could serve as a cue that J.C. Penney's target consumers prefer the way things had been done before. Perhaps the resulting changes would be a mix of Johnson's original vision and input from J.C. Penney's actual consumers. What doesn't work (and what almost never works) is steamrolling a plan out and forcing it onto consumers without adequate teaching. But in order to teach consumers, we must first have an understanding of how people learn.

Two theories of learning. It is only fitting that the notion of "how we learn" is a topic of academic debate. In one corner of the ring you have behaviorists, people who believe that learning involves actual behaviors and learning to *do* something. These people subscribe to the **Behavioral Learning Theory**, which suggests that we learn via conditioning and interaction with stimuli in our context (described below). In the other corner of the ring you have cognitivists, people who believe that all learning is actually taking place in the brain via mental representations of what is taking place in the real world. These people subscribe to the **Cognitive Learning Theory**, which contends that we learn patterns and use cognitive skills – like recall, recognition, evaluation, critical thinking skills – to actively process "information," and, in doing so, learn. We begin to acquire these cognitive skills in childhood (see Piaget's work on childhood development) and continue to refine and perfect these skills as we age, becoming smarter learners all the while. Which theory is correct? Well, they both are –

there's likely truth in both of these approaches, so we'll discuss both of them, as well as a third theory known as modeling/observational learning.

Behavioral Learning Theory. You are probably already familiar with ideas of Behavioral Learning Theory, though you may not realize it. The classic story of Ivan Pavlov and his salivating dog is the most-cited example of conditioning. The first kind of conditioning, **classical conditioning**, refers to the process by which we begin to associate an otherwise irrelevant stimulus with a particular outcome by pairing this irrelevant stimulus to a different stimulus related to the outcome. Confusing? Let's refer to the original Pavlov study for an example. Pavlov presented a dog with food, which led the dog to salivate. In this case, the food stimulus is relevant to the outcome: the dog salivating. That's a natural response for dogs (and humans, too). What Pavlov did next, however, was repeat the experiment but, this time, he rang a bell before presenting the dog with food. After a few times doing this Pavlov got rid of the food and just rang the bell. As he predicted, *simply ringing the bell* was enough to get the dog to salivate. It was as if the dog learned that ringing a bell meant food time, which then produced the natural slobbery result. Terms that often come up in classical conditioning include **unconditioned response**, **unconditioned stimulus**, and **conditioned stimulus**. In this example, the dog salivating is the unconditioned response, the dog food is the unconditioned stimulus, and the ringing bell is the conditioned stimulus.

You might be wondering what a "conditioned response" would be in this situation. Well, that's a subject of debate; technically the dog salivating to the sound of the bell is the "conditioned response" while the dog salivating to the sight of food is the "unconditioned response." "But Jim," you say, "A dog salivating is a dog salivating, right?" Kind of, but not *exactly*. Recent researchers have been able to show subtle differences between conditioned and unconditioned responses. Thus, instead of a ringing bell triggering the exact same physiological response in the dog as seeing food would trigger, it seems plausible that the ringing bell may cue that food might be coming and that this representation of food is what triggers the salivation. This, however, is complicated, heady, and beyond the scope of this book, so for now, let's stick to our simple explanation of classical conditioning and call it a day!

In addition to classical conditioning, a second type of conditioning in the behaviorist paradigm is known as **operant conditioning** (aka **instrumental conditioning**). You are also familiar with operant conditioning because you lived it as a child every time you got spanked for doing something wrong (unless your family was one of those "no spanking" families, of course). Operant conditioning concerns itself with *consequences*. According to the theory, there are three possible consequences that can come after a behavior: reinforcement (encouraging greater frequency of the behavior), punishment (encouraging diminishing frequency of the behavior), and extinction (or "no consequence," which essentially leads the behavior to fizzle out over time). Of these consequences, reinforcements and punishments can be either *positive* or *negative* in nature. These are best illustrated with examples:

Positive reinforcement: presenting a stimulus following a behavior to encourage more of that behavior. This is like giving a dog a treat for pooping in the grass instead of on the sidewalk. In the consumer world, this is providing free shipping when purchasing online instead of in a store to encourage more online purchases.

Negative reinforcement: taking away a stimulus following a behavior to encourage more of that behavior. This is like torturing someone with Kidz Bop music until they spill their secrets in a James Bond movie. In the consumer world negative reinforcement is not very common, but one example might be the way runaway alarm clocks beep loudly and literally run away from you until you get out of bed and turn it off. Or a better example might be your personal trainer yelling in your ear until you complete a full set of reps at the gym.

Positive punishment: presenting a stimulus following a behavior for the purpose of decreasing the frequency of that behavior. This is the classic "shock therapy" approach – shocking people when they think or behave in a way that is "undesirable." In the consumer world, late charges at libraries and video rental stores are an example of positive punishment: return your borrowed item late and a fee is presented.

Negative punishment: taking away a stimulus following a behavior for the purpose of decreasing the frequency of that behavior. The classic example here is taking away the favorite stuffed teddy bear of a misbehaving child to get him/her to stop misbehaving. In the consumer world, companies often like to highlight what consumers will miss out on if they are procrastinating or *not* doing something (therefore, the behavior is "dilly-dallying"). For example, a website may be programmed to alert consumers that they have not spent enough money to earn free shipping on their order. In this example, not buying enough is the behavior and the stimulus taken away is free shipping (note: this is why many companies advertise "free shipping" boldly on their website only to have an asterisk and an explanation that the free shipping is conditional on things like minimum purchase sizes or dollar amounts – they *want* you to feel like the free shipping has been taken away if you don't behave the way you're supposed to).

To keep these concepts in your head, the best way to think about it is that 1) reinforcement encourages doing more of something, 2) punishment encourages doing less of something, 3) positive means some stimulus is added, 4) negative means some stimulus is taken away.

If we were to attempt to apply Behavioral Learning Theory in the context of J.C. Penney, we may have wanted to set up a rewards program that could condition particular behaviors of consumers. Knowing that J.C. Penney consumers like sales and discounts, perhaps we could reward those customers spending more time at the "stores-within-the-store" with coupons or percentages off their purchases (positive reinforcement). Although a risky idea, the retailer could have introduced a nominal "kiosk fee" for checking out at a standard register that would be removed if consumers checked out with one of the roaming salespeople (negative reinforcement). More broadly, J.C. Penney's commercials could have eased consumers into the idea of "fair and square" pricing by pairing the idea/name with the sale/discount information consumers expected, the same sale/discount information that encouraged them to go to J.C. Penney in the first place. Over time the mention of "fair and square" pricing would hopefully elicit the same urge for customers to make a trip to their local J.C. Penney that the sales/discount info used to do (classical conditioning). See how that works?

Whereas Behavioral Learning Theory has to do with actual behavior and, perhaps more importantly, the *consequences* of those behaviors, Cognitive Learning Theory treats learning as more of an internal, brainy process. More specifically, cognitivitists focus on patterns over time and the ability for the human brain to hold information in memory, both in the short- and long-term, which then helps aid the acquisition, interpretation, and encoding of new information and allows us to draw conclusions about how the world works. Thus, the key idea of cognitive learning theory is that learning is an *internal* process and not the result of external stimuli. To understand cognitive learning theory, then, we need to review some basics about memory.

Cognitive Learning Theory and Information Processing. Unlike Behavioral Learning Theory, which concerns itself more with *doing* something and then learning from subsequent *consequences*, Cognitive Learning Theory concerns itself with information acquisition, processing, and retrieval for future use. In the previous chapter on Perception and Attention we talked about how we perceive stimuli in our context and sometimes even pay active attention to those stimuli. But if that process stopped there, we would not retain any information or be able to use the experience to help us going forward. Thankfully, our brain is capable of not just attending to that information but also *processing* that information. Thus, **information processing** can be thought of as the process in which the brain changes or works with incoming stimulus information. This goes beyond merely perceiving or paying attention to a stimulus – it means processing it. It's like when you check the status of a product order and see that it's "processing" – you know that *something* is being done to the product. In way comparable to how a computer acquires binary data, processes it, and then produces graphics, music, and other output, cognitive psychologists study learning within humans using a similar paradigm. Interestingly, what we think of as ideas and concepts are actually the product of several parts of our brain and neural circuits processing, in harmony, to produce an end result not unlike a computer. And, just like a computer, our brain can engage in this processing thanks to *memory*.

Memory. Remember when I told you not to think about a white bear earlier? It seems so long ago, doesn't it? What's weird is that until I reminded you about it again just now, you probably forgot about it. Without *deliberately* trying to forget about the bear, you forgot about him. Yet when you were deliberately trying to forget about the bear, you could not.

Memory is strange. You probably have enough of your own weird memory stories to support that statement. We have all experienced the weirdness of having something – a name, an idea, a number – *just on the tip of our tongue*, yet we cannot fully remember it. Other times, we get the strong, overwhelming feeling that we have already experienced something before, a phenomenon we call "déjà vu" (which is French for "Holy crap this feels weird!"…just kidding; it actually means "already seen"), even if we have never been in that situation before. Some people traveling abroad to a foreign city for the *first* time get the feeling they have been there before, despite that being impossible. It's all very mysterious, weird, and previous life-ish, but, in reality, it's just your brain being your silly brain.

Memory, in its simplest form, can be thought of as the process by which information is encoded, stored, and retrieved. For centuries mankind has known that memory was rooted in the brain, and very recently (in 2012) scientists at MIT started to explore memory at the level of individual neurons. By shining a light into photosensitive neurons the scientists were able to make mice recall *specific* memories. Nuts, right? Thankfully, this is not a book on neuroscience, so we'll skip the detailed neuron talk, but let's pause for a second to recognize that neural connections in the brain are involved with memory and learning in a process so complex that scientists are still making new discoveries on this front every day.

Memory is often broken down into three types: sensory memory, short-term memory, and long-term memory. These categories are primarily differentiated by the length of time. **Sensory memory** tends to be fleeting and involves the memory of a sensory experience in the few seconds after perception. The process is automatic, not deliberate, and pertains to the fleeting trace memory we have as a result of sensing something with one (or more) of our five senses – e.g., visual (iconic memory), audial (echoic memory), touch (haptic memory), smell (olfactory memory), and taste (gustatory memory). This is a bit tricky, but one way to understand sensory memory is to think about life without it. If I flashed you a computer screen containing the following letter and number sequence – N1U1S2J3M5E8V13M – for just one second and then immediately took it away, chances are you would be able to recall a few letters or numbers if I asked you to do so a moment later. If you did not have sensory memory you would have still seen the same string of letters and numbers, but as soon as the screen went blank, you would have no memory of anything your eyes just saw. Life without sensory memory would feel pretty empty.

Moving beyond sensory memory, we foray into **short-term memory**, a memory category in which we can recall information several seconds after exposure to a stimulus without elaborating upon or rehearsing information about the stimulus too much in an attempt to remember it. Short-term memory, although longer than sensory memory, is still fairly short-lived and limited in size. People often refer to the 7 +/- 2 rule with short-term memory. Anecdotally, it's the reason often given for why American telephone numbers are 7 digits long: that's the most we can remember in our short-term memory on average, which allows the maximum number of different phone number combinations while not overburdening our brains. If you're like me then you know that even 7 numbers seems like a stretch; I often look up a number, attempt memorizing it long enough to write it down, and wind up having to go back and look at it once or twice more to get it right. As such, modern scholars think a more accurate short-term memory number is more like 4 or 5 items…so either they're right or I'm getting old.

Now, the cool thing about short-term memory is that there are tricks we can use to help us hold onto memories for longer than we otherwise would be able to. One trick, **chunking**, involves chunking or "grouping" together bits of information into larger, easier-to-remember bits. For example, the number 149,217,761,983 seems like a doozie to remember. However, we can separate the number into chunks – 1492 (the year Columbus "sailed the ocean blue"), 1776 (the birth year of the United States), and 1983 (the birth year of yours truly) – which allows us to remember the original 12-digit number quite easily.

Another tool, **dual coding**, refers to encoding a concept not just as the concept or word but also as a visual representation of the concept/word. This is the strategy language-learning companies like Rosetta Stone use when they pair a foreign word with an image of that word. Instead of forcing your brain to remember that "gato" means "cat" in Spanish verbally, Rosetta Stone will place the word gato on a card bearing the image of a cat while saying the words "gato" and "cat." The idea is that as the word "gato" gets burned into your brain, your neural network is associating it semantically with the word "cat" and visually with the image of a cat.

A related idea to dual coding is the trick of **meaningful encoding** in which people link new incoming information to existing content in their memory. The cat example of the previous paragraph is also an example of meaningful encoding: we can link the word "gato" to an existing, meaningful concept in our brain – the idea of a cat. If we had never heard of a cat before then all that dual coding would be for naught. To give a different example, let's refer back to that string of random numbers and letters that I presented earlier – N1U1S2J3M5E8V13M. If we take just one second, we might be able to derive meaning from this hodge-podge of letters and numbers. Notice, for example, that the letters represent the first initial of the 8 planets of our solar system (sorry Pluto) in reverse order. If we remove the letters we might notice that the numbers proceed in the famous Fibonacci sequence in which each number is the sum of the two numbers that came before it (e.g., 1+1=2, 2+1 = 3, 3+2=5, and so on). Now that we have encoded meaning with this string of once-random numbers and letters, it's much easier to keep them in our working memory.

Meaningful encoding is also what allows experts to keep more related concepts in their working memory in a particular domain than novices. Their mental scaffolding is a much more elaborate, sturdier structure than that of the novice. For example, if we have a conversation about music and you tell me to play the following notes in this order C, E, G, D up the scale and then C, A, F, C down the scale, I can easily keep these notes in my mind, as I think, "That's a C Major 9 chord going up and an F Major chord coming down." For someone less familiar with music, keeping those eight notes in working memory in that order could be very difficult. From a consumer standpoint, think about how meaningful encoding would lead to differences in the way companies reach out to long-time loyal consumers compared to brand new consumers. For whom does it make more sense for the company to provide complex details and insider jargon/lingo to facilitate learning? The answer should be obvious.

One last trick of keeping memories accessible in the short term is **repetition** or **rehearsal**, in which information is repeated again and again to keep it salient. This is what we do when we look up a phone number and repeat the digits aloud (or mentally) while we make our way to the phone. If you're like me then you turn it into a little song (kind of like 8-6-7-5-3-0-9 for you 1980's music fans). It's also what we do when we leave the office, the gym, class, etc., and think to ourselves, "I must buy milk on the way home. I must buy milk on the way home," over and over again. Sadly, I do such a great job at this right upon leaving and then magically forget what I was rehearsing until later that night when I'm lying in bed and trying to sleep. This kind of repetitive rehearsal is referred to as

maintenance rehearsal. A different kind of rehearsal, **elaborative rehearsal**, involves repeatedly elaborating upon an idea – thinking about its meaning and trying to connect it with other known concepts – so that it (hopefully) makes its way into your long-term memory.

If we are lucky, the important things we need to remember in life managed to get stored in our **long-term memory.** Long-term memory, unlike sensory and short-term (working) memory is not fleeting but, instead, endures over time, sometimes even forever (e.g., as poetic as it may sound, I imagine few people forget their birthdays even up until the day they die). Most of the time, long-term memory is very useful – I mean, who *wouldn't* want to remember their birthday or, you know, what their loved ones look like. Other times, long-term memories can be upsetting – as is often the case when it comes to painful breakups or episodes of violent crime or war (e.g., Post-Traumatic Stress Disorder). Unfortunately, without extensive therapy (and even then) it's almost impossible to decide what we want to store in long-term memory and what we would rather forget.

Speaking of forgetting, the ability to store memories in long-term memory would be useless if we did not have a process for retrieving those memories when we need them. It's sort of like depositing all your money in a bank only to discover that the bank has no way of getting that money back to you. However, this inability to retrieve memories happens *all the time*. It's not that the memories are no longer there or that they have magically disappeared; it's just at the moment we need to remember them something in our memory machinery misfires.

Two important concepts related to this retrieval process are recall and recognition. **Recall** refers to the ability to spontaneously generate a memory or information when attempting to retrieve it. **Recognition** refers to the ability to correctly identify whether or not you have been previously exposed to a particular stimulus when it is placed in front of you. To give you concrete examples in consumer contexts, recall would be remembering the name of a book you intend to purchase when you deliberately try to remember it upon walking into a Barnes and Noble store. Recognition would be seeing the book you intended to purchase on a shelf upon entering the Barnes and Noble and having the realization that *this* was the book you intended to purchase. Sometimes you can both recall and recognize the same stimulus. Other times you might be able to recognize but not recall a stimulus. It's rare that we would be able to recall a stimulus (i.e., remember a book off the top of our head) but not recognize it unless the stimulus does not appear as we expected. You know that feeling you get when you see an old friend about whom you can recall many memories but then, when you see them, they seem totally different to you? That's kind of what it's like to recall something but not recognize it. In another example, we can all recall what love feels like but we often fail to recognize it when it's right in front of us. I should be writing a book of poetry.

Companies often measure customers' awareness of their product, service, or brand. You may hear terms like "awareness," particularly *aided* or *unaided* awareness. This is simply recognition and recall in disguise. That is, if awareness is unaided, it's that consumers are able to recall something without any prompting from a company. Aided awareness, on the other hand, involves some intervention or extra help from the company. Upon receiving this assistance, customers may then be able to recall or recognize the brand, product, or service in question.

The reason this matters, of course, is that consumers tend to limit the field of options from a broad, diverse field into a more narrow consideration set. A **consideration set** can be thought of as the limited set of products or services that a consumer actually is considering for potential purchase. Note, this concept differs from an **evoked set**, which is the set of *all* the products or services that come to mind. So, in the context of say toothpaste, I may be able to think of Crest, Colgate, Sensodyne, Aquafresh, Arm & Hammer, and Close-Up (that's my evoked set), but I would only ever consider purchasing Crest or Colgate (that's my consideration set). In order to even be in my evoked set to begin with, I likely need to be able to recall or at least recognize a brand. Otherwise, it doesn't stand a good chance of ever making it to my consideration set.

Although it would be awesome if we could retrieve our memories, whether via recall, recognition, or both, every time we try, that's simply not how the brain works. As I mentioned at the onset of the memory section, headway is still being made in the domain of memory research. To paraphrase a neuroscientist friend from Yale, people like to think that the human brain is a perfectly operating machine comparable to a computer complete with memory. In reality, the brain is a wonderful but flawed product of evolution in which bits and pieces stuck around over time as these flukes aided our survival likelihood. Thus, while useful, the brain isn't perfect and, as such, neither is our memory.

Modeling/observational learning. Beyond the reward/punishment approach of behavioral learning theory and the brainy, "thoughtful" approach of cognitive learning theory exists one of my favorite kinds of learning: modeling/observational learning – a.k.a. "Monkey See, Monkey Do" learning. The idea behind **modeling/observational learning** is that human beings are able to learn not just through self or personal experience but also by observing others engaging in behavior. If I see you touch fire, immediately pull your hand away, and scream in agonizing pain, I am able to learn that touching fire may not be a great idea. Similarly, from a consumer perspective, if I see you wearing J. Crew clothing and notice that beautiful people always surround you when you wear your J. Crew clothing, I may learn that buying and wearing J. Crew clothing could make my world look a lot prettier.

The famous academic study most cited on the topic of modeling/observational behavior is affectionately referred to as the Bobo doll study (Bandura et al., 1961). A Bobo doll, in case you don't know (I didn't), is one of those blow up dolls (…no, not that kind) that is rounded and weighted on the bottom so that if you push it over it automatically springs back up. Bandura and colleagues had young children watch an adult act aggressively (or kindly) toward the Bobo doll and then, later, after frustrating the children, measured how children in the different experimental conditions acted when asked to play with the Bobo doll. Somewhat unsurprisingly, those children who had witnessed an adult being aggressive with the Bobo doll wound up being more aggressive, both physically and verbally, toward the doll while those children in the non-aggressive condition showed less aggression. An interactive gender effect also emerged that showed the aggression effect was stronger when children witness an adult of the same gender exhibiting aggression toward the doll. That is, boys were *more* aggressive when they had witnessed an adult male acting aggressively toward the doll than an adult female acting aggressively toward the doll (this likely has to do with reference groups, which will be discussed in the chapter on Social Influence). The study was repeated two years later, but this time the adults were either rewarded, punished, or provided no consequence following the beating of Bobo. Interestingly, children were *less* likely to beat up Bobo after watching adult do so *and* get punished for doing so. Thus, by observing the actions of others, in this case adults, the children were able to learn.

Our ability to learn by observing others is rather useful and certainly adaptive. When we still roamed around in tribes, it would have been really advantageous for us to know that jumping off a tall cliff is a terrible idea without having to try it for ourselves first. This is also the same reason that if you go out to eat with me I'll often make you order something that I want to try but am a bit leery of so that I can watch the reaction on your face when you take your first bite. Don't think of it as manipulative; think of it as a teacher educating his/her pupil.

Involvement Theory. Speaking of learning, it should be no surprise that the more students are involved with a subject, the better they learn the information. That's why you are a Consumer Behavior genius right now: you are *so* involved with this book. For real. You should, like, get a room or something.

Involvement Theory in the context of consumer behavior refers to how involved consumers are with a product, service, or brand (i.e., how much effort, time, money, and/or resources we put into the process). Some products, like a new house or a new car, demand quite a lot of involvement whereas other products, like chewing gum or socks, are relatively less-involved purchases. Our involvement is also often broken down into either rational or emotional categories, with rational/emotional referring to which part of us the products primarily appeal to: our rational side or our emotional side.

Examples appealing to our emotional side with which we may have high-involvement include an expensive piece of jewelry or a vacation. These are expensive decisions not to be made lightly (hence the high involvement), and they appeal more to our emotional side than to our rational side. Examples appealing to our rational side with which we have high-involvement include selecting a particular retirement plan or stocks in which to invest. These are pricey endeavors and involve our thoughts more than our emotions. An example of a low-involvement rational product might be considering which toilet paper to buy (i.e., we want a good deal with little effort, and the toilet paper is unlikely to bring us great joy or sadness), while an example of a low-involvement emotional product might be the single rose we buy cheaply from the florist to surprise a loved one (i.e., it's a fairly easy purchase requiring little thought but has potentially strong emotional ramifications).

Understanding a consumer's level of involvement matters for many reasons not least of which includes knowing how to provide the *right* information in the *right way* that best corresponds to the consumer's level of involvement. For example, for a high-involvement rational product, like purchasing a new car for practical reasons, it would be appropriate to design print advertisements and television commercials that are chocked full of data and information as opposed to spending millions of dollars producing flashy commercials with emotional appeals. This is where knowing your target market matters, however. For a different target, purchasing a car may have more of a high-involvement emotional draw, in which case commercials with lots of data and information would be no bueno. Instead, these commercials should be flashy and cater to the emotions of the viewer. What I love about Involvement Theory is that companies get this wrong all...the...time. Overzealous ad agencies come up with a clever or cute ad and forget that the client's target market couldn't care less about emotion but, instead, are more rational. Or a company will spend loads of money on research to include factoids in its collateral without realizing that the intended target purchases products simply because they are shiny and pretty.

Measurement of Learning. In this era of "No Child Left Behind" and "teaching to the test," I would be remiss as a professor if I did not include a discussion on how we might measure the effectiveness of these efforts to educate consumers. There is no such thing as the SAT or ACT for customers, no standard metric for knowing how savvy a shopper is or is not. And the knowledge of a consumer varies considerably from product category to product category. Someone who knows a lot about purchasing household items may know nothing about how to plan a vacation.

The best way to go about measuring learning in a consumer context is to conduct research that assesses a consumer's familiarity with a concept pre-learning, teach them (or not for some consumers so you have a control group comparison), and then give them a post-learning test to see if the educational process was effective. It is important to highlight that *teaching* and *learning* are two different things. That's easy for you and me to forget because you are learning literally *every* piece of information I am teaching you (wink). Kidding aside, even when we try our *very best* to learn, sometimes not all the information sticks or, as we discussed in our conversation on retrieval, the information is there it just can't be accessed for whatever reason. When assessing the post-learning differences, then, it's important to ask questions about a consumer's involvement and engagement with the learning process: how often did they see ads with instructions? How much attention would they say they paid? How much did they enjoy learning about X? How easy is it for that customer to learn information in general? How much of a novice/expert does the consumer consider him/herself to be? If we can put numbers on these questions, we just might be able to disentangle statistically any differences between the effectiveness of the *teaching* process, the *learning* process, and interactive effects of both.

In practice, a lot of companies will say, "Well, Bob, it looks like we sold more widgets following our educational campaign, so it looks like the campaign was a success!" Maybe, Bob...maybe. But remember what I said about marketing research in an earlier chapter? Practitioners often fail to incorporate sophisticated statistical analysis into their interpretation of data, which may then lead them to incorrect conclusions. The bump in widget sales *could* have been due to the educational campaign, but it could have been due to any number of things: good weather, a different ad campaign, a sales promotion running simultaneously to the educational campaign, or just sheer luck. So if you plan to teach your consumers anything, be sure that you also plan to collect pre- and post-educating data so that you can measure the effectiveness of your educational campaign – otherwise you're just wasting time and money.

Priming and scripts/schemas. Although it is wise to measure the effectiveness of consumer learning, you may be surprised to learn that a large part of our learning is so automatic that it's nearly impossibly to measure. Indeed, a curious thing about memory is that it often guides our behavior without our conscious realization. I'll give you an example. Below there are two paragraphs. Before reading them, I want you to decide, right now, whether or not you will read the *first* one **OR** the *second* one (I don't want you to read both). Got it? Which paragraph are you reading – the first one or the second one? When you are finished, skipped to the sentence that begins with RESUME HERE. Okay, ready? Go!

PARAGRAPH 1:
Jenny works out every day. She joined a new gym near her apartment and bikes to work daily. She attends yoga classes every weekend and is thinking about joining CrossFit sometime soon.

PARAGRAPH 2:
Maria loves working in Mexico City. The people are kind, the city is vibrant, and the music is spicy. Maria is particularly fond of the tango and is thinking about taking professional Latin dance classes sometime soon.

RESUME HERE! Okay, now what I want you to do is to fill in the blanks in the word that follows to name a common food: **S _ L _ _**. Did you say salad? What about salsa? What if I told you that, depending on which paragraph you read, you'd be significantly more likely to say one or the other? "Jim," you're thinking, "Why would a paragraph unrelated to your little word game influence my response?" Go back and read *both* paragraphs this time. Paragraph 1 conjures up images of health whereas Paragraph 2 conjures up images of Mexico and Mexican culture. Because those neural associative networks are thought to be more active, logic suggests that those who read the first paragraph would be more likely to say "salad" (because of their active health associative network) and those who read the second paragraph would be more likely to say "salsa" (because of their active Mexican/Latin associative network).

The process by which exposure to a stimulus at one point in time leads to greater facilitation or ease of processing of a subsequent stimulus at a later point in time is referred to as **priming**. To remember this, think about how a painter primes walls prior to painting them; he/she gets the walls ready for something that's yet to come, something that will apply more easily as a result of the primer being in place.

Priming happens *all the time* in the real world, but given its subtlety, we rarely realize it. Constant exposure to health cues may prime us to make healthier food choices just as the logos of fast food joints may encourage us to indulge. Some research by Tanya Chartrand at Duke University and colleagues showed that even brief exposure to brand names like Neiman Marcus or Walmart led participants to make more luxurious or more budget-minded purchases in subsequent, unrelated purchasing tasks.

One of the core assumptions of priming, however, is that in order for a concept to be able to be primed, there must be some existing knowledge structure in the brain in the first place. That is, in our salad/salsa example, if you knew nothing of Mexico or Mexican/Latin culture, then mentioning these ideas to you would make you no more likely to fill in the missing letters to spell the word "salsa" when asked to identify a common food item. Thus, long-term memory and the established associative networks contained therein are essential for priming to work

Another cool concept in the context of memory is that of the **schema** or **script**. Often used interchangeably, I like to differentiate scripts and schemas as follows: schemas are simply the "way things are supposed to be" with respect to the setting, the characters, etc., while scripts refer to the way that a scene is expected to be carried out. Just as actors rely on scripts on movie sets and theater stages, scripts in the cognitive sense involve the linear, back and forth dialogue and interaction between buyers and sellers. Schemas are more like the scenery, the costumes, and all the other elements that complete the production. The key idea here for both scripts and schemas is that, over time, we *establish an expectation of how things are supposed to be*. At Starbucks, for example, where I am currently writing this chapter, I know that there are supposed to be a lot of comfy couches and chairs along with some wooden tables and less-comfortable chairs and stools. I know that there is supposed to be a relatively brown color scheme and a lingering smell of brewing coffee along with a very familiar green color that is found in the company's logo. There are also supposed to be people working on laptops and others who seem rushed and pressed for time. There must be a see-through food display case near where people order their coffee drinks, and the baristas must be wearing black shirts with green aprons and black hats featuring the mermaid Starbucks logo. That's the schema of a Starbucks café no matter where in the world I go.

I also know that when I enter the café, I must walk to where the food display case and counter are located. I stand in line behind some girl talking way too loudly on her phone about her day as if the rest of us care about her life of entitlement (pshuh!). I proceed through the line, closer and closer, until it's finally my turn to order at which point a pseudo-sincere barista grabs a permanent marker with one hand and hovers over the array of hot- and cold-drink cups as she awaits my impending order. "Welcome to Starbucks," she says, "What can I get for you?" I proceed to order my venti iced coffee (yes, venti — someone has to stay up to write this book) with a shot of sugar-free vanilla syrup and a banana. The barista scribbles down my details on the side of my cup, asks "Can I get a name for this order?" I respond in kind with, "It's Jim," despite always *thinking* about giving them a silly name like Mr. Bojangles or Jebediah St. Chihuahua, III. I laugh in my head as the barista places my cup on the counter for her colleague to fill, enters my order in the register, says the total aloud, takes the debit card I've just procured from my pocket, swipes it, hands it back to me, and wishes me a good day. I then proceed toward the end of the counter and wait for the colleague to call my name (again thinking how great it would have been had I gone with Mr. Banana Man instead of boring ol' Jim). Then I grab my drink, grab a straw and some napkins, and then proceed to sit down to do work on my laptop. That's the script of a Starbucks café encounter no matter where in the world I go…unless I'm in Paris, in which case it's the same, but in French.

So well-engrained in my mind is the schema and script for a typical Starbucks encounter that when anything out of the ordinary happens, e.g., the drink-making barista asks how my day is going while he/she is making my drink, I have this split-second reaction where I have absolutely no idea what to do. "You just broke character!" I want to tell them, but I don't because I'm not crazy. Or imagine walking into a Starbucks in a new city and noticing that the décor is pink – even the logo is a bright, brilliant shade of fuchsia instead of the typical green color. These schema/script violations would be very, very strange and, as I'll discuss in detail later in the chapter on culture, may even affect how we think and behave, potentially discouraging our likelihood of making a purchase without our conscious realization!

Indeed, schemas and scripts often make consumption much easier and, to some extent, mindless once we know what we are doing. The alternative, being unfamiliar with a script or schema, can be awkward and disastrous. Case in point, ask me about the first time I got a professional massage…*that* was awkward. Whenever possible, marketers can use these existing scripts and schemas to their benefit. In the context of the J.C. Penney fiasco, one major hurdle facing Johnson was the fact that customers had well-established schemas and scripts of their typical J.C. Penney shopping experience. This experience involved knowing the layout of a J.C. Penney store (i.e., where particular departments were located within the store), where to find employees, where to check out, how to check out, what the pricing scheme would be, the relative cost of items, and so on. Johnson *could* have used this to his advantage. Instead of treating the Fair and Square pricing plan as novel and distinct from the company's well known sales and promotional strategies, he should have integrated the new plan into the existing schema of sales/promotions with which J.C. Penney consumers were already familiar.

*   *   *

Ron Johnson's short tenure at J.C. Penney is just one example of how companies often fail to take into consideration consumer knowledge and how difficult it can be to teach "old dogs new tricks," so to speak. Another recent example is that of the famous online video streaming and DVD-mail site Netflix that you know and love. Originally started as a subscription-based DVD mail operation in the late 1990s, Netflix developed an online streaming option that eventually spun off into its own business in 2010. So far, so good. But then, out of nowhere in 2011, Netflix co-founder and CEO Reed Hastings randomly announced that the DVD mailing business would be rebranded as Quikster while the online streaming portion of the company would remain Netflix. Apparently this would make things easier internally, perhaps for accounting or strategic business units purposes. Was it *really* necessary? Probably not. Was it confusing to consumers? Totally. People weren't sure if they needed to switch memberships, pay different fees for the different services, cancel existing accounts, create new accounts – and the company didn't do a very good job explaining the change. The result? Netflix quickly canceled the Quikster plan *less than one month* after announcing the change.

In both the J.C. Penney and Netflix examples, the media described consumers as being "outraged," "angry," "upset," and even "pissed." That's some fairly strong language. But notice something else about these words: they are all emotions. Up to this point we have focused primarily on the cognitive characteristics of consumers (i.e., things we *think* about, ideas, reasoning). However, just as important to the consumption process and to our daily lives are the *feelings* and *emotions* we have as we engage with the world. We are not just *thinking* beings, we are *feeling* beings, so the next chapter is dedicated to our moods, emotions, and affect – I hope you *feel* like reading it (…I really need to stop with the casy jokes).

APPLICATION QUESTIONS

1) Say that financial analysts have picked up on a trend: Apple emails subscribers exactly 24 hours before publicly announcing new products which always leads to an uptick in the company's stock price. It gets to the point that anytime Apple sends an email the stock price immediately gets a boost. What kind of conditioning is this? Identify what in this example represents the conditioned stimulus, the unconditioned stimulus, and the unconditioned/conditioned response.

2) Involvement Theory suggests that different products and services elicit different levels of involvement from consumers and that the appeal of a product/service tends to cater slightly more to either our rational or emotional self. Think of four products or services, each one of which caters to one of the four categories (i.e., high-involvement rational, high-involvement emotional, low-involvement rational, low-involvement emotional).

3) Now think of one example of an existing consumer product or service that positions itself in one of these four ways *but* should really position itself differently based on the intended consumer target. What would the marketing executions look like for this new approach?

4) Repetition and rehearsing are good ways to keep an idea in one's short-term/working memory. In what ways do companies rely on "rehearsing" to keep their product or service in your mind? Can you think of a company that relies on *maintenance* rehearsal and a different company that relies on *elaborative* rehearsal? How do they manage to do this?

5) What is an example of a purchasing experience or a service that follows a very strict script? What is an example of a purchasing experience or service that seems to follow no script and, as such, varies each and every time you engage in that experience? Does this lack of a script help or hurt that experience?

6) Pharmaceutical salespeople used to give doctors loads of "freebies" like pens, bags, notebooks, jackets, and other items branded with the name of the pharmaceutical company. Aside from feelings of obligation or reciprocity, how might providing doctors and hospitals with this kind of paraphernalia affect their purchasing decisions (hint: maybe even without their conscious thought)?

7) Pretend you are the marketing manager for the latest Sony Playstation. Give an example of how you would use Modeling/Observational Learning as the foundation for a marketing campaign to teach an individual about your product.

8) Regional lawyers who advertise on shows like "Maury Povich" and "Jerry Springer" often created memorable phone numbers like 1-800-OUR-CASE or 1-800-LAW-GOOD. Of the various tricks and techniques listed in the section on short-term/working memory, which one best represents what these attorneys have done? Why?

9. Taglines, jingles, logos, and branding are important ideas in Marketing. How might a tagline (e.g., "Just Do It"), a jingle ("The best part of waking up is Folgers in your cup!"), logos (e.g., the McDonald's Golden Arches), and branding (e.g., Tiffany & Co.'s famous blue color) relate to the ideas of recall and recognition? Which may aid recall better than recognition? Which likely aid recognition better than recall?

10. I provided a few examples of how J.C. Penney could have used learning theories to introduce Ron Johnson's proposed changes. Consider the Netflix/Qwikster example mentioned in the chapter. In what ways could Netflix/Qwikster have used some of the learning concepts from this chapter in introducing its proposed changes?

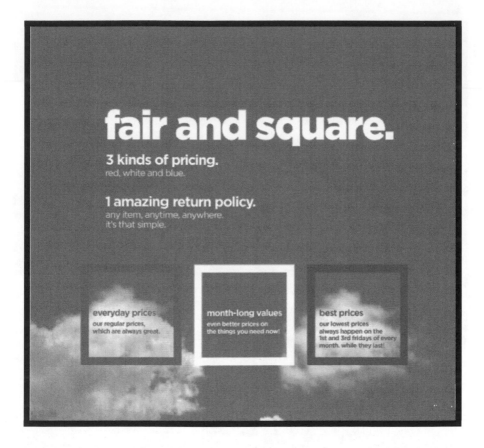

The Price Isn't Right. An "instructional" sign for Ron Johnson's proposed Fair and Square pricing plan. The plan involved using colors to identify everyday prices, month-long values, and best prices (not exactly sure what that means and the descriptions don't help). Also note the use of three unrelated cultural mantras: fair and square, clear blue sky, red/white/blue. Can it get any more confusing?

Chapter 5 | Affect, Mood, and Emotion

I hate it when people post pictures of their babies on Facebook.

Most people feel obligated to "Like" the photos and to post comments like, "Awww, so cute!" and "That's the prettiest baby I've *ever* seen." Ever? Really?

I always get the urge to post something like, "Wow! Your baby has an alien-sized head!" or, "Is it a boy or a girl? I can't really tell!" particularly when the parents have gone through the painstaking process of taping a pink bow or a blue hat to a baby's bald head, but I don't.

You see, the problem is that I just don't take a lot of things seriously. Well, that's not true. Maybe it's not that I don't take things seriously as much as it is the fact that I just view the world through this comedic lens that makes everything more humorous to me than anything. It turns out this is a very useful condition: I'm generally always in a good mood and don't have to pay for therapy.

That said, you can probably understand why there are very few things in this world that can make this stone cold heart cry. However, in 2007 I found myself on the verge of tears several times a day. And, because I am a strong man who is comfortable talking about his emotions and we're best friends at this point of the book, I'll even admit that may have actually *cried*.

"Jim! What happened?" you ask, "Bad break up? Did something bad happen to Tina Fey?!" (I would actually be sadder about something bad happening to Tina Fey than a bad break up).

Nay, friends, nothing catastrophic took place. What brought me to tears was a song that was released a decade before in 1997 when I was barely in high school.

The song? Sarah McLachlan's "Angel," but it wasn't the song that brought me to tears, it was what accompanied the song. You may know where this is going…

The American Society for the Prevention of Cruelty to Animals, better known as the ASPCA, put together a super simple commercial consisting of video clips of sad-looking puppies and kitties in shelters, on the street, and in veterinary hospitals while Sarah McLachlan's haunting song played softly in the background. Then Sarah herself appears with what is presumably her dog (or a very talented dog actor playing the role of her dog) and explains the purpose of the ASPCA and directions for how to donate (see the commercial here: http://youtu.be/Iu_JqNdp2As).

Strangely, unlike most commercials that suffer from wearout effects over time, this tearjerker seemed to become more effective over time, as people began to talk about "that commercial," the one that made them cry. The commercial wasn't just a success from a "make them cry" and word-of-mouth perspective, ASPCA managed to bring in $30 million dollars within a year-and-a-half of the ad running, including gaining 200,000 first-time donors (to put that in perspective, the company's annual operating budget is about $50 million).

Like all things, the commercial began to wear out its welcome in the long-run, probably because people did not appreciate being brought to tears in the middle of their day on multiple occasions. It got to the point that if I were in a room with a group of people and the commercial came on television, everyone in the room would scramble to find the remote and change the channel, like trying to diffuse a ticking time bomb, not because we didn't like the commercial but because our hearts just couldn't take it anymore. You hear the song, you see the puppies and kitties, and you cry.

The sad (and scary) thing is that I have seen commercials for starving children for years, *years*, and yet I had never felt more compelled to donate to a charity than I did upon seeing the ASPCA commercial. I often say that I love dogs more than most people, so that could have something to do with it, but I don't even *like* cats all that much (a.k.a. snakes with fur…unless you love cats, in which case they are truly, truly precious creatures), so the fact that I found myself willing to give money to help mangy, selfish felines was certainly telling.

Okay, while we're sharing, I'll admit that I cry all the time. Hallmark commercials have *got* to be made by some sadistic bastard somewhere who gets off on knowing he's tearing people up on the inside. Case in point, check out this commercial (http://youtu.be/XJTF77Xjqlk) and this one: (http://www.tvspots.tv/video/12745/HALLMARK-CARDS-NEIGHBOR-LADY). When you're in the business of selling sentimental cards, it's a good thing when you can capture emotion so strongly in your creative executions.

Maybe one of the worst sad commercial offenders is Anheuser-Busch. You may be thinking, "Wait a minute, Anheuser-Busch isn't known for sad advertising!" Au contraire! Every Super Bowl it seems that the St. Louis-based company lobs a tearjerker *right in the middle of the game*! So there you are surrounded by testosterone-raging friends and this gem pops up (http://youtu.be/eWEyXl3i1Ck) or this one (http://youtu.be/cwXo4PnTMYA). Then, suddenly, every guy in the room has to, "Go get a beer," or, "Go to the bathroom," or whatever else they manage to croak out between choking up. In 2013, Jeep took a page out of AB's book with this commercial, also a tearjerker: http://youtu.be/FadwTBcvISo). Proctor and Gamble produced these spots for the 2012 Olympic games, which proved to be very successful (Moms: http://youtu.be/uGJGQQVNqjg, focusing on the mothers – and Kids: http://youtu.be/zRaQRbAxXaA). Even the tech nerds at Google figured out a way to melt my old and frozen heart into a puddle of sappy goo: http://youtu.be/nnsSUqgkDwU.

Thankfully, to restore balance to the world, the yin to the yang, there are commercials that rely not on sadness but on humor. These, of course, are my favorite kinds of commercials. Some of my all-time favorites include this Ameriquest commercial (http://youtu.be/M7cUYVviK50) and this Walmart commercial (http://youtu.be/hsvAj6qfmFQ). Not to be outdone by a competing discount retailer, there is also Kmart's campaign it developed to advertise its new home *shipping* service that generated some controversy with the super conservative parent types (http://youtu.be/I03UmJbK0lA), the same parents who fear that because Ellen DeGeneres is the spokesperson for J.C. Penney, all their mom jeans will "turn lesbian."

A friend of a friend, Victoria Kelleher, won the industry award for Best Commercial Actress of the Year for her performance as the mom in these two hilarious commercials for Chef Boyardee's brilliant "Obviously delicious. Secretly Nutritious." campaign: (Spot 1: http://youtu.be/KeDjuKYzX8w, Spot 2: http://youtu.be/gaWr6riwuuQ). Take that, Progressive Flo! What's beautiful about this campaign is that the humor captures your attention and makes the spot memorable while communicating two key messages to the intended target (moms): 1) your kids will love the taste, and 2) you're a great mom if you buy this because it has a full serving of vegetables (and your kids won't even realize it). Bam. That's great advertising.

The use of humor in advertising isn't just an American thing. A brand of cheese from Egypt called "Panda cheese," has the tagline, "Never say no to Panda," which the commercials take to another level http://youtu.be/XYz3sl0LEA4). And then there's this beauty of a public service announcement from France (http://youtu.be/2gLlBv_SrZw).

From Sarah McLachlan and cute puppies to a bratty French kid and condoms, clever advertisers prey on our emotions to capture our attention, make us laugh, make us cry, make us angry, and, most importantly for companies, to sell us stuff. But what are emotions? How is it that all of us can be brought to tears by the same 30-second spot? Just how universal are these crazy things we call emotions?

*　　*　　*

Let's talk about our feelings.

If you're anything like most people, reading that last sentence probably elicited a groan from you. No one likes talking about his/her feelings, and when you have to do it in an organizational setting, there's usually some diversity HR trainer making you hold hands and do trust falls and such. I don't recommend doing a trust fall if you are reading this book by yourself.

Even though we do our best to avoid talking about our feelings, understanding the role of emotions in marketing is critical. Emotion is important to the study of consumer behavior not just because it is such a prevalent tool advertisers use but because it is the *feeling* of an urge that compels us to action. The very name of this book refers to the *feeling* of needing to do something; if we didn't *feel* urges, how or why would we consume anything?

Now, to be clear, relying on emotions in the context of marketing is not limited to advertising. No, clever marketers are in touch with consumers' emotions at every stage of the consumption process. For example, food packages for indulgent snacks are often deliberately designed to reduce the guilt you feel when you are debating whether or not to purchase the product. "Now with less fat!" or "A fat-free candy!" text appears in large letters to help attenuate those feelings of guilt. Even products and services themselves are designed to affect your emotions. Consider Southwest Airlines and their kind, humor-based approach to service or the super-cheerful and caring folks at Zappos.com, another company known for its friendly customer service. Human beings are emotional beings, so understanding how emotions affect our motivations and urges is critical to understanding consumer behavior.

Affect, Emotion, and Mood. Defining emotion is a bit tricky for most people. Is an emotion the same as a feeling? Is an emotion the same as a mood? And where does this term "affect" fit in? Although these terms are often used interchangeably, it is important to clarify how they are different so that we can be more precise in our discussion and application of each. So, let's begin with a bit of concept clarification…

Just as "marketing" can be thought of as an umbrella term encompassing advertising, logistics, sales, etc., so, too, can **affect** be thought of as an umbrella term encompassing emotion and mood. **Emotion** refers to the subjective physio/psychological experience we formulate that is *triggered* by some stimulus or event. **Mood** refers to a lingering or enduring overall sense of feeling. Mood and emotion are similar, but they differ in important ways: 1) emotions tend to be more *intense* than moods, 2) emotions tend to be *triggered by events* whereas moods may or may not be, and 3) emotions tend to be *expressed* by individuals more than mood, which often goes unexpressed to others. Just to complicate matters, some also refer to a concept known as "core affect," which is similar to mood in that it is enduring but, unlike mood, core affect tends to refer to feelings that are more primitive and not mediated by cognition – e.g., feeling tired, energetic, tense, relaxed, etc. – felt, enduring body states over a period of time.

You may wonder how the term "feeling" fits into this mix of terms? Well, the actual *feeling* itself is more the actual subjective *experience* of the emotion that you have resulting from some physiological or neurochemical actvity. For example, the release of dopamine, a neurotransmitter in our brain, creates the "feel good" physical sensations we experience that lead us to think, "Hey! I'm happy right now!" which is the emotion. One way to think about it is the sentence, "Because I feel _____, I must be _____." The first blank is a feeling, the second is an emotion. You could fill the blanks with, "Butterflies in my stomach / worried," "Empty / Sad," or, "My heart pounding / Excited." Feelings are primitive and sense-oriented, while emotions are a bit more advanced and typically mediated by our thoughts, as discussed next.

Cognition and Emotion. Cognition and emotion are often treated like salt and pepper: they *kind of* go together sometimes but, other times, are treated as differently as black and white. Cognition tends to be characterized as dry, emotionless, and consisting of purely rational thought, logic, and ideas while emotion is characterized as warm, soft, and consisting of far-less-rational feelings. Cognition is like our German or Northern European rule-following, on-time taskmaster while emotion is more our loving Spanish or Italian grandma who won't let us leave the house without eating a table's worth of food and hugging her a million times.

Despite attempts to separate cognition and emotion, however, it turns out that cognition plays a very important role in what we mean by emotion. Emotion refers not just to the *feeling* that we get but also to how we *interpret* or *make meaning* of that feeling, and when we're "making meaning" of something, we're thinking about it (i.e., cognition). Folks who study brain injuries and patients who have suffered strokes are quick to note that these patients can still *feel* in that they can perceive sensations and incoming information, but if areas of the brain responsible for interpreting these sensations are no longer functioning properly or are missing, then these people cannot experience an *emotion*.

One model linking cognition to emotion is the **Two-Factor Theory of Emotion** (a.k.a. the **Schachter-Singer Two-Factor Theory**), which proposes the following: an event takes place, we are aroused, we process this arousal cognitively, and an emotion is realized. Thus, arousal is mediated (i.e., interpreted) by our thoughts, which then leads to the experience of an emotion. To put this in the context of marketing, say you go to the grocery store and see that they are out of your non-dairy soy milk, you *feel* some void in your stomach, you *think* about how this means you are going to be gassy all weekend, and you are subsequently *angry* and a little bit *sad* (presumably because this will severely curtail your social plans for the weekend and not because you will be farting a lot, which, strangely, you enjoy). So…arousal → cognition → emotion.

Compare this with another theory of emotion called **Cognitive Appraisal Theory**, which mixes up the order a bit. In Cognitive Appraisal Theory, first an event takes place, then you process things cognitively, and finally experience arousal and emotion *simultaneously*. To use our soy milk example again this would involve going to the store and realizing there isn't any soy milk (event), thinking about how terrible this is going to be (thinking about it), and then feeling the body sensation of emptiness and realizing you are sad/angry (simultaneous arousal and emotion). So…event → cognition → arousal and emotion.

Cognitive Appraisal Theory goes one step further and suggests that we, as marketers, can influence how people experience emotions by influencing that middle step: what people are actively thinking about. That's pretty fascinating. Because, as the theory states, thought mediates the relationship between an event and our subsequent arousal and emotion, then deliberately tinkering with one's thoughts can shape their emotions. There are four useful examples in the domain of consumer behavior. The first, **agency appraisal**, focuses thought on the responsibility one's self has for the outcome of an event. This is useful for making people feel grateful, guilty, frustrated, or sad. For example, Jif Peanut Butter's famous slogan, "Choosy moms choose Jif," suggests that you, as a mother, are singularly responsible for the health and well-being of your children. If you don't choose Jif, you're a terrible mother and should feel guilty. Nice, right? The second, **anticipation appraisal,** focuses thoughts on the future. This is useful for eliciting feelings of hopefulness and anxiety. A good example of this in consumer behavior are the commercials you see during election years, which also seem to emphasize how much better things are *going to be* in the future or, alternatively, how terrible things *will be* if you elect the wrong person. The third, **equity appraisal**, focuses thought on the fairness of the event. This is useful for making people feel warm and loved or angry and bitter. For example, most retailers now like to point out how their competitors are charging you higher prices for the same products. Finally, the fourth appraisal, **outcome appraisal**, focuses thought on how an event has turned out relative to one's goals. This is useful for making people feel joy, satisfaction, pride, and disappointment. Gyms and dieting companies like Jenny Craig use this both to make people feel satisfied or sad by having them compare their actual weight to their ideal weight. The major lesson here? If you want to change the way people *feel*, it's often more effective to change the way they *think*.

Now, you might be wondering at this point, "How in the world do these two theories – the Two-Factor Theory and Cognitive Appraisal Theory – differ?" They are very similar, but the big difference involves what leads to the emotion. The Two-Factor Theory suggests that both arousal *and* thought contribute to emotion whereas Cognitive Appraisal Theory posits that the cognitive appraisal, itself, is responsible for an emotion. Neuroscience suggests that, indeed, *complex* emotions (e.g., ambivalence or mixed emotions, guilt, pride, etc.) involve cognition before being experienced. However, there are certainly some studies showing the body physiologically reacting to stimuli without cognitive intervention, so it's probably not the case that one theory is "better" or "more accurate" than the other – it's more the case that, in certain contexts, one theory may explain the process better than the other *in that particular instance.*

Misattribution of Arousal. Before today you may not have paid much attention to the role your thoughts had in your emotions. And now, my hope is that you never forget this role your thoughts play on your behavior because it is often possible to cope with your emotions by *thinking* through your emotional experiences. That is, if I find myself feeling a bit antsy, depending on how I *think* about that feeling I could wind up either extremely worried or extremely excited. Sometimes, when you feel sad, it's useful to think about the root reason you are *really* sad – more often than not you begin to realize that things you *think* are bothering you or making you feel "bleh" are actually not the root cause of your emotional experience.

But remember that emotions, like Denny's, are at play 24/7. We cannot really turn them off; our bodies were simply not designed that way. This leads to some interesting implications, then, because if we cannot always think about and categorize our emotions, then it could be the case that our arousal is sometimes miscategorized or misattributed.

Indeed, there is robust evidence of how our arousal is misattributed due to our lack of thought or incorrect thinking. My favorite example of this is the "shaky bridge" study. Picture it: a rope bridge spanning a very deep ravine and swaying in the wind. Young men were recruited to walk across the bridge and a young, female research assistant provided instructions and collected the participants' thoughts, being sure to give them her number should they have any questions. However, one group of men crossed this "extremely dangerous" bridge, while a different group of men also doing the experiment crossed a far safer, sturdier bridge. The key dependent variable of interest was the number of men from each group who would call the female research assistant. As predicted, more men in the shaky bridge condition called the girl. Why? Well, as theorized by the authors and supported in subsequent studies in different domains, the arousal of walking across the shaky bridge was misattributed to arousal toward the assistant. This is not to say that seeing the ravine floor did not evoke arousal attributed to the idea of falling, but that arousal carried over to the interaction with the assistant. Side note: next time you are planning a date with someone you *really* like, consider walking across a shaky bridge with him/her, going on a hot air balloon ride, or petting angry lions. If you are lucky, the arousal he/she experiences from these death-defying situations will turn into a lifetime of romance. You're welcome.

The bridge example is a fun one because it reminds us that consumers are constantly experiencing arousal in consumer contexts – bright colors, flashing lights, moving crowds, and more. It also reminds us that emotions are the function of not only sensation and perception but also cognition. Thus, one very useful way to apply this in consumer contexts is to make sure we reinforce arousing experiences with the right information so that consumers elicit the emotions we want them to. As consumers, it should also make us particularly aware of how companies might rely on this technique to elicit particular motivations and urges from us in consumer contexts.

This misattribution of arousal can extend to misattribution of emotions and mood, as well, which works both for and against companies. When consumers are in good moods, they tend to process things more heuristically and may be more likely to make purchases not because they *want* or *need* something but rather because they just feel good. On the contrary, customers having a bad day can be your worst enemy. Even though they are really mad about the fight they just had with their partner, telling them that a particular shirt doesn't come in their size or that the expected delivery on their order is 5 days instead of 2 is likely to be greeted with a monstrous rage.

The Risk of Relying on Emotions in Marketing. So by now we have established that emotions often involve cognition and that the former are rarely present without the latter being involved. But as any of us who have experienced a bad break up know, emotions can also affect our cognition. Indeed, while it seemed like a *really* good idea at the time to throw your ex-significant-other's things out on the lawn and set them on fire, in reality, that probably *wasn't* the best idea…probably.

Sometimes, as marketers, we don't want consumers thinking hard about the purchases they are making. "Buy this overpriced, cheaply-constructed toy," we think, "It will make your kid happy, which, in turn, will make you happy and make me money!" Thus, as consumers, we have to be careful not to let our emotions get the best of us lest we start relying too much on our heart to make important purchasing decisions.

From a company's perspective, a major risk with using emotional appeals in marketing is that, in spite of effectively eliciting an emotional response from our consumers, companies may not achieve their *business objective*. This happens each year with the advertisements we see during the Super Bowl. Ad agencies do their very best to craft the saddest or the funniest ads of the year, which often turn out to be very sad or very funny ads. Mission accomplished. However, the next day when people are talking about the ads they refer to, "That one ad with the panda bear," or, "The ad with the little old lady." They rarely say, "The ad for Panda cheese," or, "The ad for Hallmark's new line of greeting cards." If the ads are effective at eliciting emotions but not at translating to increased purchases, brand awareness, or some other company objective, then the companies have just spent millions of dollars entertaining instead of marketing.

The Basic Human Emotions. So how can marketers even attempt to elicit emotions from diverse groups of people with such different cultures? Some estimates place the number of different languages spoken to be at nearly 7,000. Imagine, for one second, a world in which each culture had its own emotions in addition to its own language. We would never understand each other! Apart from not being able to use our words, we would not even be able to read the expressions on each other's face to get a gist for what we are trying to convey or how we feel.

Few people know this, but my first language wasn't English. "Really, Jim?" you ask, "What *was* your first language?" This is when I get a smoldering look on my face, a twinkle in my eye, and reply seductively, "Love." I'm teasing, of course, I would never use such a cheesy line, but much like love and music, it turns out many human emotions are *universal*. Remember that tribe on an as-yet-undiscovered island in the tropics? The one whose tribesmen have never learned the link between a delicious, gooey warm chocolate chip cookie and an ice cold glass of milk? Well, even *these* people smile the same smiles you and I do when they are happy, the same frowns when they are sad, the same wide eyes and arched eyebrows when they are surprised. Emotions, it turns out, are *universal*. What follows is a description of the emotions for which the facial responses tend to be the same whether you're in Tahiti or Toronto:

    Anger. Anger is the emotion most-often associated with unfairness, unjustness, and outcomes that turn out in a way we did not anticipate and for which we did not hope. Negative in valence, anger typically accompanies a sense of wrongness or a violation of accepted norms or agreements. Consumer application: price gouging, insider trading.

    Disgust. Disgust is the emotion most-often associated with revulsion, distaste, disappointment, and experiences in which someone or something performs in a manner that doesn't measure up to a clearly set standard of decency, morality, and/or taste. Negative in valence, disgust typically accompanies a sense of aversion or abandonment of the disgusting stimulus. Consumer application: Political advertising, comparisons to competitors' "inferior products."

Fear. Fear is the emotion most-often associated with the unknown, risk, threat, worry, and uncertainty. Negative in valence, fear typically accompanies a sense of "not knowing" and dread. Consumer application: Insurance, warranties, etc.

Happiness. Happiness is the emotion most-often associated with joy, ease, satisfaction, and outcomes that meet or exceed our expectations. Positive in valence, happiness typically accompanies a sense of excitement, peace, and/or stability. Consumer application: Customer service, customizing products/services to meet/exceed a specific customer's preferences.

Sadness. Sadness is the emotion most-often associated with disappointment, difficulty, challenge, and outcomes that fail to meet our expectations. Negative in valence, sadness typically accompanies a sense of immobility, unease, and/or instability. Consumer application: Comfort foods, charitable donations.

Surprise. Surprise is the emotion most-often associated with excitement, feeling startled, the unexpected, and being caught off guard. Positive in valence, surprise typically accompanies the sense of not knowing something until (or after) it takes place. Consumer application: Point-of-purchase discounts, surprise perks (e.g., folded towel animals at resorts).

Now, just because these expressions of emotion are universal, this does not mean that we all laugh at the same jokes or cry at the same sad stories. You only need to watch a British sitcom to know that what one culture finds funny may not be funny to people in a different culture (for the record, I love British sitcoms but not every American does). Similarly, expressing particular emotions may be more accepted in one culture than another. In some East Asian cultures, shame and honor play a much more important role in day-to-day culture than in Western cultures. But what is interesting is that humans around the world demonstrate the same physical facial reactions when they *are* experiencing these emotions. Side note: Contempt has since been added as a seventh universal emotion, but is often considered secondary, so because it is worthless and inferior, we shall leave it off our list (…see what I did there?).

Measuring Emotion. The fact that at least six of our emotions elicit the same physical facial reactions gives us hope that measuring emotion is an easy task. Tracking changes in people's facial expressions is, in fact, one way researchers measure their emotions. Some computer programs are now capable of scanning faces and identifying emotions, which could lead to interesting applications in online shopping and customer service experiences (e.g., website avatars).

The techniques used to measure emotions are often broken down into two broad types: self-report measures and autonomic measures. **Self-Report measures** refer to questionnaires and other methods of eliciting how someone feels based on the person's own reporting. **Autonomic measures** bypass this need for someone to tell us how they feel and, instead, capture the biological and physiological responses directly to measure *and* identify how someone feels. Next, I'll walk you through some of these various approaches to measuring emotions.

Galvanic Skin Response (GSR), an example of an autonomic method, involves connecting sensors to the fingers or palms of participants to measure the skin's electrical conductance, which varies as a function of moisture. And what makes our palms moist? Arousal, of course. So GSR is really a measure of how aroused we are. This approach, also often referred to as Skin Conductance, is useful insofar as it is not particularly invasive – the nodes are easy to connect, painless, and generally accurate. However, the information we can derive from GSR is limited to arousal, in general, and not to a particular cause or type of arousal. Thus, feeling conflict, anger, fear, or other emotions may induce arousal that gets picked up by the sensors, but without further inquiry we don't really know which emotion is leading to the arousal.

Functional Magnetic Resonance Imaging (fMRI), is another autonomic method that has increased in its use in the past few decades as more people (and companies) have gotten their hands on very expensive MRI machines (each machine can cost well into the millions). Using an MRI machine we are able to see directions of blood flow within the body, which may not sound important until you know that blood flows to various areas of the brain in order to provide the brain with the energy it needs to execute particular tasks. Thus, as the theory goes, the signals that emerge from an fMRI indicate those areas of the brain implicated in doing or thinking about a particular task or object (i.e., the function). Particular "regions of interest" tend to show activation when we do or think about particular things, which then suggests a relationship between that part of the brain and the focus of our thought. With respect to emotions, researchers have become so adept at identifying which regions are implicated for particular emotions that they can predict which emotions someone just experienced based on the fMRI output alone. It's not perfect, but as is often the case with fMRI as a tool in the research world, the researchers are able to "see" information that people, themselves, might not be able (or are unwilling) to self-report.

Facial Recognition. As mentioned earlier, the fact that six basic emotions elicit similar facial reactions is helpful when it comes to identifying and measuring emotions. So consistent are these faces that computers are now able to identify these emotions in lieu of human observers. Consider, for example, how lowered eyebrows, pursed lips, and bulging eyes is a universal display of anger or how lowered corners of the mouth and slightly raised eyebrows signals sadness. My guess is that if you master these facial displays of emotion, you have no need for learning languages! Totally kidding: there is no universal face for, "I need a bathroom quickly!" and that's a sentence you'll definitely want to know.

Self-report Measures actually refers to a number of different scales and tools in which individuals provide ratings, information, and/or thoughts, which are then categorized and quantified to measure emotion. The benefit of self-report measures is that they are usually fairly easy to collect, cheaper than most autonomic approaches, and far less physically invasive compared to techniques like GSR and fMRI. The downside of self-report measures, however, is that humans are often poor judges of their own emotions. Indeed, trying to disentangle feelings of joy, happiness, satisfaction, surprise, or other positive affect may be really difficult. And sometimes I don't even know where to begin to tell someone how I feel. This is the complication of self-report: the information is only as good as the accuracy of the person providing the information which can vary as a function of an individual's ability (e.g., may not really know sophisticated differences among emotions), motivation (e.g., may be too tired or too busy to be careful when providing feedback), and/or opportunity (e.g, may be short on time).

PANAS, or the **Positive and Negative Affect Schedule**, is one such example of a emotional self-report measure. The scale, which exists in various longer and shorter versions, essentially asks participants to rate, on a scale from 1 (very slightly or not at all) to 5 (extremely), whether they feel a particular emotion at a particular period of time. Typically these emotions are categorized as either being positive or negative and are coded as such, although the emotions are randomized on the survey so that participants' response for a particular emotion is less likely to be influenced by their rating for another emotion. Examples of emotions included for positive affect include: interested, alert, attentive, excited, enthusiastic, inspired, proud, determined, strong, active. Examples of emotions included for negative affect include: distressed, upset, guilty, ashamed, hostile, irritable, nervous, jittery, scared, afraid. Although not perfect, the PANAS is a useful way to capture data on emotions quickly.

Another example of self-report is **PAD (Pleasure-Arousal-Dominance)**, in which participants fill out a survey whose questions correspond to one of three possible categories: Pleasure/Displeasure,

Arousal/Non-Arousal, and Dominance/Submissiveness. The scales corresponding to these three categories consist of positive v. negative affect, physical activity and mental alertness v. physical and mental inactivity, and control v. lack of control, respectively. Now, here's where things get interesting: using the data from the scales, points are plotted on a 3D plane corresponding to each of the three key areas of interest (i.e., Pleasure, Arousal, and Dominance). The 3D plane is divided into emotions such that if someone's PAD score is (-.51, .59, .25), this emotion is known to be "anger." Like any self-report measure, the PAD suffers from the fact that it relies on the accuracy of a participant filling it out, but the approach offers an improvement on other, comparable measures by including nuanced, varying levels of intensity throughout its measures, which helps researchers make finer distinctions between otherwise very similar emotions.

Emotional Intelligence and Emotional Involvement. Although emotion is often treated as the overly sensitive, less powerful step-sibling of cognition, the truth of the matter is that emotion is just as rich and varied as our thinking. Just as we vary in our intelligence about facts and knowledge, so, too, do we vary in our *emotional* intelligence. **Emotional Intelligence** refers to our ability to be aware of our emotions and to exert some control on our emotions. If you have ever met someone who seems to be an out-of-control hothead, chances are you have at least considered how this person may be unable to manage his/her emotions as well as the rest of us. The point is that people vary in their ability to recognize and control their emotions, which is why little kids are emotional basket cases and adults tend to have their emotions more in check.

A related idea, **Emotional Involvement**, refers to the emotions that can be elicited based on a deep personal interest that we have with a particular stimulus such that interacting with or even *thinking about* the stimulus elicits an emotional reaction. This is what happens when you think of your loved ones, your favorite vacation destinations, your dead pet, or really anything with which you have a deep personal emotional connection. If you are a die-hard environmentalist, then thinking about animals dying from pollution or seeing litter on the ground is likely to elicit very strong anger or sadness whereas people oblivious to these concerns can see the same stimuli without having a similar emotional reaction.

Although emotional intelligence and emotional involvement vary from individual to individual, emotions also have a social component. Consider, for example, the idea of emotional contagion. **Emotional Contagion** refers to the extent to which an emotional display by one person influences the emotional state of an observing bystander. This is what happens when you see someone else crying and you start crying or when you see someone else smiling wildly and you suddenly feel very happy yourself. The mechanism behind this effect may very well be adaptive, as it makes sense that being sensitive to the moods and emotions of others in our tribe might help us survive collectively – I can help you when you're sad, reinforce whatever makes you happy, etc. A few years ago researchers discovered a phenomenon known as the "mirror neuron" effect in which the neurons that typically activate for particular movement and emotions when a person *actually moves* or *feels* an emotion also activate slightly when that same person simply *sees someone else* moving or experiencing the emotion. Ever notice how yawning is contagious? There are evolutionary reasons for that, too. The brain is wired to be social, and we do not have to actually experience an emotion for our brain areas associated with those emotions to activate – simply seeing someone else experiencing the emotion is enough for our brains to say, "Hey! I know that emotion!" and to emulate the neuronal activation of that emotion.

In another example of how our emotions can have a social component, consider the group of emotions often referred to as the **Self-Conscious Emotions**. Although containing the word "self," these emotions (e.g., pride, embarrassment, guilt, shame) really refer to the way we see ourselves so that we may assess how *others* might also see us. If we lived like hermits in a world without others, would we worry about embarrassment? About shame? Would those even be emotions? Indeed, several of the emotions we have exist because we live in a social world.

Emotion and Memory. In yet another example of how cognition and emotion are finely intertwined, lots of research has shown a relationship between emotion and memory such that we tend to remember information congruent with our mood and emotions. The effect, referred to as **Mood-Congruent Recall**, suggests that it is easier to remember happy or positive information when we, ourselves, are happy, and negative or sad information when we are sad. Similarly, other research has demonstrated **Mood-Congruent Encoding**, in which the initial encoding of a stimulus with a particular emotional theme is easier when we, too, are experiencing a congruent emotion.

In the context of marketing, this is a very useful concept in the domain of media buying. Say, for example, I work for Procter & Gamble and am in charge of Pampers, the famous diaper brand. Working with an ad agency I have created a new series of advertisements that feature babies doing funny, cute things that babies tend to do. Our testing of the commercials shows that our target market, moms in the 25-30 age range with upper-middle class incomes, report feeling particularly happy upon viewing the ads. From my research, I know that the top television shows watched by these women include "The Real Housewives of Beverly Hills," "Modern Family," and

"American Horror Story." If I were to apply Mood-Congruent Encoding in my media buying decision, which show would I be most interested in purchasing time during? Yep. "Modern Family," as it is likely the case that the positive affect induced during the show would aid in the encoding of the information in my positive, upbeat, and happy advertisement. Alternatively, I could have created a fear-based diaper commercial based on, say, what happens when dirty diapers attack and placed it during "American Horror Story," but that just sounds gross.

For another example of how emotions and memory interact you need only to think about your favorite childhood brands. What kind of cereal do you remember eating as a kid? What kind of candy did you used to eat? Has any of it been discontinued? In early 2013, Hostess announced that was filing for bankruptcy. This, of course, meant that Twinkies, Donettes, and other familiar favorites would be off store shelves within weeks of the announcement. People fled to their closest grocery store to snatch up the last remaining Hostess items, and within days boxes of Twinkies were being sold for into the thousands of dollars. Why? Well, we can all remember eating Hostess' delicious (albeit fattening) snacks as kids. Certainly there are other cream-filled sponge cakes, cupcakes, and donuts in the market, some that taste just as good if not better than Hostess' offerings. But we don't just love Hostess' products because of their taste; we love them for the memories and emotions they evoke – coming home after school and having a snack waiting for us, mom or dad surprising us in our lunchbox with a note along with our Twinkie or Ding Dong.

Marketers use this emotional-memory connection all the time when it relies on **nostalgia**, the feeling that the past was somehow a better, happier time. It's the reason some music just never grows old, some fashions make reappearances, and entire markets have sprouted selling "vintage" products.

As marketers, we also deliberately try to encourage the encoding of emotions with particular products and services. Just as we have cognitive schemas about how particular situations and experiences should be carried out, so, too, do we have emotional schema. **Schema-based Affect** refers to the emotions that become stored as part of the *meaning* of a particular product or service category. Disney is known for happiness. McDonald's has tapped into surprise with its never-know-what-you'll-get Happy Meal toys. Nicholas Sparks has cornered the market on sad books. It is difficult to think of some brands or companies without experiencing an accompanying emotion.

∗　　∗　　∗

Whether driving in my car and listening to the radio, pumping iron at the gym with headphones on, or shopping in a department store whose instrumental Muzak music plays so softly in the background, I can assure you of one thing: every time I hear Sarah McLachlan's "Angel," I am going to picture cute, cuddly puppies and kitties, and then use whatever strength I have in me to keep from crying.

Human beings are emotional beings. Our emotions make life interesting – imagine an alternate world in which everything relied on thought and rationality. And those emotions affect other parts of our lives – our thoughts, our choices, our behaviors, and even our memories. Fortunately, it is rarely the case that we base our choices and behaviors entirely on emotions (imagine the train wrecks our lives would be if we were to do that! …you may know some people like this). Instead, we are a blend of attitudes *and* emotions, thinkers *and* feelers, and it is typically this interaction of our heads and our hearts that is what truly creates our urges. The next chapter addresses how our attitudes and personalities motivate our behavior.

APPLICATION QUESTIONS

1) Say your company works with a research company that occasionally provides you with data regarding several of your products' target markets. You notice in the report that one section is entitled Mood/Emotion and the section proceeds to mention only information on how consumers report feeling "in general" or "generally" while watching particular shows and reading magazines in which you are interested in placing advertisements. Why might this be a problem? What kind of information are you missing out on that could be even more useful regarding *specific* placement of your ads?

2) Recently, while sitting in the blazing sun at Wrigley Field during a very intense Cardinals-Cubs game (for real: tied game, bottom of the ninth, three men on, one strike remaining), I saw a vendor go by carrying what appeared to be the most delicious cotton candy in the history of cotton candy. I thought to myself, "Me want food! Bahhh!" Using a concept from this chapter, explain to me why I might not have *really* wanted that cotton candy.

3) The notions of Mood-Congruent Encoding and Mood-Congruent Recall are prevalent in marketing. In the chapter I gave an example of how one might apply these concepts in the domain of promotion (advertising, specifically). How might a company use these ideas in the context of one of our other 4Ps, like Placement? Give a specific example of how the distribution of a product or service could exploit Mood-Congruent Encoding or Recall.

4) In a novel use of technology, Walmart started running commercials in which they do a side-by-side comparison of costs for common grocery store items at Walmart v. a local market's grocery store (e.g., Dominicks in Chicago, Schnucks in St. Louis). What kind of appraisal does this exploit? Can you think of three new commercials Walmart *could* use that employ one of each of the other three appraisals?

5) Using a concept from the chapter, explain why companies are willing to spend millions of dollars in HR training to ensure their employees behave a certain, consistent way in all of their locations.

6) Think back to the last question, say a retailer bolsters its "happy/positive" HR training with comedy training by bringing in the world-class Second City to teach employees improv, jokes, and generally how to be funny. What is one important consideration a company must make when it relies so heavily on emotion in its interactions with consumers?

7) In a world of social networks and online reviewer comments and forums, what are some smart suggestions you would make to companies interested in starting their own company Facebook page or review site based on the concept of Emotional Contagion?

8) One would be hard-pressed to find someone who would say he/she doesn't enjoy being happy, but when might being extremely happy be a disadvantage in a consumer context? When might being angry, sad, or disgusted be an advantage? In other words, how do our emotions affect our deliberation and thinking?

9) Royal Caribbean, Amazon, and 24 Hour Fitness are among several companies who often call or email customers days after cruises, mail shipments, and/or customer service calls to ask about their prior experiences. Included in these questions are measures of satisfaction, happiness, annoyance, and other emotions. If you were consulting for these companies, what suggestions would you make regarding their approach? What would you say are the advantages/disadvantages to their approach? Why?

10) What are some common products or companies for which people have strong emotional connections? How might you rely on these nostalgic feelings to create value for and stimulate the urges of consumers? Taking it one step further, can you think of nostalgic stimuli for specific types of people (e.g., for men v. women, for people of a particular generation, for Californians, etc.)?

CHAPTER 6 | PERSONALITY, ATTITUDE, AND PERSUASION

Once upon a time, Facebook was cool.

In fact, a long, long time ago in tech industry years (so around 2005), *the*Facebook.com (yes, with a "the") was a super exclusive website open only to those at a handful of American universities. I remember my friend Lauren coming into my dorm room at Washington University in St. Louis to tell me about this "new thing" that I just had to join...we were pioneers! In that era, everyone was clamoring for a piece of the Facebook pie, a fire that the exclusive nature of the website kept feeding. You may even recall the yearning and desire you had prior to starting a Facebook account?

Eventually, *the*Facebook dropped the "the" in its name and opened up to college students at every university in the U.S., followed by high schools, followed by, you guessed it, *everyone* and his/her mother. There are probably few life moments as conflicting at the moment you see that your parents have requested your friendship on Facebook. Do you accept? Do you reject? Do you awkwardly pretend like you don't see it for as long as you can? In just a few years, Facebook managed to go from a simple idea (that really just copied already-existing sites like MySpace and Friendster) to a full-fledged global phenomenon, seemingly on a never-ending upward trajectory of success...or so Facebook thought.

In early 2013, Facebook admitted in a financial report that it was "worried" upon discovering that teenagers were using the social networking site less and less, while teen interest and engagement with competing sites like Twitter, Tumblr, Snapchat, and Vine increased. Analysts speculated about the reasons behind this beyond the obvious, "If my parents are using this site, it can't be cool anymore," reasoning. Some thought it might have to do with privacy concerns – the idea that anyone can tag your pictures and see your information. For teens, this also meant that any parties or the stupid things that teens do (of which there are many) could wind up on public display for all to see...including parents and teachers. Others thought it might have to do with the lack of intimacy; that is, some sites, like Tumblr, can be restricted to a certain group of friends, while apps like Snapchat allow users to control how long recipients can view text messages and photos. Teenagers' attitudes toward Facebook and its features (or lack thereof) simply changed; almost as quickly as teenagers "friended" Facebook, they defriended the site en masse.

Fortunately for Facebook, having billions of dollars lying around doesn't hurt. Case in point, in 2012 Facebook purchased the photo sharing behemoth Instagram for $1 billion, as Instagram had noticeably carved a niche into the younger demographic slipping from Facebook's grasp. By purchasing Instagram, Facebook could stay connected with this young, important demographic and better integrate Instagram's usefulness into Facebook's core product offerings…or so that is the hope.

As is often the case in the business world, Facebook's competition did not sit idly by. Not to be outdone, Marissa Mayer, the one-time Google powerhouse turned Yahoo! CEO, realized that to stay competitive in the social networking tech world of today Yahoo! would need to take drastic action of its own. So in May of 2013, Yahoo! announced it would be purchasing the trendy and easy-to-use blogging site Tumblr for $1.1 billion (these tech companies sure do have a lot of cash).

And back and forth the story goes as the tech giants all scramble to make sure that their social networks are the ones capturing the most eyeballs in the lucrative world of online advertising. Even Justin Timberlake jumped into the fray with his partial acquisition and redesign of MySpace.com, the one-time leader of the social media pack in the pre-Facebook days. The revamp hasn't been hugely successful, though, proving (once again) that Justin really should just stick to singing and hosting *Saturday Night Live*.

Just as our attitudes can change about the social networking "site du jour," so too can our attitudes about everyday consumer products and services. Not too far removed from the social networking market is the personal home computer market. In the 1990s, it would be difficult to find anyone who owned an Apple computer. When I was a kid in the early 1990s, we used to use Apple IIe computers in our gifted and talented class, computers that seemed dated even for that time. Suddenly, computer companies like Gateway and Dell emerged from the shadows, Gateway with its cool cow-colored boxes and Dell with its lean, "just-in-time" production processes that saved costs and, subsequently, reduced prices for the end consumer. Microsoft and Windows reigned supreme from the 1990s through the 2000s, making Bill Gates a billionaire and teaching all of us how an animated paper clip who "just wants to help" can make you murderous.

But somehow, seemingly out of nowhere, Apple crept its way back into the personal computer market. Cleverly, Apple started hawking products like the famous iPod (later evolving into the equally popular iPhone and iPad), and MacBooks became revered, trusted, and highly coveted computers. Apple positioned the Macbook laptop line as the computer of choice for younger, trendy, artsy people and the PCs (i.e., Gateways, Dells, and IBM/Lenovos) as the computer of choice for old, boring, accountant office worker types. This positioning was communicated in the famous "Mac v. PC" advertisements (you can watch just about all of them here: http://youtu.be/ByCyqSROGf0). In the spots, Apple cleverly shows the super cool personality of a Mac user v. the boring, dull personality of a PC user. The commercials were so effective that I have actually had friends apologizing for pulling a PC out of their bag when I pull out my Macbook – computer envy much?

What's even crazier is that if you were to go to a café (you may already be in a café sipping a delicious mocha while reading this book by a nice fireplace) and look around, there's a good chance that the majority of people around you working on a computer are Macbook users! Apple has so effectively positioned its computers as cool devices used by exclusive artsy, creative people that we don't even notice that the *majority* of computer users in a room are using a Mac. Samsung has caught on to this in the cellular phone market, running commercials poking fun at die-hard Apple fans who wait in line on the eve of new product releases by showing older people talking about how much they love their iPhone. The idea of Samsung's commercial, of course, is that *everyone* has iPhones, so they're just not cool anymore. Although Apple's iPhone is still dominating mobile phone sales, the various Samsung Galaxy models have achieved fairly strong sales, enough to make Apple pay attention to this rival.

So whether Facebook v. Twitter, Mac v. PC, or iPhone v. Galaxy, a company's success is not only a function of its product offerings and technical specifications but also consumers' attitudes toward the product, the brand, and even the people affiliated with the brand. And in a time when so much of our technology encourages real-time updating of our attitudes and the creation of profiles designed to capture our personalities, understanding changing consumer attitudes isn't just a luxury, it's a necessity.

*   *   *

In their quests to be the market leader, companies are obsessed with predicting the desires and preferences of consumers in the market so that they can make the products and offer the services the consumers will want the most. But if there's one constant in the world of consumer behavior it's that consumers change constantly. This is the reason smart companies, savvy marketers, and secretive government organizations (…too soon?) are always collecting data on consumers.

Although it is useful to track consumers' *actual* behavior and purchases, which most companies do, by that point it is often too late for a company to make any big decisions that might give it an edge in the market. So, instead, smart companies do their best to measure other features of consumers that might predict what these same consumers are likely to do and where their preferences are likely to go. What are these mysteriously predicative tidbits of information, you ask? Why, they are personalities and attitudes!

This is where you, dear reader, should get really excited: we are actually about to spend an entire chapter talking about people's weird personalities and sassy attitudes. In short, we are going to gossip. We are going to gossip about who people *are* and how they *express themselves* (personality), as well as gossip about how people *evaluate* and *judge* objects, ideas, products, issues, and other people. It's kind of like a trashy talk show without paternity tests or bleeped out obscene language (...although we can do a [bleeping] paternity test if you [bleeping] want to). The chapter begins with an introduction of the more enduring notion of personality, transitions to a discussion of finicky attitudes, and finally concludes with how we, as marketers, might go about changing or shifting those attitudes using a tried-and-true, old-fashioned technique we call persuasion. Let's get this talk show started.

Personality. **Personality** can be thought of as the combination or totality of an individual's thoughts, feelings, and behaviors. In our daily lives, we describe people's personalities as being anything from kindhearted to abrasive, sociable to standoffish. Personalities are relatively enduring, so when we label someone as having a particular personality, it's typically because they demonstrate that personality consistently over time.

For your trivia night purposes, you should know that the word "personality" derives from the Latin word "persona," which means "mask." This is fitting, of course, as our personalities are essentially a reflection of how others see us, how we see ourselves, and the lens through which we see the world. And, just like a mask, our personalities are our "front" – although a function of all the thoughts, feelings, and behavioral tendencies we have inside, our personality is the outward manifestation of our entire self.

Personality, as you can imagine, has been around for a looooong time, probably since there were three microscopic living creatures: one with a personality and the other two to talk about the first one. The Ancient Egyptians and Greeks are credited with the earliest known formal study of personality. Their approach, **Humorism**, proposed that each human being's body consisted of a mix of four "humors" (i.e., bodily fluids) – black bile, yellow bile, phlegm, and blood – each of which corresponded to particular characteristics – despondency and irritability (black bile), angry and temperamental (yellow bile), calm and neutral (phlegm), invigorated and sociable (blood). Philosophers believed that each human's personality was a function of some mix of these four "humors." Even Hippocrates, the guy for whom the Hippocratic Oath is named, was an advocate of the Humorist theory, and when a guy *that* important endorses your Humorist theory, well, that's no laughing matter (…groan).

Beyond Humorism (which, it turns out, isn't how personality actually works), modern researchers shifted to other explanations of personality. Sigmund Freud is famous for proposing his **Psychoanalytic Theory** of personality, which suggests that human personality is rooted in suppressed desires and instincts bubbling below our conscious awareness. Our personalities, Freud claimed, were merely those deep-rooted desires attempting to get out. Every now and then one of these urges breaks free and sexcapes, something we refer to as a Freudian slip.

Modern psychologists, however, tend to focus their efforts on the **Trait Theory of Personality**. A **trait** can be thought of as a distinguishable characteristic that describes an individual's tendency to act in a relatively consistent manner. Thus, the **Trait Theory of Personality** suggests that there are many traits – shy, outgoing, warm, relaxed, imaginative, etc. – and that for each trait there exists a continuum so that you and I might differ to the degree with which we possess each trait. Now, this may sound familiar to the Humorist approach earlier in that our overall personality is really just a combination or mix of a number of traits. That's kind of the idea here: personality is really just the combination of varying levels of ingredients we call "traits." So if I tend to contain heaping levels of "shy" and "introverted" and just a pinch of "outgoing" and only a dash of "extroverted," one might predict that my personality would *not* be that of a party animal.

One technical detail we need to get out of the way is the assumption underlying the Trait Theory of Personality. Specifically, this theory assumes a nomothetic approach to traits. The **Nomothetic Approach** believes that there are few traits that span across *all* people and that an individual's personality depends on how much (or how little) of each of these traits he/she possesses. Because of the shared pool of traits from which each individual creates his/her unique mix, it is possible to compare people based on their personalities (apples to apples). Furthermore, it is possible to use standard surveys and scales to assess differences among people. The alternative view to the nomothetic approach, the **Idiographic Approach**, believes that each person's personality is his/her own unique structure of traits and that some traits are likely to be specific to that individual only. Because of the extreme focus on individual difference in this approach, it is often impossible to compare people based on their personalities (apples to oranges), and highly individualized research methods must be used (e.g., journals, diaries, individual interviews). *Most* researchers today lean toward the nomothetic approach and the use of the Trait Theory of Personality. Because of this, it is much easier to measure personality and particular traits using surveys and scales, which makes life particularly easier for marketers. It also makes it possible for us to compare personalities, which is what makes *TMZ* and *Access Hollywood* worth watching and life worth living.

Measuring Personality. Because we are big believers in the nomothetic approach, it is possible for us to design surveys that can measure people's scores on a variety of traits and dimensions in our quest to uncover their personality.

One approach you may have heard of is the Big Five Personality Traits. The **Big Five Personality Traits** approach includes five traits – Openness to Experience, Conscientiousness, Extraversion, Agreeableness, and Neuroticism (just think "OCEAN" to remember the five traits). Each of the five traits is measured on a continuum (e.g., Extraversion: outgoing v. reserved) and the resulting scores provide a personality profile for the user. Another popular personality trait approach is the **Myers-Briggs Type Indicator (MBTI)**, which breaks down personality according to four dichotomies: 1) Extraversion/Introversion, 2) Sensing/Intuition, 3) Thinking/Feeling, 4) Judging/Perception. If you're curious about your Big 5 score or your MBTI results, check out the following links: Big 5 – http://www.outofservice.com/bigfive/ (apparently one of the better options), and MBTI – http://www.humanmetrics.com/cgi-win/jtypes2.asp (Note: several varieties of these assessments exist, so feel free to try others, as well). If you're curious, I'm an ENTJ – and I've scored the highest extraversion score *twice* in my life. There's no filter on this guy.

Although it's fun and interesting to talk about traits in a general sense, kind of like doing one of those "What kind of lover are you?!" quizzes in Cosmopolitan (…not that I have actually done one of those or anything), we marketers have our own set of "consumer traits" that we see manifest at different levels in shoppers. Those traits include:

- **Value-Consciousness**: tendency to seek out best bang for your buck, cost/benefit
- **Materialism**: tendency to seek out luxury or exclusive branded products
- **Innovativeness**: tendency to seek out novel, cutting edge products
- **Need for Cognition**: tendency to seek mental stimulation, thinking-it-through
- **Competitiveness**: tendency to vie against other consumers or a company to win

- **Impulsiveness**: tendency to act on instinct/urges with little thought
- **Anxiety**: tendency to worry and fret over making choices and taking action
- **Bargaining Proneness**: tendency to haggle or negotiate for better trade or value
- **Frugality**: tendency to avoid spending money, be thrifty, preserve resources
- **Superstitious**: tendency to follow rituals, habits, self-imposed rules

These consumer traits certainly do not encompass *all* the many characteristics that describe consumers, but they should provide a reasonable understanding of how an individual can be thought to vary on a continuum for each of these traits. You can imagine how a consumer might have a "consumer personality" based on the varying levels he scores on these traits. Having this information about an individual consumer or noticing trends at an aggregate market segment level can be useful for developing marketing communications.

One caveat to the trait theory approach is that just because two people both score high on a particular trait *does not mean* that they will both perform the exact same way in the real world. There is a difference between possessing a particular personality trait and *expressing* that trait. **Trait expression** refers to the fact that two or more people may share similar traits or trait profiles, but the actual expressed behaviors of these people may differ. The reason their behaviors may differ can be due to a variety of causes – self-moderation, situational factors, etc. One person who is characteristically sad may express this by moping around glumly and complaining all the time whereas another person who is also characteristically sad may express this by shutting down and becoming quiet. Someone who is the life of the party at a club during the weekend may be equally cheerful but more reserved when in class on Tuesday. So while many similarities exist among people whose personality profiles are comparable, it is naïve to assume they will always be *perfectly* identical in their behaviors. Still, personality gives us a good sense of who people are and, importantly, who they are likely to continue to be.

Personality and Self-Image: One and the Same? As I mentioned, the word personality derives from the word "mask" and can be thought of as the mask we wear by which others come to know us. But just as some people get all fixed up to go out on the town for a Saturday night and *think* they look really, really good even though they look like crap, so, too, can our own sense of our personality differ from how others see us.

The notion of **self-image** refers to the mental representation that we have of *ourselves*. Knowing a consumer's self-image is useful because people often actively pursue choices and behaviors that reinforce their perceived self-image and avoid pursuing choices/behaviors that are incongruent with their self-image. To give you an example, if I see myself as a young, urban professional (a.k.a. a Yuppie) then I am more likely to pursue consumer choices reflecting this (e.g., eating at "seen and be seen" restaurants, driving a flashy sports car) and to avoid engaging in behaviors that do not reinforce that image (e.g., shopping at a thrift shop, living in a dreaded suburb). Fortunately, my self-image is more that of a very smart homeless person or that of kind old widower who takes in stray pets and lives for *The Price is Right*.

Further complicating matters is that, in today's world, the internet and our many online profiles (e.g., Facebook, Twitter, Yelp, Match.com, FamersOnly.com), allow us to express our personality and our sense of self through a variety of media, which also means we have to manage that self-image across this variety of media. This also means that we can selectively differentiate our personality depending on the medium. The notion of a **virtual self** involves any representation of our 'self' in a virtual or simulated setting. This could be via a username on a website, an avatar, a Sims persona, or even your personality as it comes across on a personal website, blog, or user review posting.

One issue often raised when discussing a consumer's virtual self is that of anonymity. In some instances, from a marketing perspective, anonymity can be very helpful, as consumers feel like they can provide honest feedback without any fear that their comments will be traced back to them. Other times, however, the anonymity or separation between one's "actual self" and "virtual self" gives consumers the liberty to post nastier feedback than they would have provided otherwise, which can be harmful. For this reason, collecting data online or trying to make sense of user reviews or ratings can be tricky. Given the many ways we can now express our 'self,' marketers must be cognizant of how each medium may influence how that personality is expressed.

Brands can have personalities, too? A lot of marketing consulting firms have made good money selling the idea that brands, like people, can have personalities. MTV is young and hip whereas VH1 is a bit older and more nostalgic. Fox News is conservative and angry (when Obama is President) whereas MSNBC is liberal and angry (when Bush was President). Axe Body Spray is masculine and playful while Old Spice is masculine and classic. The list goes on and on; you can construe a personality for just about any brand you can imagine. The dimensions of brand personality marketers discuss most often include Sincerity, Excitement, Competence, Sophistication, and Ruggedness, each of which incorporates its own traits (e.g., Ruggedness: strong, outdoorsy). When it comes to famous clothing brands, Hollister Co. is a bit more rugged and less sophisticated with its "worn" jeans and frayed hems while J. Crew is more sophisticated and a lot less rugged with its perfectly cropped dresses and slacks and preppy design styles.

Thinking about brands and companies as having personalities is useful, for sure, as it helps facilitate conversations when conducting market research with consumers, helps to develop the creative content for branding and advertisements, and helps to keep all marketing communications "on target" or "on brand" more easily (… "Is this too old for MTV?"). However, I would be remiss if I did not mention some pretty cool research by my Ph.D. advisor, Carolyn Yoon. Carolyn, who often incorporates neuroscience in her research, discovered something quite interesting: the neural areas recruited when we think about or process *human* personalities are <u>different</u> from the neural areas activated when we process *brand* personalities. What this means, in simple language, is that although brand personalities are a useful way to think about brands and companies, they are not exactly *identical* to human personalities. Throw this factoid out next time some boastful jerk of a marketing manager tries to say there is no difference between actual human personalities and brand personalities.

From Personalities to Attitudes. Knowing and understanding someone's personality is useful because it allows us to make predictions about how they will feel about certain issues (if we want to talk politics), what kind of products they will like (if we want to buy them a gift), and what kind of person they will be (if we want to put a ring on it). In short, our personalities, which are enduring, are often predictive of our attitudes, which *can* be enduring but can also shift.

Attitudes. When we say that someone "has an attitude," we tend to mean this in a negative way, like, "What a jerk!" In reality, however, an **attitude** refers to any relatively enduring overall evaluation of an object, product, service, company, issue, or person (a.k.a. an "attitude object"). The "relatively enduring" piece comes into play because an attitude tends to span some period of time; that is, it's not a snap judgment based on a stimulus that suddenly appears and then disappears. Attitudes are learned over time as we are exposed to and interact with stimuli and form our evaluations. Because we learn attitudes it is important to note that attitudes *can* change over time due to new information, new experiences, and new beliefs, which is actually very important for persuasion.

Understanding attitudes is useful to marketers for many reasons, but perhaps the most important is the fact that *attitudes are often predictive of actual behavior.* The reason for this is that our thoughts and emotions sort of culminate into our attitudes, so if we are able to accurately measure and assess consumers' attitudes, we can make some reasonably accurate predictions about what those consumers are likely to do in the market based on synthesized information about their thoughts and feelings.

One reason our attitudes are so strongly predictive of behavior is because human beings tend to prefer that their attitudes are consistent with their behavior. For example, if I have strong negative attitudes toward smoking and positive attitudes toward my health, then I'm probably very unlikely to engage in smoking behavior. If I did smoke, I would probably feel rather uncomfortable given the misalignment of my attitudes toward smoking and health and my conflicting behavior. We refer to this uncomfortable feeling resulting from this disconnect between our beliefs and our behaviors as **cognitive dissonance**. When our beliefs do not align with our behaviors we feel a sense of uncomfortable arousal, and it turns out that this motivation to avoid feeling uncomfortable often leads us to shift our attitudes to be in line with our behaviors (or vice versa). In the case of our smoking example we would either 1) think of examples of how smoking isn't really that dangerous, say an 80-year old relative who smokes like a chimney and is in good health (i.e., shifting beliefs to align with behavior), or 2) stop smoking (i.e., shifting behavior to align with beliefs)

Another example of this innate human tendency to strive for "balance" is a theory known as...wait for it...Balance Theory (clever name, right?). **Balance Theory** refers to a natural preference in which our 'self' and two other associated stimuli exist in a balance of positive or negative relationships. Let me explain with an example. I love Tina Fey. Love. If she weren't married with children, we would elope. I also love chocolate-covered strawberries...like with a passion. If I find out that Tina Fey also loves chocolate-covered strawberries, all is right in my world: there is balance. However, if I find out Tina Fey does *not* love chocolate-covered strawberries, we've got problems. This is that feeling you get when you find out your new crush, whom, at first, seems to see every part of the world *exactly* the same way you do tells you that he/she hates dogs (which you love). Crushing! Balance Theory is most often depicted as a triangle, with the self in one corner and two stimuli at the other two corners. Positive and negative signs then indicate the relationship any two self/stimuli or stimuli/stimuli combination has with one another. Balance Theory can be useful for persuasion, as discussed later, because (like cognitive dissonance) we prefer to keep the internal peace in our mind. So if Snapple launches a new flavor of tea that I know nothing about, but I *do* know that Tina Fey loves the new flavor (because she said so in a television commercial), and I *do* know that I love Tina Fey, then my brain says, "Jim, you must also love the new flavor of tea because that will keep the world in balance!" It's all very Zen, really.

Balance Theory works like positive and negative numbers: the product of two negative numbers is a positive (e.g., -1 x -1 = +1), so in order for there to be "balance" there needs to be all positive links, one positive link and two negative links, or two negative links and one positive link. All negative links is not "balanced" – I can't stand Taylor Swift, Taylor Swift doesn't like One Direction, I don't like One Direction…suddenly Taylor Swift and I agree on something?! Never! So when drawing your Balance Theory triangles, think back to basic math to know whether or not a particular triangle is "balanced."

As the cognitive dissonance and balance theory examples suggest, our attitudes and preferences are related ideas. However, "attitude" and "preference" are *not* one and the same. Although similar, attitude is best reserved for *general* evaluations of a product, service, or some other stimulus, while *preference* goes one step further and indicates what you *want* or have otherwise ranked based on your likes and/or needs. If we think about it in the context of Balance Theory, our attitudes are the positive or negative signs along the edges of the triangle while our "preference" is whether or not we would buy or consider buying the product or service at the triangle's corner. To give a more general consumer example, I can have attitudes about the various kinds of air fresheners one can buy at the store (e.g., "They're too small," "The aromas are nice," "They wear out too quickly."), but I may not have particular preferences about the same air fresheners ("I prefer citrus scents," "I like clever designs," "I opt for Glade because it's a familiar brand."). Attitudes are valenced (i.e., positive or negative) evaluations; preferences are expressions of wants (or rejections).

Structural v. current view of attitudes. It is tempting to think that attitudes are these perfectly structured, crystallized ideas in our brains that we can readily call to attention in a moment's notice. However, that's quite a simplification of how attitudes actually work. Attitudes are not perfectly defined structures nor are they entirely static and unchanging. Instead attitudes are more *abstracted* evaluations consisting of a mix of cognitive, affective, and behavioral components. The former approach, known as the structural view, tends to take a backseat to this current view of attitudes.

Because the current view of attitudes incorporates these cognitive, affective, and behavioral components, as well as allows for factors like context and situation to influence attitudes, several models have been proposed that include these components so that we, as marketing researchers, can attempt to measure consumer attitudes. A few of these models are discussed next.

Multiattribute Attitude Models. There are many different ways to measure attitudes with each method having its own strengths and weaknesses. Some marketing researchers will simply ask, "How would you rate your overall attitude toward ADVERTISEMENT X?" with three, 7-pt. scales anchored by bad/good, unpleasant/pleasant, and dislike/like. The researchers then average those scores and make predictions using the attitude measure…it ain't great, but it's not *terrible*.

However, people often have a very difficult time articulating their attitudes for a variety of reasons: we may not actually know how we feel about something, we may be too embarrassed to say exactly how we feel, we may feel social pressure to respond in a particular way. One smart way to sidestep these problems is to elicit attitude measures *indirectly* through the components that make up those attitudes. To this point, a series of **Multiattribute Models** that incorporate these subcomponents of attitude often provide a better way of capturing or measuring attitudes.

One such model, the **Attitude Toward the Object Model (ATO)**, asks consumers to consider attributes of an attitude object (e.g., a product, service, or brand) and then to evaluate both 1) the strength of the belief that the target object possesses a particular attribute, and 2) the attractiveness or goodness of a particular attribute. So instead of asking directly for an attitude measure, the ATO model gets at overall attitude via the evaluation of attribute goodness and the belief that the target attitude object in question possesses that particular attribute. Here's the equation:

$$A_o = \sum_{i=1}^{N}(b_i)*(e_i)$$

A_o = Attitude toward the object
b_i = Strength of the belief that the object possesses attribute i
e_i = Evaluation of the attractiveness or goodness of attribute i
i = Attribute
N = Number of attributes

To give you a concrete example, say you are assessing your attitudes toward two car options: a sporty Audi or a practical Volvo. Three attributes you consider important include high price, car design, and safety. You rate the attractiveness or goodness of each attribute on the following scale:

-3	-2	-1	0	+1	+2	+3
Very bad	Bad	Slightly Bad	Neutral	Slightly Good	Good	Very Good

Following this, you rate each product (in this case the two cars) on how much you believe that they possess each attribute. For example:

Q: *How unlikely/likely is it that the Audi possesses a high price?*

-3	-2	-1	0	+1	+2	+3
Extremely Unlikely	Unlikely	Slightly Unlikely	Neutral	Slightly Likely	Likely	Extremely Likely

After all evaluations have been completed, it is often useful to organize the data in a chart like the one below:

Attribute	Evaluation of Attribute's Attractiveness/Goodness (e_i)	Audi: Belief that Audi possesses attribute i (b_i)	Volvo: Belief that Volvo possesses attribute i (b_i)
High Price	-1	+3	+1
Car Design	0	+2	+2
Safety	+2	+1	+3

To come up with an overall attitude toward each of our two objects we simply insert the numbers above into the equation. So for Audi, the math looks something like this:

$$A_{Audi} = (+3)*(-1) + (+2)*(0) + (+1)*(+2) = -1$$

And for Volvo we get:

$$A_{Volvo} = (+1)*(-1) + (+2)*(0) + (+3)*(+2) = +5$$

So, using these (totally arbitrary…) numbers (…don't sue me, Audi), it seems that this person has a more favorable attitude toward the Volvo than the Audi. Looking at this person's evaluations, it's clear that he/she prefers safety and is not a fan of high prices. Because this person believes Volvo has high safety ratings and Audi a high price, it makes sense that the math led to Volvo coming out on top.

The Attitude Toward the Object (ATO) Model is a useful way for marketers to estimate attitudes toward a particular target object without simply asking the ambiguous question, "What is your attitude about Product X?" a question many consumers wouldn't even know how to begin to start answering. However, we are interested in knowing about attitudes because we said earlier that attitudes are often predictive of behavior. Yet, if we look at the ATO model, nowhere do we see any measure of behavior or behavioral intentions. Never fear: here comes the Behavioral Intentions Model.

The **Behavioral Intentions Model** (a.k.a., the **Theory of Reasoned Action, BIM**) is another attitude model that focuses more on *behavioral intentions* and *actual behavior* than beliefs and evaluations about a target *object*. The BIM proposes that attitudes toward performing a particular behavior, combined with one's perception about what *others* think about engaging in that behavior, will predict behavioral intentions, which is a close approximation for *actual* behavior. Furthermore, the importance of one's own attitude toward the behavior and others' attitudes toward performing the behavior are weighted, as some people care more/less about the opinions of others and more/less about their own opinion. The equation is as follows:

$$B \cong BI = (w_1)^*(A_{behavior}) + (w_2)^*(SN)$$

B = Actual behavior
BI = Behavioral intention
$A_{behavior}$ = Attitude toward performing the behavior
SN = Subjective norm
w_1 and w_2 = empirical weights

Let's consider a real example to make this idea more concrete. Say you are out with friends and you're thinking about singing karaoke. The behavior here is getting up to sing karaoke in front of your friends and a room full of strangers. Let's say you're kind of shy so your attitude toward singing karaoke in public on a scale from 1 (mortifying) to 10 (amazing) is a 3. Your friends, on the other hand, are crazy and love attention, so your friends' subjective norm regarding karaoke on a scale from 1-10 is a 9 – singing karaoke and public embarrassment is *totally* normal to them. You like to think of yourself as an independent person and, as such, you have a history of weighting your own advice more than that of your friends (say 80% self, 20% others). This gives us...

$$B \cong BI = (.80)^*(3) + (.20)^*(9)$$

So on our weighted score of 1-10, we have a behavioral intention of 4.2, slightly less than the midpoint. From the looks of that score, it does not seem like karaoke is in your future tonight.

But let's have a little fun, shall we? Let's say I am the owner of the karaoke bar. I worry that not enough people are singing karaoke, so I decide to run an advertising campaign convincing you that friends give much better advice than we give ourselves and that you should really start listening to your friends more often. Maybe this would change the weights to say 40% self, 60% others:

$$B \cong BI = (.40)*(3) + (.60)*(9)$$

Now your behavioral intention score is a 6.6 out of 10; you're letting the subjective norm influence you more than yourself. Let's say I run a different marketing campaign in which I ask people to "remember the last few times you sang karaoke and how much fun you had getting up in front of the group even though you didn't think you would have fun." Perhaps bringing back these memories changes your attitude about the behavior to a more positive one:

$$B \cong BI = (.40)*(7) + (.60)*(9)$$

These revised numbers give us a behavioral intention score of 8.2. Suddenly, you went from definitely not singing karaoke to almost definitely singing some "Don't Stop Believin'" or "Sweet Caroline" simply because we shifted 1) the weighted importance of the subjective norm (which, in this case, favored singing karaoke), and 2) your attitude toward singing karaoke.

It is important to pause here and to point out that this "subjective norm" component is quite critical to consumer behavior. Think back to the Facebook example at the beginning of this chapter. One of the primary reasons Facebook has decreased in popularity with teenagers is because using the site is *perceived* to be uncool among one's friends and age group. According to the BIM, if a teen *believes* that no other teens are using Facebook, he/she is going to be less likely to use it, too. It doesn't even matter if teens are *actually* using Facebook less, just that they are *perceived* as using it less.

So, if you were a marketing manager at Facebook, what would you do? You might start by shifting the perception of the subjective norm so that a teen thinks Facebook use is actually much more prevalent among other teens than he/she currently thinks. You could try to shift a teen's weighting of his/her *own* attitudes higher and the weighting of the subjective norm lower if the perceived subjective norm is anti-Facebook and the individual's personal view of using Facebook is more favorable. You could also try to increase the individual teen's attitude toward using Facebook. Of course, an integrative approach in which you combined a few of these strategies could be even better.

Although other models for measuring attitudes and subsequent behavioral intentions do exist, the Attitude Toward the Object (ATO) Model and the Behavioral Intentions Model (BIM) are among the most prevalent. Although these two models are somewhat similar, they differ in three important ways. First, ATO focuses on attitudes whereas BIM focuses on intentions to act. Second, ATO has no social component whereas BIM incorporates a consumer's perception of what others think they should do. Finally, ATO focuses on attitude toward the object whereas BIM focuses more on the attitude toward the behavior of buying. While both models are useful, one criticism of ATO is that it is *less* predictive of behavior because it does not account for potential situational factors like BIM does. That is, one's "attitude toward an object" does not incorporate how this attitude may vary in different situations in the ATO model. The BIM incorporates situation into its model and, as such, may better predict behavior.

One final attitude theory, the **Theory of Trying to Consume**, tweaks the Behavioral Intentions Model slightly and suggests that *behavior* should be replaced with *trying*. The motivation behind this is that our actual behaviors or outcomes are more distal to our current thinking compared to our thoughts about *trying* to do something. To give a concrete example, my attitude toward driving a sexy sports car is nice, but before I drive that sexy sports car, I have to engage in this lengthy process of conducting research, visiting dealerships, taking test drives, adjusting my finances, and much more. As such, our attitudes about something (e.g., driving a sexy sports car) are likely affected by more proximal considerations like how much control we believe we have, our expectations of succeeding or failing, our attitudes toward trying or making an effort, how recently and frequently we have tried before, and our thoughts about what others think about our efforts.

Attitudes through the lens of Consumer Behavior. The Theory of Trying to Consume raises an interesting point: our attitudes are sometimes evaluations of an end target but can also be the evaluations of the *process* involved to reach the end target. Consumer researchers have realized that people often form attitudes for *functional* purposes. Indeed, the **Functionalist Theory of Attitude Formation** proposes that attitudes are formed to serve one or more of four primary functions:

- **Utilitarian:** The utilitarian function refers to the simple idea of maximizing gains and minimizing losses, so we tend to develop positive attitudes toward those things that lead to greater gains and negative attitudes toward those things that lead to losses. For example, we may have a favorable attitude toward Doritos because they make us feel full whereas we may have a negative attitude toward rice cakes because we find that we are still hungry after eating 1,000 of them.

- **Knowledge:** The knowledge function refers to organizing the complex information of the world around us, and attitudes are able to help make the acquisition, interpretation, and organization of that information easier. For example, I have an attitude toward animals that anything incapable of responding to its name when spoken aloud cannot be trusted. This excludes dogs but includes just about everything else (…this is where cat people say things like, "I know most cats don't respond to their names, but *my* cat does…"). Now, when I encounter any new species or critter, my attitude toward non-dogs allows me to classify the critter quickly into the appropriate "good pet" or "not a good pet" bucket.

- **Value-Expressive:** The value-expressive function involves forming an attitude to reflect or to portray your values or identity to others. Say, for example, you consider yourself to be a loyal member to the Republican or Democratic party; chances are you have developed attitudes espoused by these groups, maybe not entirely because you believe those ideas 100%, but rather because holding those attitudes communicates your belongingness to this particular group.

- **Ego-Defensive:** The ego-defensive function involves forming an attitude to save yourself from reality or ego-threatening information. My *favorite* example of this occurs when a deeply insecure person takes on attitudes of extreme *superiority*. Most bullies also rely on ego-defensive attitudes to compensate for deeply-rooted insecurities. In a consumer context, imagine a shopper who holds strong negative attitudes about T.J. Maxx and Marshall's. Despite *knowing* that the stores offer the same quality of clothing as department stores at much lower prices, someone concerned about his/her image or new acceptance in a wealthy group may take on dismissive attitudes toward the stores.

Beyond thinking about how attitudes serve functional purposes, consumer researchers also think about how different consumer experiences take place at different levels of involvement and how this may effect the order in which consumers *think* (cognition), *feel* (affect), and *do* (behavior). This model, known as the **ABC Model of Attitudes** (a.k.a. the **Tri-Component Model**) breaks down attitudes into three components–Affect (A), Behavior (B), and Cognition (C)–and proposes a **Hierarchy of Effects** (i.e., the order in which we think, feel, and do) depending on the kind of purchasing context we are in at the moment. Here are a few examples:

- **Low-Involvement Hierarchy:** C → B → A. This is a "think, do, feel" approach in which we first think about our purchase and then buy immediately, only reflecting on our feelings after the fact. Examples of this include routine, boring purchases like toilet paper. "I need toilet paper. (Buys toilet paper). This feels as it should."
- **High-Involvement Hierarchy:** C → A → B. This is a "think, feel, do" approach in which we first think about our purchase, then assess our feelings, and then decide to either purchase or not. Examples of this include more complex decisions like purchasing a television or a new car.
- **Experiential Hierarchy:** A → B → C. This is a "feel, do, think" approach in which we first have an emotional arousal or stirring that leads us to do something (purchase, not purchase), and we only think about it after the fact. An example of this is having a strong feeling of desire upon seeing dessert come by on a dessert tray, grabbing and eating the dessert, and then thinking about the calories only later after you've eaten the dessert and gone home.
- **Behavioral Influence Hierarchy:** B → C → A. This is a "do, think, feel" approach in which you do something impulsively and only think about it and assess how you feel about it after the fact. Examples of this include ordering another round of drinks without any forethought or mindlessly grabbing a magazine or candy at the checkout counter. Then you think about what you've done and subsequently develop a feeling about it.

The hierarchical approach to attitudes may be an oversimplification of how attitudes are actually formed in the brain, but for marketers it is a useful tool because it suggests effective ways for intervening in the attitude development process. That is, if we know that our shoppers are making "high-involvement" decisions, it would be wise to focus on their thought process and to provide them with logic and reasons up front whereas doing the same strategy in the context of "experiential" decisions would be pointless, as shoppers in that context focus on feelings and behaviors well before thoughts. Yet again, we see how understanding and breaking down attitudes into its various components can provide insights on how we, as marketers, might be able to persuade consumers.

*   *   *

Persuasion. Persuasion is one of the more infamous marketing buzzwords, one that suggests some nefarious, subtle manipulation tactic in which we, as marketers, make consumers do our evil bidding so that we can earn suitcases full of cash, spread them on a luxury hotel's bed, and roll around in an ocean of money. Fair enough.

Although you may not have noticed, we actually have already talked quite extensively about persuasion in this chapter. In fact, I've already provided you with several tools you can use to persuade others up to this point in the chapter. Yet you have not sold your soul to the devil yet nor have you forked over your entire life savings to some Nigerian prince via email. What gives?

Persuasion refers to any attempt to shift or change attitudes. Remember our discussion of Balance Theory and how using someone we idolize as a spokesperson may lead us to like a product we've never even seen or tried simply because we love the celebrity and have an innate bias to keep balance? Persuasion. Or how about the example where the Ad Council tells us our behavior of sitting for four or more hours does not jibe with our beliefs about the importance of health? Persuasion. Shifting an attribute's evaluation of goodness/desirability or the belief that a product possesses a particular attribute? Persuasion again. Reweighting the importance we place on our own attitudes or the subjective norms of others regarding a particular behavior? Yep. Persuasion.

What is beautiful about the way we currently think about attitudes is that the different approaches give us a guide for which levers we might pull (i.e., beliefs, evaluations, attitudes, weights) when we want to persuade an individual or a group. As a marketer, this should be exciting to you. Heck, as a human being interested in having some sway over someone else, this should be equally as exciting...methinks someone is going to attempt using these tools in their social time this weekend, eh?

Now, before I go into more detail on persuasion, I want to share a story with you:

One time I escaped from a cult.

Okay, well, it wasn't like a wear-brightly-colored-robes-and-drink-a-mysterious-fruit-punch kind of cult. Well, that's not entirely true – it totally could have been that kind of cult, but I didn't stick around long enough to find out. The people were definitely crazy, though. And before you think that I deliberately joined a cult, you should know that my involvement with these folks was the result of one big mistake.

Now you might be asking yourself, "How did you *mistakenly* wind up at a cult meeting?" That's a fair question. You see, when I was working as a consultant in Los Angeles, one of the new products we were planning to develop was a leadership retreat for corporate executives. As is the case with any business product, it's important to benchmark against your potential competitors, so the owner of the company for which I was working at the time decided that four of us, himself included, would participate in a weekend "leadership retreat" sponsored by an LA-area university. That sounds innocent enough, right? Well, it turned out later that this "university" was actually owned by a private organization (i.e., the cult) despite having an extremely misleading title that used the name of a local city in its name.

Side Note: I'm deliberately avoiding any specific mention of this organization, the faux university they own, or any other identifying information, as this particular cult, like most cults, is sue happy, meaning they would drag me into court and accuse me of some ridiculous charge for exposing their insanity to the world. I will gladly tell you in person, however, and before signing up for any leadership retreats in the greater Los Angeles area, please consult me first.

Now to be honest, the group's "beliefs" were mostly benign. From what I can remember they had some theory about metaphysical energy that originated in the heart and then projected outward from the body. Of course, as the trained scientist in the room, I repeatedly raised my hand to ask questions about the science behind these "energy" theories after the leaders repeatedly said, "Several studies have *proven* these ideas," which was funny to me because science *proves* nothing; it merely *supports* theories, some that persist over time and others that are replaced by newer, better theories. So it wasn't so much that I thought the group's beliefs were *dangerous*, per se, as much as I thought their deceptive and misleading approach was uncomfortably sneaky, like this weekend was maybe a "recruitment" into something potentially more dangerous.

Early on in the weekend I noticed that things were a bit off. First, you had to be checked in on a list at the street door before coming in. Then a man immediately locked the door. Creepy. Then you were directed to this large, windowless room with no clock. In the back of the room about 5 or 6 "volunteers" stood about two feet apart from one another, each sharing the same "lights are on but nobody's home" glassy stare you often hear about in cults. Even stranger, one "volunteer" was typing everything that happened in the room into a computer as it happened. Strange. I also noticed that several of the volunteers were wearing a particular symbol around their necks, which, upon my inquiry, I learned represented the Aramaic word for "human." Aramaic? In 2009? Weird.

The sessions ran from early morning until the late evening with few breaks except for mandatory breaks in which all the participants had to leave the room but the volunteers could stay. One woman, who was also an unwitting participant in the weekend, forgot her purse in the room during one of these "mandatory breaks" and, upon reentering the room, was shocked to find the volunteers all huddled in the middle of the room, each making physical contact with one another in what she described as some sort of prayer. We were also discouraged from engaging much with others from the outside world (e.g., family and friends) during the weekend.

The strangest part (that I feel comfortable writing without having to look over my shoulder for the rest of my life) involved the two leaders of the weekend. One man, an African-American man in his late 30s or early 40s, reminded me of Tim Meadows from *Saturday Night Live* and, as such, did not creep me out. His partner, on the other hand, was a 50-something year old Caucasian woman who clearly had a solid education but mentioned, on several occasions, a fairly nasty divorce that she had gone through. I noticed a theme in that *all* the volunteers seemed to have some extremely tragic event that took place in their lives or otherwise indicated themselves to be *aimless* at some point during their lives.

The female leader made use of a very interesting tactic when dealing with participants in the audience. The leaders would ask for volunteers to discuss challenges in their lives, and then the leaders would deliberately poke and prod the sharing participants about the *reasons* for their misfortunes. Without fail the leaders would ask, "What is it about *you*? What did *you* do that led to this misfortune?" Even in situations where the individuals could not have possibly caused an event – a natural disaster, the cancer death of a friend, a wife's miscarriage – the "leaders" would attempt to shift the blame back to the individual.

Right in front of my eyes I watched as the leaders broke down participants, exposing their vulnerabilities in front of a group of strangers. I watched as even the people *I* knew started breaking down – my business partner crying in front of the group and blubbering about the need to feel loved, a friend who admitted his suicidal tendencies in front of the group. At some point, I had Googled information about the group and found that they had been labeled a cult organization in Europe, a region of the world that does not play games when it comes to such matters. "Of course!" I thought, "That explains the long days, the windowless room, the lack of a clock, the preying on vulnerable people, the guilt and blame attribution followed up by the, 'Let us help you with our method,' approach." It all became crystal clear.

I remember calling my parents to tell them all the craziness I saw expecting them to get on the next flight to LA to drag me back to the Midwest. However, my mom encouraged me to take a different tactic: she suggested I go undercover and let the other innocent participants know what was *really* going on, how this "leadership retreat" was really a front for a spiritual organization. As a lifelong lover of spy movies, she didn't have to tell me twice. Oh, side note, she also called me really stubborn, which is why she wasn't worried about the group's attempt to persuade me…thanks, Mom. I love you, too.

So I returned the next day determined to tell as many people as I could about what was *really* happening. I deliberately partnered with a different partner during each paired activity. I would start by saying, "Oh, this activity sounds fun!..." then I'd lean in closely and whisper, "Okay, here's what's really going on right now…" My goal was to tell all the other participants in the room without either of the leaders or any of the volunteers catching on. I had one close call when I realized that one of the participants, a doctor in the area, was actually a plant in the audience; i.e., someone on the inside who was working for/with the leaders and volunteers. This was some CRAZY stuff!

For a full day and a half I managed, slowly and secretively spreading the word about the group. The straw that broke the camel's back for me, however, was a fairly dangerous exercise in which participants in the room were to partner up with one another and "role play" such that you had to be whomever your partner wanted you to play. The potential danger here, friends, is that we were in a room of people who had suffered domestic abuse, sexual assault, and other horrific things, so attempting such an exercise without the expertise of a trained, certified professional did *not* sit well with me. I alerted the leaders I would be respectfully "peacing out," and proceeded to find my way to the locked exit, get let out, and make my way to a Starbucks down the street. My duty there was done.

I share my cult experience with you for three reasons: 1) it's a crazy $#@% story, 2) it illustrates the power of persuasion at play, albeit in a nefarious, manipulative way, and 3) to *really* put in perspective how marketing, despite what critics may say, is *not* an evil, deceptive, misleading, scary, imposing, and uncaring beast. Marketing is like the pit bull of the business world: people assume it's dangerous and deadly when, in reality, whether or not it is good or menacing depends entirely on how it is raised and nurtured (cue Sarah McLachlan's "Angel" here…suddenly you feel the urge to give money to your dog or cat…hmmm).

You see, cults are characterized by several distinguishing features: unquestioning commitment to its practices (check – see: volunteers), punishment of dissent or questioning of its methods (check – I was reprimanded several times for this), leader dictating how members should think, act, feel (check – the "leader" of the group developed his method after being visited by a "spiritual being"), the leader is not accountable to others (check – the history on this guy is that he's an ego maniac), leaders induce feelings of guilt, blame, or shame to influence participants (check – the leaders made participants blame themselves for their life's ills), there is an established hierarchy that encourages advancement through more participation in group events (check – you could pay to participate in more seminars and "move up" in the ranks). *And that's just a few!*

When we talk about Harley-Davidson riders and Apple fanatics as being cult-like tribes, we are simply relying on an expression that we do not mean *literally*. The important distinction is that the majority of companies are genuinely concerned about fulfilling the needs and wants of their consumers to *improve* their lives in a *transparent* way. Religious cults are more concerned about *controlling* lives in an *opaque* manner. When you go forward as marketers, keep this distinction in mind, as it is the difference between the ethical marketer and the unethical crazy person.

Still, if you ever hear your boss or a team member talking about your customers as a "cult" and asking how you can increase purchasing among this adoring consumer segment, I want you to answer, "Lock them in a room with no windows, deprive them of sleep, and make them feel bad about themselves and *then* we sell our product as the solution." ...Totally kidding. You can't do that. Well, you *can* do that, but you probably shouldn't. Instead, let's return to some other, less questionable persuasion techniques.

Positioning, Repositioning, and Persuasion Tactics. When it comes to changing attitudes in the marketing world, this is where one of our 4Ps pays us a guest visit: Positioning. The concept of positioning our product or service in the marketplace and, if need be, *repositioning* our product or service in the marketplace is really just an exercise in persuasion: here's what you think now, here's what we want you to think, let's do what it takes to get you from point A to point B.

To position or reposition a product or service (or brand, even), marketers often rely on a few common tricks or tools. One tactic is to *change the motivational function of consumers*. The reason for this is that the motivation or reason we pursue a product or service directs our attention to particular, relevant attributes. However, products and services often serve many functions, address many needs, and are pursued for various motivations. Thus, if we know people eat at Panera both because the food tastes good and because it is a healthier option than most quick service restaurants, but we also know that a particular consumer segment often overemphasizes taste over health, we might shift them to focus on the healthy reasons they go to Panera particularly if doing so enhances or increases their attitudes toward the restaurant.

Another (re)positioning tactic marketers use involves *associating the product with a group, cause, or event.* This approach relies on somewhat of a spillover effect: concerts tend to make people happy, excited, and enthusiastic, so if I am a new brand just starting out, I want to give out free samples at that concert to get people happy, excited, and enthusiastic about my brand and product. Similarly, sponsorship of major events, like Relay for Life, can both communicate a company's goodwill and also focus attention on the beliefs and evaluations of the *event,* which then gets applied to the product or company because of its association. There is also a bit of Balance Theory at play, particularly when a product is associated with a group that you may already like.

A third (re)positioning strategy relies on exploiting (and resolving) conflicting attitudes. We saw examples of this earlier in the context of how marketers cleverly use cognitive dissonance and Balance Theory as tools of persuasion because of our innate human preference for balance, consistency, and conflict resolution. If I believe myself to be a healthy person but the Ad Council tells me sitting for more than four hours a day is making me obese, well, I will probably stop sitting for four hours a day. If I cannot stand Kanye West and I learn that Kanye West loves Reebok shoes, then I may have to hate on Reebok shoes. Exploiting simple, innate preferences for consistency and balance is a simple way to shift attitudes.

My personal favorite (re)positioning strategy involves altering components of one of the multi-attribute models. In the case of ATO this involves shifting the attractiveness of an attribute, adding more attributes for a consumer to consider (or removing attributes with unfavorable scores), and adjusting the degree to which a consumer believes a product possesses a particular attribute, dialing up in the case of good scores and dialing down in the case of bad scores. In the case of BIM this involves altering an individual's perceived subjective norms, the individual's attitude toward performing a particular behavior, or adjusting the weights placed on his/her own attitudes and the attitudes of others in a way that favors your product, service, brand, or company. What I love about this approach is that it provides a simple way to produce psychological and behavioral changes and even suggests the *specific* messages your marketing executions should include.

One final (re)positioning tactic marketers often exploit has little to do with themselves and everything to do with the competition: repositioning the competition. Although we discussed the ATO model at length earlier, one thing we did *not* yet discuss was how the ATO model could be used to affect attitudes about our competition. Let's pretend we are the marketing team at Dunkin Donuts wondering how we can increase our relative position in the market compared to Krispy Kreme, our competitor.

Although we could try to increase the beliefs and evaluations of our *own* donuts, we could just as easily launch a marketing campaign that shifts the beliefs and evaluations of our competitor's donuts *downward*. Competitive advertising makes use of this approach all the time.

Components of Communication. So now that we have these different approaches to positioning or repositioning (i.e., changing or shifting the attitudes of consumers, a.k.a. persuading), the next logical thing we have to consider is *how* to communicate this information. Various communication models exist, but the most common is one that includes five components: the **sender**, the **receiver**, the **medium**, the **message**, and **feedback**.

I won't deep dive too far into this other than to tell you that the key takeaway here is that our earlier discussion on STP, the 4Ps, the 5Cs, and Integrated Marketing Communication applies directly here. That is, we need to know our target audience (i.e., the receiver) as best as we possibly can because knowing this consumer inside and out will dictate the media through which we reach him/her (i.e., the medium), the copy and word choice we use as well as the artistic style and/or tone (i.e., the message), whom we should use as the source of this information (e.g., a person, a newspaper article, an advertisement, the company; i.e., the sender), and the measurements in place to know how our consumers have changed, how our competitors are reacting, and how the general market climate is affected (i.e., the feedback). Good communication can break down at *any* stage of the process, so although each piece of the communication chain is inextricably tied to the next, thinking about them as being distinct components can be helpful when it comes to identifying particular trouble areas.

The best piece of advice I ever received regarding persuasion is simple: don't just say it, *show it*. That is, when communicating an idea to an audience, don't rely on them to take the extra step of mentalizing or visualizing your vision…SHOW them. Produce a mock-up, a prototype, a storyboard, projected results if they follow your advice, etc. This may seem subtle, but it is easily the best, most effective advice when it comes to active persuasion.

But not all persuasive communication needs to be so well articulated. Although we will discuss subtle, incidental cues in a later chapter, I'll introduce one communication tactic that can influence your attitudes outside of the more formal communication chain. This tactic, known as the **mere exposure effect**, involves simply repeating a stimulus multiple times in the presence of a consumer. Regardless of whether or not that consumer *actively* attends to the stimulus, research has shown that we tend to evaluate a stimulus more positively after it has been repeatedly exposed to us. This is one reason companies still spend lots of money on banner ads and product placement in movies and television shows. Even politicians rely on mere exposure: we also tend to believe things are "truer" the more we hear them. This is one reason so many people insist President Obama is a Muslim (he isn't), was born in Kenya (he wasn't), and has a secret gay relationship with Chicago mayor Rahm Emanuel (we doubt it). Yet despite plenty of evidence to the contrary, people *still* believe these ideas…*a lot* of people, which is a worrying feature of democracy: these people vote.

Social Judgment Theory. One problem with assuming that communication is a perfectly straightforward process is evident in a theory known as Social Judgment Theory. **Social Judgment Theory** essentially states that we compare all incoming information to our *existing* attitudes. If we are huge fans of Hostess products – like Twinkies and Donettes – then any incoming information about the nutritional facts or quality of these products is going to be processed differently than people who do not share our affinity for Hostess snacks, people who hate Hostess snacks, or people who may have never even heard of Hostess. The theory derives from work on physical experiments in which researchers realized that participants differed in their ability to assess the physical characteristics of a stimulus depending on their starting point or "anchor." For example, if I am used to seeing huge portion sizes (which, as an American from the Midwest, I totally am), Denny's new and improved "Bigger Grand Slam" breakfast may not likely change my attitudes regarding the size or value I am obtaining from the new menu offering. However, if I were from Europe, a place where portion sizes are moderate and delicious, the same stimulus would be interpreted very differently because my starting anchor point is very different. Incidentally, this is also why I am always self-conscious eating in front of my European friends.

Social Judgment Theory produces another robust effect: if information coming in confirms what we already know or is at least similar to what we already know, we are much more likely to accept it. If, however, incoming information is very different from our established anchor of what we already know or believe to be true, we may flatly reject the new information. As marketers, this is important to know: sometimes we cannot just say what we want to say but, instead, we have to say what we want to say in a way that our intended audience is *willing to hear.*

Persuasion Strategy. I just brought up two, very different approaches to persuasion: a very thoughtful, reason-based communication model in which we craft verbal and visual messages sent through specific media to our end receivers and, conversely, a very automatic, incidental, and thoughtless approach that involves simply exposing an audience to a particular stimulus repeatedly over time. Which approach is more effective?

Well, it depends.

You see, although we like to think we are fully in control of how we are processing incoming information, this simply is not the case. Sometimes we are motivated, able, and have the opportunity (MAO) to process incoming information at a deliberate, analytic, and critical level. Other times we lack the motivation, ability, or opportunity to process information in this way, but that does not mean that our sensory system still isn't picking up cues and stimuli. Two clever researchers, Richard Petty and John Cacioppo, caught onto this in the 1980s and developed what is referred to as the Elaboration Likelihood Model (ELM).

The **Elaboration Likelihood Model (ELM)** suggests that our elaboration is a continuum on which we either process information more deeply (greater elaboration) or barely at all (little to no elaboration). Broadly speaking, the model proposes two "routes to persuasion," the central route – which involves the more attentive, rational, analytic style recruiting cognitive processing – and the peripheral route – which involves peripheral cues, situational factors, and other stimuli unrelated to the message content itself that evade cognitive processing. To give you a concrete example, a television commercial enumerating reasons you should switch to AT&T for your cable and internet needs is appealing to central route processing while the beautiful spokesperson and catchy music of the commercial is appealing to the peripheral route.

Indeed, marketing executions can (and often do) appeal to both the central and the peripheral route. After all, even people who like to think and work through persuasive arguments logically sometimes get tired or busy and lack the resources to process at this higher level of elaboration. That's when the commercial's pretty spokesperson and music work their magic. Sometimes specific product or service categories predispose people to engage in greater/lesser elaboration. Buying an expensive new television is more likely to recruit greater elaboration given the price tag and the involvement of the decision, whereas purchasing a pair of socks is a lot less involved, requires much less elaboration, and, as such, is probably better served by peripheral appeals.

This idea that our depth of elaboration on incoming information and attempts at persuasion can vary is extremely important because, as marketers, we can make more efficient choices and avoid wasting money by appealing to our intended audience in the way that is most likely to be effective. However, to do this we have to have a strong understanding of not just the consumers and their respective "Self," we also have to have a strong understanding of the contexts and environments in which they find themselves – a.k.a. their "Situation." Remember my cult story? That room consisted of a group of about 50 people, mothers, fathers, a prominent Los Angeles doctor, a Harvard MBA, a college freshman, and others, people who lead normal lives and who probably question claims they hear on television like, "This is the best possible price," and, "Your life will be better for using our product." And yet, despite being smart, functioning, and critically thinking people, I watched as, one by one, they began succumbing to the claims and appeals of a strange group with even stranger, non-scientific beliefs. Removed from the outside world and the support of their social networks, deprived from sleep for several days, limited in the time they had to eat, blocked from knowing how time was passing outside in a windowless room with no clock, their long-held attitudes and views of the world went from being set in stone to being flexible, pliable, and moldable, capable of being sculpted by a group who had questionable, ulterior motives. Although our Self matters when we sense and interpret information in the world around us, our Situation turns out to be just as important, and the interaction of the two critical to understanding how we, as human beings, think and behave.

*   *   *

The world of social networks, much like any world in the tech space, evolves at the speed of light. Case in point, when the Pew Research Center asked teenagers which social network they used the most in 2007, 85% said that MySpace was their most-used social network site (Madden, 2013). How many teens report MySpace as their most-used social network site today? Just 7%.

In a follow-up report in August 2013, the same research center pointed out that Facebook is still *the* dominant social networking site for teenagers despite beliefs to the contrary: 94% of the teens they interviewed who have social network profiles have a Facebook account. However, Zuckerberg and colleagues are likely wise to be concerned given the emergence of competing sites and services. It only took MySpace 6 years to see its teen use drop 92% and that was with fewer players in the market. And, certainly, there is the pervasive belief among teenagers that their peers aren't using Facebook. So even if teens all actually have accounts, we know from the Behavioral Intentions Model that this "subjective norm" belief that their peers are not on Facebook can have a profound influence on a teen's behavior, particularly at that age when what others think often weighs more heavily on the mind than one's own beliefs.

This leads us to an important point: so far in this book we have focused primarily on those motivations that are internal to the individual. However, throughout this section on the Self, we have repeatedly encountered examples in which triggers or stimuli *external to the self* affect our thoughts, emotions, behaviors, and even change our attitudes. Indeed, we don't live in this world as separate, isolated human islands never interacting with other human beings or a changing, dynamic world. Quite the opposite, we are innately *social* beings, even possessing a neurochemically-induced motivation to bond with others (...sometimes even sexually). We are physical bodies designed with sensory systems like vision and olfaction and touch so that we can take in information about the changing world around us. The presence of other people and our ever-changing, rich surroundings strongly influence our choices and behaviors. Thus, the next section of the book, The Situation, is dedicated to these very ideas and more.

APPLICATION QUESTIONS

1) A young, inquisitive child learning about the world asks you to explain the difference between "personality" and "attitude." How do you describe this difference so simply that even a child can understand?

2) Say you conduct research on your consumers and find that the vast majority of them tend to score high on introversion. How can you take this information and doing something with it in the context of a retail experience? With respect to advertising?

3) Why would knowing someone's Big 5 scores be useful in the context of guarantees, warranties, and insurance sales? How could you raise more money or avoid wasting money with this knowledge?

4) Let's link a concept from a prior chapter in which we said comparing one's actual self to one's ideal self can be motivating. Bearing this in mind, how do you think a difference between one's self-image and others' objective image of that person affects an individual? How could you apply this in a retail or business context?

5) People often form extremely strong bonds with their cars, sometimes going as far as giving their vehicles actual names! You probably have a friend like this (or may even be that kind of person). How would you intelligently console a friend if his/her car died and he/she said to you, "You don't understand! I lost a true friend today?!"

6) Although understanding attitudes is important to marketers, we tend to talk about attitudes predicting behavioral *intentions* and not

simply behavior. Why is this an important distinction?

7) Jenny was raised in a culture where only boys play rough sports, but lately she has been participating in a women's rugby league. She's thinking about quitting before it gets too dangerous, but she's also beginning to think those old-school beliefs about men, women, and sports is kapooey. What psychological phenomenon is Jenny experiencing?

8) Someone has a crush on you (ooooh!). He/she sees that you are always getting frozen yogurt at Forever Yogurt and, despite never have eaten frozen yogurt, seems to now eat it all the time like it's essential for life. What phenomenon explains this?

9) Now, let's say you've made it clear to your admirer that it's not gonna happen. Suddenly, he/she finds frozen yogurt revolting. Besides the treat reminding him/her of your callous, cold, and unloving heart, what phenomenon may explain the sudden dislike?

10) You work at a major consumer packaged goods (CPG) food company as the marketing manager for pudding cups. You just got back a research brief showing that you are losing ground to your competition. It turns out that consumer attitudes toward you product aren't favorable. When customers think about your pudding they think of two things: the taste, the color. When customers think of other puddings they also think of size, texture, smell, and convenience. Knowing this information, how could use the Attitude Toward the Object (ATO) model to potentially improve attitudes toward your pudding?

11) You own a company that makes toys for cats. You focus on customers who love their pets as if they were children and, as such, who enjoy giving toys to their kitties. However, there is a movement by animal psychologists to discourage overstimulation of pets because it fosters a sense of entitlement. As such, there is a growing belief among pet owners that *too* many toys is a very bad thing...yet people may still love giving toys to their animals. Using the Behavioral Intentions Model as a starting point, what marketing actions would you take to make sure your business does not suffer?

12) In politics, one of the hardest things to do is to change the attitudes of a voter once he/she had made up his/her mind on an issue. Think about different issues on which a voter is likely to have a strong attitude and then, using the Functionalist Theory of Attitude Formation, explain how each attitude might be serving one of the different four functions (e.g., someone may believe global warming is a hoax to avoid dealing with the ego-threatening reality that he/she knows nothing about science, weather, and/or geology).

13) Teavana, a store known for selling high-quality teas, features a sleek design, lots of information regarding the various teas it sells, peaceful music playing, strong smells of fresh teas and scented products like candles also sold in the store, as well as free samples of its products. If we consider each of these cues to be persuasive in encouraging shoppers to purchase tea at the store, how would we classify each one according to the Elaboration Likelihood Model (ELM)?

14) You noticed lately that Target has been purchasing banner ads on major search sites like Yahoo! The ads are simple, just the famous Target bull's-eye, and don't seem to encourage the web surfer to do anything. Using a concept from this chapter, what might Target be doing?

15) Motivation, Ability, and Opportunity (MAO) are important with respect to our ability to attend to information. Greenpeace volunteers are out in full force in your neighborhood, standing on street corners and trying to get your attention. Using MAO, explain why you are likely able or unable to engage with the Greenpeace volunteers and do something for the organization. How could Greenpeace change its approach/strategy to help facilitate MAO so that you are more likely to get involved?

PART II:

THE SITUATION

Although it is easy to think that we are each the center of the world, the fact of the matter is that we are each merely players in a play unfolding around us. Even the field of psychology was biased in focusing on the self for decades before finally acknowledging the role of situation, environment, and context, thus starting the 'social psychology' movement. How we think and behave in one context can vary quite drastically in other contexts. How you behave in a classroom may differ from how you behave in a club or bar. The choices you make privately or anonymously may differ from the choices you make publicly or in an identifiable situation. To understand how our "situation" – our context, surroundings, and/ or particular point in time – affects our decision-making and behavior, the following chapters are dedicated to situation-related characteristics: social influence, culture, subcultures, context, environment, and situation.

Chapter 7 | Social Influence

Everyone in Los Angeles is beautiful.

Okay, not *everyone*, but when I began consulting in LA I noticed that LA consists of a disproportionate amount of good-looking people. This makes sense, of course, as LA is the heart of the entertainment industry and, as such, attracts good-looking people hoping to become the "next best thing" all the time. How *I* wound up there is anyone's guess, but I knew that if I wanted to stay in LA and, importantly, to *fit in*, I, too, would have to jump on the fitness bandwagon.

Now, I have never been an overweight person. Quite the contrary, I have always been a skinny, beanpole kind of a guy, with my skinny body somehow miraculously able to support the weight of my abnormally large head that I inherited from my father. Thanks, Dad.

Before moving to LA I had gone to the gym only a handful of times. Once, freshman year of college, I remember getting decked out in workout attire only to learn 1) people do not get "decked out" to go to the gym, and 2) you feel really, really sore for days after going to the gym for the first time in your life, so sore, in fact, that going back just feels impossible...so I didn't.

The other hang up I always had about going to the gym is that people would watch me and judge my apparent ignorance regarding what to do. All I knew is that there were a lot of weights, some running machines, and weird, metal machines that combined pulleys with weights that seemed to be meant for specific body parts. In short, I was gym illiterate and feared the judgment of the meatheads working out nearby who, based on their bodies alone, clearly knew what they were doing.

So on that fateful day in late 2007, I was invited to go workout with my business colleague at the time to a place called Barry's Boot Camp. Although militaristic in name and design (the gym has a camouflage motif complete with dog tag signs and more), the gym was not *too* imposing. I use the word "gym" loosely to describe a place where one works out, as Barry's Boot Camp is actually more of a room no bigger than a decent-sized living room. There are about 15 to 20 treadmills on one wall featuring a mirror and then about 15 or 20 "spots" on the floor consisting of makeshift benches with several full sets of weights on the other side of the room featuring another mirrored wall.

That there are mirrors everywhere at Barry's Boot Camp is fitting: everyone in attendance that Saturday morning was beautiful – the men and women there all had model-esque bodies, classically good-looking facial features, and perfectly white teeth. I started feeling that bit of insecurity I always felt regarding the gym, but I brushed it off so that my colleague would not catch on to my nervousness.

I should pause here to tell you that, prior to arriving at the gym, my colleague had me take a (perfectly legal) pre-workout supplement – No Xplode – which hails itself as an "Extreme Pre-Training Energy and Performance Igniter." No Xplode comes as a fruit punch-flavored powder that you add to water, shake, and then drink. It's probably delicious if you like fruit punch – I do not. Now, my parents always taught me never to take edible things from strange people, but my colleague was a Yale- and Harvard Business School-educated dude, so I obliged…then again George W. Bush *also* went to Yale and HBS. Hmmm.

The clock was nearing the hour, and I noticed people getting on the treadmills "warming up" with light jogs. Taking my cues from those around me, I, too, jumped on a treadmill and began running. The problem, friend, is that I *hate* running. *Hate* it. I include running in my workouts now because I realize cardio is important, but I think I'd rather be punched in the face than run a mile. Because I hated running so much and, therefore, avoided it at all costs, my colleague mentioned that my breathing made me look like a, "Fat Girl Scout running down the street after eating 1,000 boxes of my own cookies." He's a really, *really* nice guy.

As I was warming up, I noticed that the guy running on the treadmill next to me looked familiar…like *really* familiar but not in a, "This is LA and you're a celebrity," way. Instead, he seemed to be someone from my past, from my days growing up in southern Illinois, who just so happened to be in LA, as well.

As I trudged along on my treadmill realizing that, despite already being out of breath, the *real* workout hadn't even started, someone walked by my familiar-looking neighbor and said, "Hey, Bob."

Bob? Bob who? And then it hit me. It was Bob Harper, the celebrity trainer featured on the NBC television show *The Biggest Loser*. Yes, next to me was a man whose job consisted of making very overweight people run for miles, and there I was, Skinny McSkipperson, barely able to breathe while jogging at a snail's pace. This was going to be a long hour.

Just then, the lights changed from normal ceiling lights to red lights like those you see heating food at fast-food restaurants, the fans were turned off, and the entry door was closed. The trainer, this insanely ripped guy named Joey Gonzalez (who, by the way, is awesome), started talking on his headset, instructing people to take a place on the floor or at a treadmill, and then this heavy bass club music started pumping out of the speakers. Today was going to be 15 on, 15 off, meaning people on the treadmill would run for 15 minutes and then switch with people on the floor so they could lift 15 minutes, and then repeat the process.

I remember thinking, "It's just an hour, Jim. You got this," but if you picture me masterfully running the 11 mph sprints or doing 50 bicep curls until exhaustion with the greatest of ease, you have the wrong mental picture. The workout was intense, grueling even, yet near the end of the hour I realized that I had somehow managed to survive. This militaristic theme was *not* false advertising, although I think a church theme would be just as fitting, as it was only through some holy act that I survived that hour.

The last five minutes of the class consisted of a "cool down" session in which everyone stops where they are and participates in stretching exercises to calm their heart rate. For whatever reason, my body was fine when it was racing at 11 mph or curling 35 lb. weights, but when things actually slowed down I think my mind got the best of me. Suddenly, I felt that uncomfortable gurgle-gurgle grumbly feeling in my stomach; you know, the feeling where you realize that *something* is about to happen to your body, you're not quite sure what, but you realize you have little-to-no control over it. An "uh-oh" moment, if you will. I was gonna toss my cookies.

Not wanting to be judged by the beautiful people around me, I did this weird, automatic mental math calculation based on my position in the room, the distance to the exit, and just the right pace I'd have to keep to get from Point A to Point B without running but fast enough so that I didn't throw up in the middle of the room. I should have never drunk that disgusting fruit punch-flavored supplement, that devil's drink, because I could tell that's what my body was doing its absolute best to hold in. It turns out that trying to keep down something that has the word "explode" in its name isn't super easy.

In a cool-but-hurried dash, I managed to make it just outside of the building where I saw a potted planter. Yes, friend, my first Barry's Boot Camp class ended with me hunched over, hands on my knees throwing up into a potted planter. Super embarrassed, I hurried to get it all out of me before my classmates made it outside. Nope. I was too late. People were already grabbing their bags and parading out of the building with their perfect abs and sculpted features shining in the golden California sun. I. Was. Mortified.

And yet, strangely, when people saw me puking my guts out their reaction was not one of disgust or judgment. Instead, people said things like, "Great job, man – that's when you know it's a good workout!" or,

"Way to push yourself, bro!"

That's when I knew LA was a really, really weird place.

*   *   *

Barry's Boot Camp, which has now expanded to New York City, London, and Miami, is but one of many fitness programs that include social influence in their design. Perhaps the best-known example of this "social fitness" phenomenon is CrossFit. Started in 2000, CrossFit now consists of over 6,000 gyms (or "boxes") in which its members, working as a sort of supportive family, swing from gymnast rings and endure intense WODs (workouts of the day) in their quest to get healthy and/or ripped. Other examples of this social fitness craze include group obstacle course races like Tough Mudder, the Spartan Race, and even Run for Your Lives, in which you and your friends pay to run away from people pretending to be zombies…because that's not at all horrifying.

This "social fitness" trend is not limited to gyms and endurance races. Dieting companies, like Weight Watchers, have long believed in the power of peer support, incorporating group support meetings into their respective programs. And, of course, gyms have had yoga, aerobic, and spinning classes for years, which, although not *exactly* as close-knit as CrossFit's social group, are still more social than doing deadlifts alone in the corner.

If you have ever tried lifting heavy weights at the gym while someone is watching compared to when no one is watching, then you know that lifting the weight in one instance often doesn't feel the same as it does in the other instance. Similarly, downing a pint of Ben & Jerry's ice cream in the privacy of our home *feels different* from downing a pint of Ben & Jerry's ice cream in the presence of others. So why is this the case? Why should it matter that other people are present? Why can't I just lift a weight or eat my Ben & Jerry's and enjoy it? This chapter is dedicated to the notion of Social Influence and will address why the presence of others, either real or imagined, affects our decision-making and behavior.

The Birth of Social Psychology. Despite the fact that social interaction is such a pervasive part of our daily lives, early psychology mostly concerned itself with studying individuals, deciphering cognitive processes, and trying to figure out how the individual mind worked. Although interesting and important, this early work failed to address one thing: an individual does not live in a vacuum. On the contrary, most of our lives are spent interacting with other people. In fact, "interacting with people" is kind of essential to the propagation of our species, if you know what I mean (wink, wink).

So psychologists around the 1900s started branching off into a new, distinct field of psychology addressing how the presence of others might affect an individual's thoughts and behaviors. In other words, these psychologists put the "social" in social psychology. As it turns out this notion of "others" does not even have to involve *real* others; no, even the *imagined* or *implied* presence of others can shape the way we think or behave.

An example of this comes from a memorable study in which researchers put a poster in a company's coffee break room that featured either eyes (in the experimental condition) or flowers (in the control condition). The dependent variable was how much money workers at the company put into the communal coffee fund over a specified period of time. The researchers predicted that the mere presence of eyes would subtly simulate the presence of another human being and, in turn, elicit more contributions to the coffee fund as if "someone were watching." Quite amazingly, during the period in which a poster with eyes was hanging in the room, employees at the company unknowingly put almost three times as much money in the communal pot compared to the period in which the poster with flowers was hanging in the room. Even simulated social presence seems to matter.

But the presence of others doesn't just affect how pro-social we are in a given situation. Sometimes even our *performance* at a task can vary based on whether or not someone is watching. I'm sure you have been in a situation in which something you do routinely becomes either easier or more difficult to do depending on *if* someone is watching you and, if so, *who* is watching you. **Social Facilitation Theory** proposes that an individual performs easy tasks better (and harder tasks worse) in the presence of others. So doing five jumping jacks in front of CrossFit buddies is probably super simple, while attempting to do one-arm pushups may actually feel harder when you think about these peers watching you.

Evaluation Apprehension Theory takes matters one step further and suggests that it isn't merely the presence of others that affects our performance but rather our realization that their *evaluation of our performance* will affect our social rewards (e.g., inclusion) or punishment (e.g., getting shunned). Deciding which clothes to wear in high school is a good example of how evaluation apprehension theory affects our consumer choices. We fear that wearing the wrong brand or style of clothing might lead to negative evaluations from the group to which we hope to belong. This, in turn, can make the clothes shopping experience much more stressful than it would otherwise be (and may explain why my grandma, who is at the age at which she couldn't care less what others think, dresses the eccentric way that she does).

Conformity. Speaking of high school, one idea rooted in social influence is the notion of conformity. **Conformity** refers to the process in which one matches his/her thoughts, emotions, and/or behaviors to those of others. High school is all about conforming – whether with respect to fashion, music, what's cool or not cool – many of our preferences are shaped not by what *we* actually prefer but what others around us prefer.

This urge to conform likely stems from an underlying need we discussed at the very beginning of the book: the innate need for love, belonging, and affiliation. In fact, I imagine that this need for belonging is driving most of these social effects. Social belonging was likely adaptive in human evolution: it's a lot easier to survive when you can divide labor among a tribe or when the rest of the tribe doesn't want to kill you, so yeah, those of us still around today are likely the ancestors of the lucky ones who were motivated to "play well with others."

Let's consider conformity in the context of music. Oftentimes, people decide what to like or not to like based on what others around them seem to be enjoying. This is my theory on how/why people like Taylor Swift, Kanye West, Katy Perry, and Ke$ha are famous. Music producers believe this, too, as massive amounts of money are pumped into making you *believe* an artist is beloved by the masses, which, in turn, enhances their popularity. Does this mean these "artists" are good musicians? Hardly. Although, to be fair, at least Swift *can* actually play an instrument...it's her permanent hybrid look of bewilderment and anguish I have a problem with. In any case, when someone has an intense, emotional reaction to a Ke$ha song, well, I just feel really $ad for them and wonder how their de$ire to $tay connected $ocially might influence their mu$ical preferences in the ab$ence of actual knowledge of mu$ic or mu$ical theory (side note: for *true* talent check out Jon McLaughlin, Sara Bareilles, and Matt Nathanson).

So powerful is our urge to conform that *even in the face of obvious evidence to the contrary* we often still conform. Dr. Solomon Asch put this idea to the test in a very famous series of experiments in the 1950s. To test conformity, Asch recruited participants to take place in a study in which they would be shown a line of a particular length on a card and then shown a second card featuring three lines, each of a different length, labeled A, B, and C. Each participant's job was to identify which line of the three matched the length of the original line. Participants would complete this task 18 times.

Unbeknownst to participants, Asch had recruited seven "confederates," people working for him (sort of like spies) who *pretended* to be participants who knew nothing about the task but who, in reality, both knew the task *and* how to reply. Asch instructed the confederates to answer *incorrectly* 12 out of the 18 trials and to answer consistently with their fellow confederates. The participant and confederates were seated such that the participant would always give his response last after hearing everyone else's response. To avoid arousing suspicion right away, the confederates answered the first few trials correctly but then began answering incorrectly around the third trial, subsequently sprinkling in some correct responses on later trials to keep the ruse going.

Keep in mind that it was always *very obvious* which line of A, B, and C matched the initial line of each trial, yet participants in the experimental condition chose the incorrect line 33% of the time, opting to agree with their supposed "fellow participants" instead of what they actually knew to be the correct answer. Over 75% of the participants in the experimental condition provided at least one wrong answer, meaning that 3 in every 4 participants conformed at least once to the group. Compare this to the control group in which there was no secret collusion and participants were incorrect less than 1% of the time. Sometimes, the drive to be a part of the group can make us do seemingly irrational things.

Reference Groups. Despite our surprising tendency to conform to group or social norms, it is not the case that we are *always* conforming to *every* group and to *every* norm. To understand how groups of people may influence our tendency to conform, let's consider two different types of reference groups. The first, **Normative Reference Groups**, refer specifically to those groups of which *we would like to be a member.* As such, this drive for acceptance motivates us to align our attitudes, beliefs, and behaviors to those of the group. These groups are also referred to as "associative groups." **Comparative Reference Groups**, on the other hand, refer to groups that an individual compares himself to for the purpose of calibrating and making evaluations about relative position with respect to attitudes, beliefs, and behaviors. A key difference, then, is that an individual *wants* to belong to a normative reference group but not necessarily to a comparative reference group, which is used for comparison or benchmarking purposes instead. One specific type of a comparative group, a "dissociative group," is a group that we actively want to avoid being a part of (e.g., a Republican not wanting to be associated with Democrats and vice versa).

To make this concrete with an example from consumer behavior, consider the case of "Beliebers," the die-hard fans of Justin Bieber. If I had to guess, I would say that the majority of Beliebers are young, tween girls who idolize the Canadian crooner. These girls probably compete on some benign level to have the most Bieber posters hanging in their rooms, the most re-Tweets of the singer's ridiculous Tweets (e.g., "Live life full," "We work hard."), the most posts on online fan forums, and more. If fellow Beliebers start hating on someone, such as one-time Nickelodeon star Josh Drake who often makes fun of the Biebs online, then the aspiring Belieber, wanting to be a part of this normative reference group, would also hate Josh Drake.

Although it is likely the case that a lot of these Beliebers are equally as infatuated with the British boyband One Direction, the Brits actually have their own loyal fan group: Directioners. Just as young girls fall ill with Bieber Fever, so, too, can they be diagnosed with One Direction Infection…it *is* all sort of sickening. Still, it is likely that a lot of Beliebers compare themselves to Directioners. Who's the better fan? Who attends more concerts? Who dresses better? Who's smarter? Thus, Beliebers and Directioners may be comparative reference groups for one another, comparing each others attitudes and behaviors to have a relative sense of their own without necessarily wanting to belong in each other's respective group.

Consumer-Related Reference Groups. Reference groups include more than just rival teen idol groups, of course. Several categories of consumer-related reference groups exist including:

- **Friendship groups**: we cannot help but compare ourselves to those people with whom we choose to associate on a daily basis: our friends. Friendship occurs for many reasons, not least of which is the tendency to like the same things, so it is only natural, then, that we assess the preferences, beliefs, and behaviors of our close friends and compare them to our own. Similarly, our "non-friends" and even enemies often serve as a point of comparison, as we may want to actively avoid whatever they are doing to ensure no one mistakes us for them. Marketers have become particularly interested in tapping into the influence of friendship reference groups thanks to sites like Facebook and Pinterest where customers basically tell marketers, "Hey! These people are my friends!"

- **Shopping groups:** other people often buy the products we also purchase, but that does not necessarily mean we are friends with these people. Shopping groups refer to groups of people who share a common bond because they make similar purchases. Thus, as an avid fan of Starbucks, I find myself inextricably tied to my fellow Starbucks drinkers against whom I may compare my loyalty and my purchase frequency (normative) and with whom I may compare our satisfaction to the local mom n' pop café-goers (comparative). The fancy lounges at airports for loyalty members, like American Airlines Admirals Club Lounge, brings together like-minded shoppers who may not be friends but who share their shopping in common.

- **Work groups:** Because we spend the majority of our time slaving away behind our desks or in "scenic" cubicles and (if we're lucky) corner offices, it turns out that we often rely on our colleagues as a reference group. Now, we can approach this from many perspectives – comparing ourselves to others in our same position, comparing ourselves to colleagues above/below our position, comparing ourselves to employees at our company in general v. employees at another, competing company, etc. The point is that our colleagues provide a natural means for comparison.

- **Virtual groups:** With the increase of online communities, as perpetuated by Facebook, Pinterest, and company-created online engagement sites, we are able to interact virtually with people from all over the world. Mommy blogs are a great example of this. New moms can go online, talk about raising children, and criticize each other's approaches anonymously from the comfort of their armchairs.

- **Consumer-action groups:** Consumer-action groups consist of people sharing likeminded views on consumption, such as environmentalists or proponents of clean energy. Another famous consumer-action group is PETA, or People for the Ethical Treatment of Animals, who often flock together to throw red paint on any celebrity wearing fur. If you belonged to an advocacy or consumer-action group, chances are you would find yourself comparing your attitudes, beliefs, and behaviors to those of groups like PETA.

- **Indirect reference groups:** The preceding examples, from friendship groups to shopping groups, work groups to virtual groups, all represent **direct reference groups**, or groups with whom you can have actual face-to-face or real-time contact. **Indirect reference groups** refer to people with whom you identify but with whom you do not share face-to-face or real-time interaction. Examples of indirect reference groups include actors, actresses, athletes, and other famous people.

Reference groups can change depending on the product or service in question. For example, when I think about clothing, I tend not to use my colleagues as a reference group because although academics are super smart, very few are what I would call "fashion forward." Instead, I am more likely to peruse the latest Facebook photos of my European friends who always seem to be one step ahead of us on the fashion front. However, when I am looking for a new book to read or a new documentary to see, my work group is a great reference because they enjoy the same nerdy, intellectual things that I like. Mark my words that there is a lot of money to be made in the domain of Virtual Groups whereby companies filter more accurately by "people like you." Amazon.com does this to some extent, "People who have viewed this product also looked at x, y, and z," but a surefire way to make recommendations and feedback sections of websites more useful is to allow the user to filter reviews to refer to people who share a similar profile. Although Fern, a grandmother of 7 in Kansas, may have also purchased the fancy alarm clock I am thinking about purchasing, I would rather know what the 20-something urban dude who works out routinely and considers himself knowledgeable of pop culture has to think. If anyone wants to start this with me, just let me know.

Social Appeals. We naturally compare ourselves to others in just about every domain of life, but we also look to others for guidance and direction. Marketers know this, of course, and make use of others as a *source* of information. The most common example of this is the use of **celebrities**, which, to be completely honest, has always sort of baffled me. But, to be fair, I couldn't care less about celebrities (the one exception being Tina Fey, but that just sort of goes without saying). Still, when Alec Baldwin talks about Capital One credits cards or Beyoncé sings about Pepsi the masses think, "I must get a Capital One card! I must drink Pepsi." It's weird. This likely derives from many influences – Balance Theory, a halo effect of positive thoughts emanating from the celebrity, familiarity, etc. Consumers always seem to forget about the multi-million dollar deals behind these celebrity endorsements. Pepsi allegedly paid Beyoncé $50 million for her latest endorsement of their products – silly, Pepsi, they could have hired me for $49.9 million, and I would have gladly worn suggestive clothing and sung praises of Pepsi Max. I can twerk...I think. Do hear that Pepsi? I'm offering.

A related idea to the use of celebrities is the use of **trade/spokespeople**. Although these people aren't "famous" in that they have multimillion-dollar film, television, or music careers, these people often *become* famous as the icons or representatives of the companies and products they are hawking. The most famous example of a spokesperson today is probably Flo the Progressive Insurance lady. My mom *hates* those commercials and thinks Flo is pretty annoying (I'd have to agree), but we would all have to agree that the Flo character has helped earn Progressive loads of attention and awareness. In fact, according to friends in LA, the actress who portrays Flo is doing quite well for herself: she earns royalties each and every time you see a Progressive commercial. Another infamous spokesperson is the now-defunct ShamWow! guy, Offer "Vince" Shlomi. Known for his extreme energy and outrageous products, Shlomi fell off the radar after getting into a physical altercation with a prostitute in Miami in 2009...ShamWhoops.

Beyond celebrities and spokespeople, marketers know that consumers place a lot of value on the opinions of **experts**. If you are thinking about purchasing a new food processor or some other piece of kitchen machinery, I imagine that you would care more about what a chef at a Michelin three-star restaurant has to say about the product than my opinion of the machine. The chef may not have any celebrity status, but because he/she is an expert, we are more likely to believe what they have to say than a novice.

But novices are not without their own power. Indeed, sometimes we actually prefer hearing about the **common man**, what the Average Joe thinks about a particular product or service. This was true in the 2008 U.S. Presidential election when Joe the Plumber became a household name after weighing in on the plight of the small business owner. It was also true in the early days of Subway's famous Jared commercials. Jared was an overweight, regular dude who, by eating a diet of strategically selected Subway sandwiches, lost a considerable amount of weight. The appeal of the common man, of course, is that they are objective, honest, and give us hope: if they can do it, we can do it.

Another tactic marketers use is recruiting company **employees and executive spokespeople** to appeal to customers. Southwest Airlines includes its employees in television commercials. Pilots, flight attendants, and technicians deliver the safety information in American Airlines' takeoff video. The Hair Club for Men president reminds us that he is, "Not just the President of the Hair Club for Men," he is, "Also a member." The strategy here is that companies can make themselves come across as more personable, more caring, and more human, thereby mitigating the likelihood of being seen as cold, money-hungry, and out-of-touch.

Family first. Although celebrities and experts, spokespeople and salespeople are all likely to influence our consumer choices, there exists an even stronger social influence on our consumer behavior: family. Unless you were raised by a pack of wolves (which is totally possible; no judging) chances are you grew up in a house with your parents, grandparents, foster parents, or some other guardians who, at least in the earliest years of your life, were probably responsible for making all the major household purchases: food, cleaning supplies, toilet paper, detergent, clothing, etc.

To this day the brands I buy (e.g., Bounty paper towels, Tide detergent, Ritz crackers, Jif peanut butter, etc.) are *exactly* those that my parents, primarily my mom, purchased. The reason for this is likely due to the fact that these are the products you get used to first and, as such, that serve as the anchor points for evaluating any other new products. For me, Kraft Deluxe Mac & Cheese is what I think of when I think macaroni and cheese. There may very well be other artisan brands out there selling deliciously tasty macaroni and cheese, but my reference point will forever be Kraft

Deluxe. Aside from these products serving as reference points, there are certainly positive associations we place on these brands *because* they are nostalgic, remind us of home, and evoke thoughts of our family.

Companies are wise to this familial influence and, as such, exert a considerable effort in identifying the person responsible for making certain purchases within the family. In some households, moms do most of the shopping. In other households, dad is the shopper. For some product categories, mom wins. In other product categories, dad dominates. In my house growing up my mom was the primary purchaser of most of the consumer products even the ones my dad would argue that we did not need. The exception to this involved car-related products, hardware for fixing things in the house (tools, washers, pipes), and junk food, which my father is particularly adept at finding despite not being at all overweight.

Even though he'll probably be upset at me for including this in the book, my father's wardrobe is entirely purchased by my mom...except the all-white tennis shoes he buys for himself (my mom has far better fashion sense than to buy someone all-white tennis shoes post-1985). I include this example to highlight an important idea: sometimes a product's *consumer* is not the same as the product's *shopper*. My parents are both the proud owners of iPads and AppleTV, but I'll give you one guess as to who helped make those purchases happen. Indeed, knowing who does the purchasing of particular products in the household is critically important for the efficient use of marketing dollars.

It turns out that each member of a family takes on a consumer role within the household. These roles often include influencers, gatekeepers, users, decision-makers, and purchasers. Sometimes one person can play several roles; other times an individual plays just one role. **Influencers** are described as people who recognize a need and communicate a purchase possibility to other family members (e.g., "Our entertainment options are limited; maybe we should look beyond cable."). **Gatekeepers** are the folks who control information flow into the household (e.g., my father doesn't always share the mail advertising from cable alternatives so that we don't realize what else is out there). **Users** are the people who actually use the products or services in question (e.g., everyone in my family watched television growing up). **Decision-makers** hold the authoritative last word on what gets purchased and what does not (e.g., my mom decided that we would switch cable companies to one with a better package). **Purchasers** are the folks who actually engage in the buying of a product or service (e.g., my father cancelled the original cable company subscription and paid for a subscription to a new and improved service). Knowing who serves what role, therefore, is important for marketers: you want to make sure your message is reaching the right target.

Family Life Cycle (FLC). The funny thing about families and family consumption roles is that they evolve over time. There was a time in my life as a child when my mom literally made every purchase for herself, my father, for my siblings, and for me. Nowadays, I love that I can buy nice things for my parents – like a Roomba vacuum for my mom or a wireless outdoor speaker system for my dad. But buying these products would have been impossible for me when I was a kid, partially because I would not know how to engage in purchasing behavior and primarily because I had no money. This is why 5-year olds *make* gifts, like buckets full of weeds and dandelions or abstract art crayon drawings.

Various Family Life Cycle models exist, but they generally all include similar stages. Here's the version we'll go with:

- **The Nurtured Stage:** This refers to the time in life where you are being taken care of from morning until night. At this stage, you probably make almost no decisions regarding purchases, as your primary caregivers take care of everything.

- **The Rebellious Youth Stage:** This refers to when you start making some of your own choices and decisions with respect to clothing, entertainment, and how you spend your time. Your primary caregivers are still actively involved in your life and decision-making, however; you just have a bit more freedom than you used to.

- **Young, Single, and Looking to Mingle Stage:** This refers to a period of great independence when you are actually making the majority of your own choices. For most, this is when they go away to college or move out on their own in the real world.

- **The Ring-On-It Stage:** This refers to the period in which you have found the potential love of your life and stop making decisions based only on your own needs but, instead, based on the needs of you and your partner. Note: not everyone enters this stage, which is also important for marketers to know: people often shop differently based on whether they are single or in committed relationships.

- **The Baby Chicks Stage:** This refers to young couples who have young children themselves in the "nurtured stage." Money is no longer a luxury spent on oneself or one's partner but, instead, is now primarily devoted to the needs of the young child or children. These young families are a primary target for home sales (or upgrades).

- **The Pesky Pigeons Stage:** This refers to the period in which your children are in that "rebellious youth" stage, making some of their own decisions but still relying on you for financial support, guidance, and parental instruction. Like pesky pigeons, they always show up when there is food around but, at other times, can be very flighty. They seek their own independence and want to believe they are a lot more grown up than they actually are.

- **The Empty Nest Stage:** This refers to the period in which your kids have ventured off into the world and you now have your freedom (and money) back for yourself. These couples tend to be the target for cruise companies and other lifestyle services catering to crowds with disposable income and time on their hands. Variants of this include parents of Boomerang Kids, adult children who move back home, and Giving Grandparents, grandparents playing very active roles in the raising of their grandchildren.

Although there is no set certain path that every family follows, nor is there one definition of "family," you can see how thinking about the evolution of a family can matter to marketers. The needs of the single bachelor are simply not the same as the grandfather of seven. Knowing where your consumers are in the general scope of a Family Life Cycle can affect how you market to them. Expensive vacation companies probably won't have much luck targeting new parents, just as video game companies attempting to sell their games to young children need to figure out a way to communicate their appeal to the moms and dads who will likely be the purchasers of the product, as the kids cannot purchase the games themselves.

In my family, my parents are now grandparents of my nephews—Caleb, Cooper, and Liam—and have entered into a modified Empty Nest stage of the Family Life Cycle. My siblings and I are all gainfully employed adults who own their own homes, but because we are a close family, the "empty nest" is rarely "empty" as much as it is a gathering place. I, too, have shifted into a new role as uncle, which is a great role because you can spend all day playing with adorable, energetic little kids but, at the end of the day when they get tired and cranky and are smelly and dirty from playing outside all day, you get to pass them off to their parents, in this case, my sisters. I also have found that I pay much more attention to advertisements for children's toys, but this could also be a cover for me as I do my best to disguise the fact that I am truly a child posing as an adult.

Power and Social Influence. Up to this point we have talked about how others can have an influence on us because we aspire to be like them (or to avoid being like them) or because we are related to them, but another way in which the opinions and attitudes of others matter to us has to do with the *power* others exert over us. Indeed, whether it's because we want something or fear certain consequences, the fact that others wield power over us can affect our choices and actions.

Several kinds of **social power** influences affect us daily. First, **referent power** refers to the power that members of a group to which we want to belong possess. This is the kind of peer pressure nonsense that happens when a member of the "cool kids" group in high school encourages us to drink.

Another type of power, **legitimate power**, is power that exists because of a structured design, like a boss wielding power over an employee. In the infamous news bit known as the London Whale, a trader at JPMorgan Chase made a risky bet that wound up costing the company anywhere from $2 billion to $9 billion despite the company posting a much smaller loss. Yet the trader did not get in trouble for posting the fabricated smaller number because it turned out that his boss was the one who coerced him into doing it, an example of someone knowing the right thing to do but, fearing the power of a superior, performed a drastically different behavior.

Expert power refers to the willingness to alter or change behavior because of the expertise of another or in service of acquiring expertise from another person. This happens around the gym all the time when individuals wind up doing crazy things, like jumping rope on one foot, not because it's something they would normally do but rather because the expert trainer is imparting his/her wisdom for getting fit.

A related idea is that of **reward power**, which, in spite of its name has little to do with obtaining a reward. Instead, what reward power refers to is the process in which we are more easily influenced by an individual who has been rewarded or exalted by others. It's as if saying, "Everyone else thinks this person is doing something right, so maybe we should, too." This is the only way I can think of to explain how the Kardashians can have their own product lines: others seem to have exalted them to celebrity status (for no apparent reason), so others see this exaltation as a broader social acceptance and, as such, let the Kardashians influence their behaviors…probably not a great idea.

Finally, **coercive power** is perhaps the most notorious of the social powers as it involves the use of threats, fear, and/or physical or psychological punishment. A comical use of this is the old "Slim Jim" beef jerky commercials in which viewers were warned they would be "snapped" if they didn't "snap into a Slim Jim." But coercive power can be extremely dangerous. In the world of modeling, for example, it is not uncommon for casting producers and agents to warn models about their physical state – being too fat, not fit enough, etc. – and threaten exclusion from consideration for modeling gigs, which can then encourage unsafe eating practices, fitness addictions, and disordered eating.

Sensitivity to Social Influence. If you remember from the Behavioral Intentions Model from the previous chapter on Personality, Attitudes, and Persuasion, people differ in the extent to which they weight their own attitudes and the perceived attitudes of others. The concept of **self-monitoring** proposes a continuum in which people vary to the extent they actively monitor their "self" and update their behavior depending on their social situation. High self-monitors pay active attention to themselves and update their behavior in real time according to their environment kind of like chameleons. Low self-monitors, on the other hand, are less affected by their context and environment, typically being essentially the same person at any point in time and in any setting. As a high self-monitor I notice that I am so sensitive to others and my situation that I'll even take on the accent of friends if I am hanging out with a group of French friends or Russian friends...it's weird and happens automatically. You can actually take the 25-question self-monitoring scale developed by researcher Mark Snyder to know how much of a self-monitor you happen to be: http://personality-testing.info/tests/SM.php

My Self-Monitor Scale score is a whopping 23/25. To amuse you with a marketing example of how being super sensitive to the opinions and influence others can manifest in daily life, I'll share a story with you. I remember one time during grad school after a particularly long week I was looking forward to nothing other than staying home on a Friday night, watching a new episode of *Dateline* (I live for that show, which is problematic because now I worry I am going to die a painful, mysterious death at the hands of a jealous millionaire), and ordering in Italian food (another favorite). However, as I was looking up the menu I thought to myself, "These people are going to think it's totally lame for a twentysomething year-old guy to be stuck at home on Friday night watching *Dateline*," so I did what any normal thinking person would do: I ordered *two* meals and *two* drinks so that the delivery person wouldn't think I was alone. I ate the second meal for lunch the next day. Now I'm not sure what sad moment of desperation and fear of social judgment led me to that tragic moment in my life, but the point is that some of us are so keenly aware of what others may think of us and, whether we admit it or not, that the *imagined* presence of others is more than capable of affecting our choices and behaviors.

Another measure for assessing one's sensitivity to social influence is the **Attention to Social Comparison Information (ATSCI)** scale. Developed by Bearden and Rose in 1990, the thirteen-item scale includes items like, "I usually keep up with clothing style changes by watching what other people wear," and, "I try to pay attention to the reactions of others to my behavior in order to avoid being out of place." Similar to the Self-Monitoring Scale, the ATSCI is a way to measure just how sensitive we are to the influence of others.

Marketing and Social Influence. Although we may vary to the extent to which we are sensitive to others, we all, at some point in time, let the opinions and/or presence of others affect our choices and behaviors in the marketplace. Whether we make an expensive purchase in an attempt to impress someone or order an extra meal to avoid others thinking you're leading the lame life of a graduate student, our choices are simply not determined with no regard for others.

Because of this marketers have several strategies that rely on this innate inclusion of others in our decision-making process. One popular strategy for marketers is to focus on **word-of-mouth**, which refers to consumers talking about our products and company to their friends, family, and coworkers. The idea here is that the positive messages talked about among friends are less scrutinized than the messages conveyed in advertising. Plus, word-of-mouth benefits from being associated with the referent groups of friends, family, or colleagues, as people may think, "If Johnny likes it, and Johnny is someone like me, then I'm probably going to like it, too."

A related strategy involves the use of buzz marketing. **Buzz marketing** refers to deliberate tactics designed to facilitate discussion among consumers. Whereas word-of-mouth marketing is more about crafting the talking points likely to be communicated among like-minded consumers, buzz marketing focuses more on creating creative campaigns *worth being talked about*. The M&Ms "Great Color Quest" campaign discussed in the chapter on Perception and Attention is a good example. Although people certainly talked about this campaign with their friends and colleagues, the marketing execution also garnered significant press coverage. Whereas word-of-mouth feels more organic, buzz marketing need not be…it just needs to be talked about, to "create buzz."

A bit less honorable in the world of social influence is the notion of stealth marketing. **Stealth marketing** is marketing that relies on the underlying reasons social influence is so powerful in a way that *seems* like it is organic and natural but is actually tightly controlled by a company. Consider, for example, the case of a cell phone company that paid actors to walk around Times Square and chat about their great new phone as if they were real people who just so happened to be lauding the amazingness of their new phone in public. Or, in a rather tragic example, consider the case of Chik-Fil-A that, when being criticized by consumers for its support of anti-gay marriage measures, thought it would be a good idea to create a fake Facebook profile and proceed to post on the Chik-Fil-A page in support of the company. Consumers aren't stupid, however; they figured out that "Abby Farle," was not only *not* a real person but was actually someone in the marketing department at Chik-Fil-A attempting to do damage control. Talk about making matters worse, Chik-Fail-A. Consumers *do not* like to feel manipulated, so stealth marketing, although potentially successful if kept off the radar, can certainly backfire.

Finally, marketers recognize the value of using an opinion leader strategy. **Opinion leaders** are revered folks, famous or not, whose thoughts and preferences tend to influence the thoughts and preferences of others. Perhaps the greatest example of this is Oprah Winfrey who, when she started her monthly program "Oprah's Book Club," singlehandedly changed the book market. Each month the book Oprah selected immediately shot to the top of the book bestseller lists. Beyond this, Oprah's annual "Favorite Things" episode became a pop cultural phenomenon, as companies and consumers tried to get their products placed on the show and tried to get their hands on the products demonstrated, respectively.

But it turns out you don't have to be Oprah to be an opinion leader. Marketers often rely on what is commonly referred to as the **Adoption Process** to break consumers down into five key categories: Innovators, Early Adopters, Early Majority, Late Majority, and Laggards. Mentally, picture a normal distribution with the x-axis representing time and the y-axis representing the number of people purchasing a product or service. When a new product is launched, only a very small number of people take the risk of purchasing the product. These folks are the "innovators." From there, the slightly more risk-averse people in the market, early adopters, follow the innovators' lead. Following the early adopters, things really take off: the early majority group starts purchasing a product en masse. This is when a company is likely to achieve its largest audience. As demand tapers off the company gets some purchases from the late majority and, finally, laggards who are totally late to the game may make a few purchases. Each group differs with respect to its risk assessments, its product and/or industry knowledge, and its ability to be persuaded. As such, solid marketing research actively seeks to identify who the innovators are in a particular product/service category and may even lead to the development of a marketing plan timed to amp up production, launch creative executions, and facilitate interactions among the different adoption groups to make marketing spend more efficient.

To give you an example, Disney's D23 weekend caters to die-hard Disney fans who are innovators and early adopters in the market for Disney movies, products, and vacations. By providing these die-hard consumers with enough buzz, Disney can rely on these loyal fans to spread the word about upcoming Disney products to early majority members, people who enjoy Disney but are not ahead of the pack on the company's latest offerings. Another tactic Disney employs, particularly for the late majority and laggards, is the use of a "limited-time only" technique they created called the "Disney vault." Popular Disney films are likely to be purchased right away by innovators and early adopters, but by warning customers that the movie *Tangled* is going to be "locked away in the Disney vault forever!" Disney motivates these laggards to take action before it is too late, this, of course, only if Disney's early adopters and innovators have not already spread the word about how great the movie *Tangled* is (which, it turns out, is great).

And, of course, the motivation to be viewed as an innovator in a particular product category can be motivation unto itself. I am a comedy junkie, so when the networks launch *previews* of their new shows (not even the full shows themselves), I am already telling people what I think will be funny and what looks terrible. It is important for me to be seen as an innovator in this category and in music because people who know me know that I grew up performing improv and music. Similarly, some people actually *prefer* being seen as laggards most typically in product/service categories that are deemed as risky. While some people get excitement out of risky stock market investments, other, more conservative investors get value out of being seen as hesitant, particularly when the innovators lose lots of money on their risky bets and the laggards, having learned from the innovators what *not* to do, wind up doing better in the long run.

Risks of Social Influence. Although social acceptance and affiliation are both important, fundamental human needs, sometimes the presence of others can actually lead to some problems. The most famous story concerning this topic in psychology is the woeful tale of Kitty Genovese. Aside from having what may be the coolest name ever (that's the upside), Kitty Genovese is also known for being stabbed to death in the borough of Queens in New York in the 1960s (that's the downside). The reason Kitty's death lives on in the study of social psychology is that her neighbors *actually saw her getting murdered* (allegedly) and yet they *did nothing*. Can you imagine? One of your neighbors is being brutally murdered, and you don't call the police, you don't scream for help, you don't intervene to help your neighbor?

The Kitty Genovese story is an example of what psychologists refer to as the **Bystander Effect**, in which a person is less likely to help someone if there are other people present. A related idea, **diffusion of responsibility**, is used to explain the effect by suggesting that as the number of people in a particular situation increases, the likelihood of any one person doing a particular something *decreases*. In the context of poor Kitty Genovese, had only *one* neighbor seen the murder going down, she might have lived to see another day. However, because each neighbor allegedly saw other neighbors witnessing the crime, each opted to do nothing, perhaps assuming someone else was already taking care of it, perhaps thinking that someone else would know something better to do.

It turns out that this diffusion of responsibility effect is not limited to violent crimes. Research has shown that in a game of tug-o-war the more people you add to your team, the less each team member pulls. So if my effort is a 9 out of 10 when there are just two of us, adding a third person might reduce my effort to 6 out of 10 – not exactly a great strategy for tug-o-war. Similarly, in a room with a large audience, individuals clap *less* for a performance than if there were fewer people in the room. Crazy, right? It's as if we assume, "Hey, these other people are here; they can pull some weight so I don't have to do as much." As many of us know, this also happens on group or team projects, which is why smart managers and professors tend to limit teams to 4-6 people or, in the case of mean managers, to provide more work for the team to do.

If we consider these potential downsides to the presence of others in the realm of consumer behavior, we might be curious as to whether or not it's a good idea for charity telethons to display that there are many other people also watching and donating to the cause. The audience sitting at home might think, "Well, there are clearly plenty of other people taking action. What good will my drop in the bucket do?" On the other hand, if a telethon showed almost no one donating, one might think, "Hmm, I guess it's not a very popular or worthy cause?" Sometimes all it takes is one person to change our behavior, sometimes several people, sometimes many, and sometimes even the *imagined* presence of others, but if you think the people around you aren't constantly affecting your choices and behaviors, well, you'd truly be alone with that thought...unless there's a poster with eyes behind you.

*   *   *

Whenever I visit Los Angeles, I make it a point to attend Barry's Boot Camp, not because I'm a glutton for punishment but because I realize that I rarely work out nearly as hard when I work out alone. Even if I deliberately "push myself" at the gym when I am alone, the level of intensity that automatically consumes me at Barry's Boot Camp far exceeds even my best intentions flying solo. There's just something about the social pressure of being around super hot people that makes you try harder...maybe if we voted hotter people into Congress something would actually get done?

Of course, any great workout is bound to make you tired, and when you're tired you yawn. All vertebrates, from snakes to salamanders, yawn, but only three vertebrates – humans, dogs, and chimpanzees – share something special in common: our yawns are contagious. We all have experienced seeing someone open their mouths wide, stretching, and inhaling that famous yawn inhale only to find ourselves emulating the *exact same behavior* automatically. In fact, sometimes even reading about yawning is enough for people to feel the urge to yawn. I once incorporated several different animals yawning into a print advertisement and, sure enough, people viewing the ad were likely to yawn. With any hope, you are yawning right now!

Why is yawning contagious only among our ancestors and man's best friend? Scientists are not entirely sure. Some suggest it promotes social bonding via empathy, much like emotional contagion discussed in the chapter on Affect, Mood, and Emotion. Others propose it helped aid survival in pack/tribal groups, as contagious yawning would help "spread the word" through the group that someone was physically exhausted and that the group needed to rest lest it continue on and lose some of its members to fatigue.

Whatever the reason, the fact that yawning is contagious is just one of the many examples suggesting that human beings are *programmed* to pay attention to others automatically. From fitness to fatness, yearning to yawning, people around us influence almost everything we do, so choose your friends wisely.

APPLICATION QUESTIONS

1) You are slated to give a huge presentation on the latest marketing campaign you and your team have developed. You find out minutes before going into the room that the CMO is also going to be in attendance. You freak out – you're a genius at giving presentations, but knowing that the CMO is there still bothers you. What's going on?

2) Your great-great-aunt is hanging out at the bingo parlor with her buddies Edna, Veera, and Thelma. She notices they are reading magazines like UsWeekly and the National Enquirer. Across the table are the "Mean Dudes," Fred, Alfred, and Ned. They are reading magazines like The Economist and National Geographic. What kind of reference groups do these two groups represent? How is it likely to affect your great-great-aunt's magazine readership?

3) You work for a company that makes fruit snacks for kids. You have a finite amount of money with which you can develop your ads and buy media time. Your partner suggests spending the ad money on a flashy commercial with a young, cool endorser and media time on Disney, Nickelodeon, and HUB. Using consumer roles, explain to him/her why this seemingly good idea is flawed.

4) You own a beverage company and find in your research that your target customer scores, on average, very high on the self-monitoring scale. What sort of marketing engagement could you develop or produce to instill an urge in this target to buy more of your drink?

5) A new restaurant is opening in your neighborhood, and to celebrate the occasion the owner is throwing an open house for the residents nearby. You think the new restaurant is a nice addition to the neighborhood, but aren't sure if you are going to go or not. From what you've heard, others sound like they're definitely going. The open house comes and nobody shows up…explain.

6) Sometimes we don't want to consume the things we *ought* to consume. Use a concept from this chapter to explain why, as children, we eat the broccoli and other green veggies on our plate when a parent is nearby. Is there another example of forced consumption in the adult world that is the result of this same concept?

7) Why might real estate agents consider partnering with jewelry stores? Use a concept from this chapter to answer the question.

8) From a marketing perspective, why might it be reasonable to think that songs with accompanying dances (e.g., "Gangnam Style") or songs with controversial lyrics (e.g., "If U Seek Amy") are deliberate?

9) What is the benefit of those commercials you see in which it is clearly stated on the screen, "Real user. Not a paid actor."?

10) One of the challenges confronting Facebook and other social networks is an inability to monetize its offerings beyond that of ad sales. Using "Social Influence" and the concepts contained herein as your foundation, come up with one or two specific ways Facebook or another social networking site could monetize the power of social influence.

Chapter 8 | Culture and Socio-Cultural Influence

Early on a Saturday morning in October 2012, a long line stretched around the corner of a block at 5th Avenue and East 56th Street in New York City. Although it was only 9:00am, the people waiting in line had clearly been standing for some time, as those near the front of the line had begun to lean against the wall, to squat, or even to sit down on the sidewalk. These people were determined; it was clear that they would *not* be leaving New York without the goodies that awaited them within this store.

"The Apple Store?" you're thinking, picturing the long lines of Apple fanatics who often spend the night (or night_s_ in the case of some die-hard Apple loyalists) waiting in line for the next great Apple product. You, however, would be mistaken: the Apple store is located two blocks north on 5th Avenue between 58th and 59th Street.

"That cupcake place from *Sex and the City*?" a friend of mine guessed when I mentioned this story. That "cupcake place," Magnolia Bakery, has several locations throughout New York City, none of which is located along 5th Avenue.

No, the popular store that drew such a large crowd early that Saturday morning was…wait for it…Abercrombie & Fitch.

"What?!" you're thinking, "Abercrombie & Fitch isn't cool anymore! That brand was big in the 1990s and early 2000s at best. Today's kids are wearing Hollister and Urban Outfitters. Nobody wears Abercrombie anymore!"

Au contraire, mes amis. For, you see, A&F is still the clothing brand du jour of one particular fan base: Europeans.

Now, let's not be naïve, not *every* European wears or even likes Abercrombie and Fitch, but now that the American market has saturated and is shrinking (A&F has plans to close 180 stores in the U.S. by 2015), the American casual clothing company is looking across the pond for its growth: the company has opened over 60 stores in Europe in the past five years and has plans for more as the European economy slowly recovers.

Part of the appeal for those Europeans standing in line early on that Saturday morning was the lower price for A&F clothing in the U.S. compared to the same clothing in Europe. Additionally, although A&F stores continue to open in Europe consider the fact that, as of this book's writing, there is just *one* A&F store in all of France on the Champs-Élysées in Paris. That's like having just one Abercrombie in Chicago for the entire U.S.

Abercrombie and Fitch is not the only clothing brand whose audiences are shifting between Europe and North America. Consider European brands like Diesel (Italy), Zara (Spain), and Ben Sherman (England), which have surged in popularity stateside in the past several years. But if you've ever traveled to Europe or, if you're European, if you've ever traveled to North America, then you know that fashion trends and tastes can differ drastically between the continents. Here are some examples:

- Cargo shorts: Distinctly an American trend and, even then, a waning one. In fact, although it is possible, finding a European wearing shorts is like finding a needle in a haystack.

- Scarves in seasons other than winter: Europeans have adorned their outfits with scarves for some time, both men and women. Although this trend is increasing in popularity in the U.S., it's still nowhere near as prevalent as it is in Europe.

- Athletic shoes as casual shoes: In the U.S., people casually wear athletic or running shoes as day-to-day shoes. In Europe, it's rare to see people wearing athletic shoes for anything other than running or participating in some sport.

- Slim-fitting clothing: While this may be one to chalk up to the difference in obesity rates, "European cut" clothing tends to be slimmer and taut to the body whereas Americans often wear looser clothing. Case in point, dress shirts at Banana Republic tend to have slightly baggy, extra fabric compared to European-made dress shirts.

- Sandals and flip flops: While it's certainly possible to see Europeans wearing sandals, flip flops and thongs (the shoe kind) are less prevalent.

- Socks: One surefire way to identify Europeans and Americans in a crowd is to sort the group by white socks v. non-white socks (e.g., grey, black). Europeans tend to wear darker socks relative to Americans who seem to prefer white socks.

- Beach attire: Americans are often surprised at the beach culture of Europeans. Ladies sunbathe topless like it's no big deal (because it isn't there) and the men roam around the beach in their skimpy speedos. American women keep their tops on stateside while their male counterparts like to cover the ol' tiddles and bits with more than just a speedo – boardshorts and swimming trunks are far more popular in the U.S. You can thank the Puritans.

- Baseball caps and cowboy hats: Of course the iconic cowboy is a staple of the U.S.'s Old West culture, but Europeans are also a lot less likely to be seen wearing caps of any kind. The French may have their berets, but trucker hats have yet to cross the pond.

Now let's put the caveat out there: just because there are some "general" fashion differences between Europeans and North Americans at a broad level does *not* mean that every European or every American follows these generalizations. Certainly there are Americans with dark-colored casual socks and speedos just as there are Europeans who wear baseball caps and flip flops. But fashion, like many things, is a cultural phenomenon. And that's the funny thing about culture: sometimes the world's cultures share a lot in common with one another, and other times they couldn't be more different. But one consistency is that *every* culture influences the thoughts, preferences, and behaviors of its people, which means that understanding cultural influences on consumer behavior will always be in fashion.

*   *   *

How would you answer the question, "What is culture?" You might say "American culture" or "French culture." You might think of something like "pop culture" or fashion or music. Culture might evoke images of food, ethnic food and otherwise. The word "culture" might bring to mind what it means to be "cultured" – sophisticated, worldly, knowledgeable, experienced.

These are all correct answers, as culture is quite an encompassing, robust concept. When I think of **culture**, I tend to think of it as the learned way a particular group of people go about living their daily lives: what they eat, what they drink, the music they like, the clothing they wear, the styles they prefer, the language they speak, the mannerisms and gestures they use, and more. In short, culture is the "how-to" guide for our day-to-day lives.

These "how-to" guides can differ by country. For example, whether it is appropriate to tip and how much to tip a service provider differs from country to country. Perspectives on the rightness and wrongness of purchasing counterfeit products can also differ by country. Even something like belching in public is accepted and even encouraged in the how-to books of some cultures but certainly not in others.

Thinking of culture as "how-to" books is one way we can try to understand how culture guides and shapes our behavior. This chapter is dedicated to presenting different perspectives on culture and to understanding how situations that we are born into, like culture and socio-economic status, can influence our thoughts and actions.

Dimensions of Culture. Because culture is so robust, studying culture can be a challenge. Thankfully, a very smart Dutchman by the name of Geert Hofstede decided to break culture down into six dimensions that make studying and understanding cultural differences more manageable. Hofstede's dimensions – Individualism v. Collectivism (IDV), Indulgence v. Restraint (IVR), Long-Term v. Short-Term Orientation (LTO), Masculinity v. Femininity (MAS), Power Distance (PDI), and Uncertainty Avoidance (UAI) – are based on the results of a global survey conducted with IBM employees almost fifty years ago. More measures have been collected in the interim, of course, and these measures are used to give countries (and their respective culture) "scores" along each of the six dimensions:

Individualism v. Collectivism: this dimension measures the extent to which people pursue individual goals and identities or, instead, pursue relational and relationship goals, seeing their identity as inextricably tied to others. Cultures that tend to be more individualistic include many of the traditionally Western cultures (e.g., the U.S., the U.K., Australia, Canada, Scandinavia, Germany) whereas collectivism tends to be more characteristic of Eastern, Latin, African, and Middle Eastern cultures (e.g., southern Europe, China, Korea, India, Brazil, Mexico, etc.). In consumer behavior, knowing a customer's predisposition to focus on the self or on the self as seen in the context of others matters. An advertisement for a cologne or perfume, for example, could emphasize the wonderful way it makes *you* smell or, alternatively, the way that *others* will smell and notice you. It should be noted that although cultures tend to be more individualistic or collectivistic by default, it is possible to shift individuals to be more individualistic or collectivistic in the moment. Furthermore, regional differences can exist *within* a country (e.g., northern Italians and northern French tend to be more individualistic than southern Italians and southern French).

Indulgence v. Restraint: this dimension is relatively new to the mix (there were originally five dimensions) and focuses on the tendency for a culture to permit its people great freedom in expression and doing whatever they feel like doing or, alternatively, to restrict freedom of expression and behavior through very strict cultural expectations and social norms. This is comparable to a comparison of progressive v. restrictive cultures. Examples of cultures high on indulgence include the Scandinavian countries, the U.S., the U.K., and most Latin countries and several Asian countries (e.g., Korea). Countries high on restraint tend to include highly religious cultures or cultures thought of as being traditionally less "free" in comparison to other parts of the world (e.g., Iran, Egypt, and, lately, Russia). From a marketer's perspective, one must be very sensitive to positioning products and services to the extent that individual expression is encouraged. Even former Soviet-era countries in Eastern Europe are just now getting used to the freedom of expression their capitalist economies now permit. Imagine doing focus groups in countries where decisions were always made for you for decades!

Long-Term v. Short-Term Orientation: this dimension has to do with the perspective of time and how this changes focus and importance of outcomes. For example, a short-term culture is focused on norms, immediate results, and spending whereas a long-term culture is more open to the idea of change, creative or different thinking, and saving. There tends to be an East/West divide where the U.K., the U.S., and other strongly capitalist economies are focused on the short term whereas China, Japan, and South Korea often emphasize a longer-term view. This different perspective of time may affect willingness to invest in riskier projects for a quick gain or longer-term projects with lower risk in financial contexts. Similarly, there may be different cultural expectations about how long a product should last, which could have implications for customer satisfaction, warranties, and insurance.

Masculinity v. Femininity: this dimension is a bit sexist in my view but it is what you would probably guess. Masculine cultures are those that are achievement and status oriented in which competition is embraced whereas feminine cultures are those that are more cooperative, helpful, and modest. Here we see a surprising difference between otherwise similar cultures. For example, although the U.S. and Scandinavia share many cultural similarities, the U.S. tends to be more masculine and the Scandinavian countries more feminine. Advertising messages that promote competition or boasting are likely to play well in masculine cultures but far less likely to do so in feminine cultures.

Power Distance: this dimension is a measure of the hierarchy within a culture and the expectation that such a hierarchy has on the interaction of the people within that culture. Cultures with high power distance (e.g., India, China) have longstanding traditions in which there are clear authority figures and clear worker bees – think of the old caste system. A lot of these cultures have distinct family roles, as well, where the elderly command a lot of respect. Cultures with low power distance (e.g., Denmark, Germany) have fairly level playing fields in which everyone is considered relatively equal. Remember our discussion on "social power" in the Social Influence chapter? Imagine how much stronger these social power influences are in cultures like India and China, where culture mandates very strict hierarchies establishing power compared to more power equal countries. From a business-to-business (B2B) perspective, this could very well shape the way you do business abroad: influencing key decision makers at the top is a must for high power distance cultures whereas decision-making is likely more organic in low power distance cultures.

Uncertainty Avoidance: this dimension is a measure of how comfortable or uncomfortable people in a culture are with uncertain situations. A high uncertainty avoidance score indicates cultures whose people prefer to know outcomes, have little risk, and avoid spontaneity (e.g., Germany, Italy). A low uncertainty avoidance score indicates cultures whose people are okay with not knowing, not planning, or having risky outcomes (e.g., China, Sweden). The example cultures highlight an important idea about Uncertainty Avoidance: just because you have a lot of rules (e.g., Germany), it doesn't mean you follow all of them (e.g., Italy). It may very well be that attempts to persuade in a high uncertainty avoidance culture work better when they are rational and appeal to logic and rules compared to messages that are less clear.

If you want to have some fun and compare countries' Dimensions of Culture, have a look at Geert's website: http://geert-hofstede.com/. Any company even *thinking* about conducting business in a different culture should definitely consult these dimensions. I learned about Hofstede's work in high school, and I still find it to be one of the best, most useful, and most practical measures of human behavior in existence.

Country-of-Origin. Culture has a funny way of shaping our behavior based on what we learn to value and how we learn to behave growing up, and attempts to measure some of the most important, high-level variables within culture produce useful tools like Hofstede's Dimensions of Culture. However, culture also has a funny way of shaping our expectations about consumer products, services, and companies that may not at all be rooted in fact or upbringing but, instead, rooted in the perceptions we have about a particular country or culture.

Let me ask you this: if I told you I was going to send you delicious, fine chocolate at the end of this book (which I totally could do), and then gave you a choice of chocolate from one of two countries, either Switzerland or Afghanistan, which would you choose? The choice is fairly obvious. But even if I were to make the comparison a bit more apples to apples, say Switzerland or Sweden, you would probably still pick Switzerland. Why? Well, we have learned cultural associations that suggest to us that Switzerland is known for its delicious chocolate. Switzerland is also known for cheese, dairy, cuckoo clocks, quality watches, efficiency, good engineering, cows, and the adorable Swiss Miss. Sweden, on the other hand, is known for high quality design, trendy furniture, Ikea, ABBA, good music, great seafood, progressive thinking, stylish fashion, and beautiful people. Thus, although Sweden has many wonderful things and probably even has its own delicious chocolate brands, we still probably would prefer chocolate from Switzerland.

This effect, known as the **Country-of-Origin Effect**, occurs when we attribute positive (or negative) characteristics to a particular product, service, or company based on preconceived perceptions about the source of the product, service, or company. This is why we associate "Made in China" with poor quality, pay more for wines made in France and Italy (even if wines made in North Dakota taste better), and trust a ballet instructor more if he/she has a last name like Romanov instead of Rodriguez. In fact, when I was an eager undergraduate business student at WashU I did an independent study with Dr. John Branch (the guy responsible for duping me into doing a Ph.D.) in which I looked at how country-of-origin affected one's perception of service and satisfaction levels. We certainly have learned associations that affect these choices and evaluations – Russians and French with ballet/dance, Scandinavians with design, Latins with romance and socializing – yet we are often oblivious to how these associations automatically influence our decisions.

Another subtle way that culture influences our behavior is via a process I call **cultural fluency**. Having moved up in the world in terms of research training and study design, I developed an idea after visiting France in which I noticed a young Parisian woman lighting a cigarette without any concerted conscious effort involved. No, her behavior was so engrained and hardwired that she carried on her conversation with her friend with almost no regard for what her hands and fingers were doing. Now, I knew that many of our behaviors often become so routinized that we learn to do them without needing to think about doing them; the additional "a ha" moment came when I thought about how culturally different an act like smoking still is between Americans and some Europeans of my generation. The idea became, "If culture truly operates and guides behavior at a very implicit, automatic level, then it should be the case that experiencing something that is *disfluent* with one's own culture should arouse more deliberative thinking, whereas exposure to culturally *fluent* stimuli should encourage one to simply, 'Go with the flow.'"

To give you a concrete example, imagine that on the 4th of July in the U.S. I give you a plate for an outdoor barbecue buffet that has stars, stripes, and firework patterns on the plate. Now let's say, at a different barbecue also on the 4th of July I give people basic white plates that are identical to yours in every way except they feature no design. And let's say there's even a third barbecue where I give people Halloween-themed plates. If I measured the amount of food (by weight) people put on their plate, what do you think happens? Think it through. Have a guess? Well, we ran a version of this very study at a *real* 4th of July picnic and found that, on average, people put significantly *more* food on the culturally fluent plate (i.e., the stars, stripes, and fireworks plate) and significantly *less* food on the culturally disfluent plate (i.e., the Halloween plate) compared to the white control group plate. We know that putting more food on the 4th of July plate was *not* simply because the plate was more festive – the Halloween plate was equally as festive – no, what mattered was the cultural fluency and disfluency of the stimuli. No one said anything about the plates nor did anyone report thinking there would be a link between the kind of plate they were given and the amount of food they put on the plate, but that's exactly what happened.

My coauthors and I have replicated this cultural fluency effect using a variety of other cultural contexts: weddings (in the U.S.), Chinese New Year (in Hong Kong), Valentine's Day (in China and the U.S.), and even funeral obituaries (in the U.S.). *Every time* cultural fluency leads people to "go with the flow," to be more likely to buy a random consumer product, and not to think at an analytic, deliberative level. Cultural disfluency, on the other hand, leads people to stop and think, to hesitate, to think twice before consuming a random consumer product, and to think more carefully and deliberately about questions posed to them.

To summarize, culture certainly influences the way we view power distance, time, our relationships with others, and even our freedom to express ourselves based on learned norms growing up. But culture is so pervasive and so prevalent that it often operates at a much more implicit, automatic level; serving as a guide to our depth of processing and even our behavior with no need for thought.

Learning Culture. Anyone who has experienced the joy/challenge of living or studying abroad knows that "learning" culture is not necessarily a straightforward process. That is, you cannot simply *sit* in a classroom and learn a culture. Instead, a large part of learning how to "do as the Romans do" while in Rome, is simply to exist within the culture, to immerse yourself entirely in the food, the music, the people, the language, the fashion, the hobbies, and more.

This should not be surprising to you, as this is exactly how we learn our *own* culture. You and I were born into a particular culture in which we were surrounded by particular foods, specific kinds of music, people dressing a certain way, gestures and words of the languages around us, and more. When you are a baby you do not attend a school to learn this information (…wouldn't that be a sight?).

This acquisition of one's own culture is known by a fancier term, **enculturation**, while the learning of a culture other than one's own is referred to as **acculturation**. For an effect like cultural fluency to work, it is required that one has learned the established norms of the culture in which he/she currently is. For example, I know very little about the culture of Botswana. I bet there are many rich traditions and cultural practices that the people there have had for generations, but if I were to go there, their culture would not guide my behavior in the same way that my culture guides my behavior so effortlessly in the U.S. – knowing which side of the street to walk on, how much distance to keep between myself and someone nearby so they still know I'm friendly but not a creeper, etc. (i.e., the products of my early enculturation of American norms). What was once effortless before is now very effortful.

But contrast this with Spain, France, or Italy, places where I have spent a considerable amount of time and whose cultures I know well from my own parents' upbringing. Although I'm sure I was a super-awkward American traveler on my first trip to France, I now navigate daily interactions with such fluidity that I feel as comfortable in Paris as I do in Chicago. Over time, I acquired the cultural know-how necessary to live as a French person lives (i.e., acculturation). Sure, there are still some awkward or confusing situations, but I've come a long way, so much so that the last time I was in France this little old woman came up to me and started going on and on and on about her day in very fast French. I suppose I either looked the part very well or the old lady was crazy, either way, I'll chalk it up to my acculturation of the French culture.

The notion of enculturation and acculturation is particularly important in today's mobile world. Consider the growing Latino population in the United States, for example. The "Hispanic market" actually encompasses *many* cultures – Mexican, Puerto Rican, Cuban, Dominican, Panamanian, Honduran, and many, many more. Sure, there exist *some* similarities among these different groups, but I assure you that there's nothing we dislike more than being lumped together into one "Hispanic market." There are *very* important differences among these cultures. Consider, for example, that Cuban-Americans tended to be very politically conservative as are many immigrants (and subsequent generations) from socialist-leaning countries. That demographic is shifting more liberal recently, but the assumption that Mexican-American voters would vote the same way as Cuban-American voters is as incorrect as assuming both groups would want the same consumer products.

To the point of differences in acculturation, consider differences within my *own* family in which my grandmother insisted that Spanish not be spoken in my mother's house growing up despite my grandfather being a native speaker. The reason? Acculturation. My grandmother did not want my mother and her siblings to be set apart from non-Hispanic-American students at school. This is a very common approach many immigrant families take to help encourage the acculturation of their children. Fortunately, my mother's abuelo and abuela often spoken to my mom in Spanish, so it wasn't a total loss of culture, but my Spanish is severely limited as a result (...at least I know grandfather and grandmother).

The enculturation and acculturation processes are reinforced through things like **language**, **symbols**, **myths/rituals**, and other **markers of culture**. Obviously, language is an important feature of culture. Language researchers now know that the sounds to which we are exposed during the early months of infanthood, phonemes, are essential to our ability to speak and even understand a language with great fluency. Have you ever had that experience with a friend who speaks a different language where they teach you how to say something in a language you don't speak, you repeat it, and no matter how much you *think* your pronunciation is correct your friend tells you that you're not saying it right? This is the story of my life with my German and Chinese friends. I swear that I repeat what they tell me to say *exactly* as they are saying it, but pronunciation is so nuanced that they can sense a difference where I believe there is none. Remember our earlier discussion on perception and just noticeable differences? Yeah, their JND threshold is *much* lower than mine, apparently.

The importance of understanding language in the context of consumer behavior need not even cross into *different* languages. Consider the slight differences between British English and American English. Words like bathroom, elevator, and gas in America are loo, lift, and petrol in the mother country. Obviously, crafting a marketing message for the British market would mandate a review of the language, but something even as subtle as the *spelling* of a word could change our attitudes about a product.

For example, thinking back to country-of-origin effects, it's reasonable that I would find a pub's food better or more authentic if I saw words like colour and flavour instead of color and flavor.

Beyond language, cultures are replete with unique **symbols** that reinforce the culture even through mere exposure to the symbols. Consider, for example, the popular hammer and sickle that served as the symbol for the U.S.S.R. and, by extension, Communism. Even colors carry significant symbolic meaning; there's a reason flags of predominately Muslim countries often feature green, Communist countries feature red, and democratic countries bear red, white, and blue in some combination. Similarly, symbols like the yin yang, most often associated with Eastern cultures, often express something characteristic about the cultures in which they are found. Eastern cultures, for example, are often referred to as "dualistic," meaning that the cultures tend to view the world as consisting of two opposing forces, a belief reinforced in the cultures' religions, laws, and institutions. Sound familiar? The yin yang is a visual symbol of this concept of duality. Are you familiar with the flag of South Korea? If not, go Google it. Look familiar?

And, of course, our daily **rituals** and **traditions**, as well as the **myths** and cultural stories we tell, reinforce cultural norms and help teach culture to young children and new immigrants. From handshakes in the U.S., bowing in Japan, and kissing each side of another's cheek in many western and southern European countries, even the simple act of *greeting* another person varies by culture. Stories we tell our children, like The Little Boy Who Cried Wolf, meant to teach American children about the ills of telling too many tall tales (the lesson being that when you *really* tell the truth or need help no one will know and, as such, you will be eaten by a wolf), are clever ways of reinforcing broader cultural ideas about honesty, truthfulness, and social interaction. A Chinese equivalent about a king (*King You of Zhou*) tells a similar tale of a king who misused warning beacons (that were *supposed* to only be used in case of an attack) to make his bored lover laugh. The army began to ignore the warnings as King You continued to misuse the beacons, which ultimately led to his demise when a neighboring kingdom attacked as the generals continued to ignore the warning beacons. Ahh, the things we do for love...

Beyond stories, however, our daily practices such as setting a table, driving on the road in a particular way in a particular direction and following specific rules, addressing adults with a particular salutation (Mr. or Mrs., Prof. or Dr., vous or tu, usted or tú) are all ways of reinforcing the values and norms of our respective cultures. In some cultures, it is forbidden for men to associate with women whereas that idea is absurd in other cultures. In some cultures, there is an expectation that elderly family members will be taken care of by their children and younger generations whereas the reverse is true in other cultures. The stories, symbols, rituals, and traditions that emerge in our cultures are both reflections of and reinforcements of our cultures.

From a marketing perspective, you may be interested to learn that DeBeers is often considered to be responsible for associating diamonds with love and commitment in its "A diamond is forever" campaign. The idea that an engagement ring should cost at least two months of a proposer's salary also did not appear out of thin air and is further perpetuated via cost calculators on jewelry company websites. Cultural traditions like lavish weddings have turned into a multi-*billion* dollar industry ($40+ billion annually), and even simple cultural rituals – like brushing, flossing, and rinsing with mouthwash – have changed the way people shop for products (e.g., the emergence of whitening strips and professional dental tools you can use at home). Or consider how Taco Bell has attempted to create the concept of "fourthmeal," referring to a late-night meal (the fourth meal of the day after breakfast, lunch, and dinner) to encourage more late-night sales of its tacos and burritos. Smart marketers know they have the power to create and shape culture, which is hopefully a power they wield carefully.

Global v. Local strategies. Because most companies now operate in many international markets or start in a particular market and subsequently expand abroad, many marketing managers are forced to make a decision whether or not to keep the brand "global" or to localize the brand. The **global v. local** strategy essentially involves keeping one same look, message, and feeling about your brand (global strategy) or differentiating the brand so that it is customized to the local preferences of a particular market (local strategy).

McDonald's, quite surprisingly, is only the world's *second*-most prevalent restaurant chain since it was surpassed by Subway a few years ago. Still, McDonald's is the largest restaurant chain by way of revenue and has managed to appeal so broadly due largely in part to its blend of global and local strategies. Some McDonald's staples, such as the cheeseburger and french fries, can likely be found in every McDonald's around the world (…at least they have been found in McDonald's locations in Paris, Berlin, and the Bahamas in my experience…not that I dine at McD's that often, particularly when abroad). However, what is *not* found at any McDonald's in the U.S. but *is* found at McDonald's stores in Paris are fresh-baked macarons, the delicious, brightly colored French cookies that taste like heaven in a cookie. Similarly, I was surprised to learn that Starbucks in Paris has fresh-squeezed orange juice (a personal favorite) on its menu and a *far* superior selection of food items; I guess when you're in a city known for its delicious pastries, you better get it right.

Even as of this book's writing, the annual Apple rumor mill is circulating about the possibility that the famous tech company will, for the first time, add a gold phone option to its high-end mix (while simultaneously launching a variety of colors at a lower price point). The speculation is that Apple, cognizant of the ever-expanding Chinese consumer market, is looking to tap into the local preferences of the Asian market where the color gold is a symbol of prosperity and influence. Going with gold seems to be a wise option, then, but the company may also explore a high-end red phone, as the color symbolizes joy and good fortune in Chinese culture.

Companies vary in the degree to which they customize or tailor their products to fit the local preferences and cultures of consumers, but the point is that marketing managers doing business in multiple markets often have to weigh the benefits and costs of customizing products to particular markets.

Core Values and Trends. American core values are fairly well known to those of us who were born and raised in the U.S. of A. Indeed, phrases like, "Life, liberty, and the pursuit of happiness," "Freedom and justice for all," and, "Living the American Dream," are all fundamental beliefs engrained in the American brain since childhood. We are taught to believe that everyone has equal opportunity, that individualism is valued and encouraged, and that we have the freedom to say *whatever* we want to say. Although some naysayers may disagree to the extent that each of these core values is actually expressed in our culture, relatively speaking to some of the world's cultures (e.g., North Korea), there's simply no question: America is the epitome of freedom, liberty, and equality. And we are not alone in these core values: most of our closest political allies – France, the U.K., Germany, Australia, EU nations, etc. – espouse very similar beliefs.

Whereas some beliefs and values are enduring, others change almost as frequently as the direction of the wind. Consider, for example, the shifting American cultural view on health and fitness. Perhaps tired of being the joke of the world with respect to obesity rates, the fight against American obesity and for personal fitness has led to a huge growth in markets for diet programs (e.g., Weight Watchers, Jenny Craig, MediFast), gyms (e.g., Curves, CrossFit), and fitness classes/videos (e.g., Zumba, P90X, and even Carmen Electra's Aerobic Striptease, which, btw, she totally ripped off from yours truly – I once taught a class called Sexercise well in advance of this "Aerobic Striptease" nonsense). For the first time Mexico surpassed the United States in its obesity rate in 2013. Even Michelle Obama has made healthy eating and fitness her top priority as First Lady.

So while certain elements of culture are more permanent, long-lasting mainstays that have endured decades and even centuries, other elements of culture – like food, music, and fashion – are trends that come and go, sometimes to reappear, sometimes to disappear forever. Neon, once thought to be lost to the 1980s, now adorns the tanktops that frat bros and sorority girls wear for Greek events. Boat shoes, popular in the early 1990s, have reemerged as *the* shoe men must wear in the past few years. Even spandex-as-pants, a terrible idea also from the 1980s era of way-too-tight clothing (prior to the baggy clothing craze of the 1990s) has, quite unfortunately, managed to work its way back into American culture…kind of like how Abercrombie has managed to hang on in Europe despite it falling out of favor within American culture.

Even consumer products/services like online dating are cultural phenomena. As I mentioned earlier in the Needs, Wants, and Motivation chapter, American culture once considered online dating desperate and even extremely *dangerous*. Who would have thought that now, not even ten years later, online dating is one of the most common forms of dating, with Americans even beginning to have more favorable views about meeting potential life partners online compared to in bars. Shifting cultural attitudes are not limited to products and services, however; think of the shift in the support of same-sex marriage in the U.S. and abroad in the past five to ten years. Remember that at one point in the history of American culture it was illegal for people of different races to marry one another, a belief (quite fortunately) overturned in the landmark and aptly-named case *Loving v. Virginia*. Some cultures mocked the American reluctance to interracial marriage then and its modern reluctance to same-sex marriage now, whereas others criticize our shifting views on same-sex marriage, an idea still considered taboo in their culture.

Socio-Economic Status (SES). One of the important core cultural values in America is the idea of **social mobility**, the belief that it is entirely possible for someone born into one socioeconomic status to, by means of hard work and focus, improve his/her socioeconomic status. My siblings and I are all first generation college students, for example. While I don't imagine we will be purchasing personal jets or small private islands in the Caribbean any time soon, we are all certainly in better, more secure socioeconomic groups compared to my parents who, in turn, were in a better position than their parents. This was due entirely in part to the hard work of my parents who, as hard-working, middle class Americans, worked *multiple* jobs – from truck driver to janitor, secretary to office cleaning person – to provide for their four children the opportunities that they, themselves, never had. Rest assured it is never lost on me the real reasons I was able to attend college, to travel the world, to live in exciting cities like Chicago and Los Angeles, and to write this book for you, as I speak to those two reasons on the phone on a daily basis.

The reason I include socioeconomic status in the chapter on culture is that, much like the default culture into which we are born, the default socioeconomic level into which we are born profoundly influences our consumer behavior. There are certainly perks being born with a "silver spoon" in one's mouth affords you compared to being born to a family receiving public assistance, but, even then, there are often challenges along with these perks like feeling a pressure to "Keep up with the Joneses." One of my favorite stories from my undergraduate statistics professor who also did some financial advising work on the side involved him telling us to "picture the mansions surrounding WashU" and then to imagine the "size of the owners' bank accounts." He then held up his hand, made a zero with his thumb and pointer finger, and said, "Zilch. Every dime they make goes to paying for their lavish lifestyles." Professor Gordinier was also a huge supporter of the NRA, so when that guy told you something, you did not question it.

Still, pressure to "Keep up with the Joneses" may pale in comparison to the struggles some families have to pay for food, housing, or childcare so that they can work jobs to raise money to pay for these needs. Indeed, our innate needs for resources and security are extremely motivational but they can also get us into trouble. Consider, for example, the prevalence of payday loan companies and other insanely high interest rate companies preying on low-SES individuals most often in impoverished neighborhoods. The interest rates for these "no background credit check" loans are so high that borrowers stand no chance of ever paying off the companies. The same strategy applies to "ambulance chaser" lawyers who exploit low-SES people by suggesting they take part in what are often frivolous class-action lawsuits to make money quickly. Die-hard capitalists would say, "Hey, there's clearly a market for these services if these businesses exist," but, ethically speaking, one has to wonder if a line should be drawn.

Socioeconomic Status is actually a function of one's income, employment (occupation), and education and, as such, is a broader, more comprehensive construct than simply "income." How SES is measured and labeled takes on many forms, but one of the most common is a six-class hierarchy that positions "upper-upper class" and "lower-upper class" at the top, "upper-middle class" and "lower-middle class" in the middle, and "upper-lower class" and "lower-lower class" at the bottom. Some researchers will simply use income as a measure for classifying people whereas others use metrics that combine income, employment level/status, and education level as interactive terms, as there is information to be had in knowing someone has accrued great wealth but is currently unemployed and may not have an advanced degree. Similarly, there is something different about a highly-educated, gainfully employed person who makes very little money because he/she works for a non-profit that may not have the resources to pay well compared to an unemployed, low-educated individual also making little money.

Although each SES approach's cutoffs and designations may seem arbitrary (and, to some extent, the particular cutoffs *are* certainly arbitrary), several studies have found significant relationships between SES level and important outcomes like mortality and health. While one might assume that different SES could affect availability of resources, the fact that one's SES can significantly affect one's health status should be alarming. Unlike different SES approaches, the definition of poverty in the U.S. is actually set by the U.S. government and is currently (as of 2012) defined as being a total income of $23,050 for a family of four. If that is alarming to you given your family's experience or situation, don't panic: a majority of Americans will spend at least some time under the poverty level at some point in life.

Wait, what? Re-read that last sentence: a majority of Americans will spend at least some time under the poverty level at some point in life. If that seems hard to believe then you are going to be super upset with what I am about to share. Michael Norton, a colleague of mine who is a professor at Harvard Business School (and who is, incidentally, one of my favorite people in our field), has some really interesting research involving wealth distribution in the United States. Basically, Mike and Dan Ariely (of Duke University and of *Predictably Irrational* fame) asked people two questions: 1) how do you think wealth is distributed in the U.S.?, and 2) how do you think wealth *should be* distributed in the U.S.? Participants slid bars along a continuum, basically identifying the cutoffs of their own perceived and ideal SES cutoffs. Mike and Dan captured all the data and then plotted this information as it compared to the *actual* distribution of wealth in the U.S.

The result? Consistently, across age groups, political beliefs, gender, etc., participants plotted "ideal distributions" that were far more equal than their "perceived distributions" of reality, but the true shocker was the difference between "perceived distributions" of reality and actual reality. Whereas participants' perceived distributions were roughly equal in size, slightly skewed in favor of the wealthier groups (e.g., the top 20% owning just under 60% of the wealth), the *actual* distribution showed that the top 20% own nearly 85% of the total wealth...85%. In fact, the bottom 40% own *so little* of the total wealth that they don't even show up on the chart.

Because a large part of consumption involves having the resources needed to consume in the first place, understanding how socioeconomic status affects consumer choices and behaviors is essential. Whether you're a marketer at a large consumer packaged goods company focusing on food or a medical professional giving a patient a list of options to treat a health problem, understanding consumer choices from the different perspectives of varying SES matters: some people won't even *consider* health treatment because they cannot afford it – or, to state it differently, some people would rather *risk death* than put their family in a financial bind. If you have not understood the importance SES can have on consumption up to this point, I bet you can now.

Implicit Associations and Stereotyping. In our discussion of culture and socioeconomic status, I mentioned how these default, innate factors, characteristics so tightly woven into our identities that we often take them for granted, exert almost invisible forces on our choices and behaviors. Although we may not see it *even if we deliberately try* to think of the way our culture and socioeconomic status affect us, trust me that it happens.

If you don't trust me then trust my colleagues who use a now famous methodology known as the **Implicit Association Test (IAT)**. The IAT consists of a task in which experimenters present words or images on a computer screen and instruct participants to click a certain key on the keyboard corresponding to a certain idea or valence. There are usually several stages. The first stage might involve presenting words or images of mammals and reptiles where participants must click "A" for mammal and "N" for reptile. The second task may then consist of positive or negative words (e.g., happy, miserable) and ask participants to click "A" for positive words and "N" for negative words. The third task then combines stimuli so that mammals, reptiles, positive words, and negative words are shown and participants click "A" for "mammal OR positive word" and "N" for "reptile OR negative word." The fourth task is a repeat of the first task with the "A" and "N" reversed such that participants click "A" for reptile and "N" for mammal. The final task is a repeat of the third task in which *all* the stimuli are shown, but the letter combos are mixed such that "A" is for "reptile or positive word" and "N" is for "mammal or negative word." Confused yet?

You should be. The point of the IAT is to test for *implicit* associations among constructs that are related in our brain. You may be able to recall from our chapter on Learning and Memory that knowledge is theorized to be stored as associative networks in the brain, such that when I think of "dog" it becomes easier for me to think of "cat" compared to say "carrot." The IAT deliberately challenges us so that it can test, using time as a proxy, how closely associated certain concepts are in our brains. Thus, if my IAT score from the example above showed that I repeatedly responded to mammal much more quickly when it was paired with "positive" and much more slowly when it was paired with "negative," and the opposite for reptile (i.e., I responded faster when reptile was paired with "negative" and slower when reptile was paired with "positive"), then it is likely that I have an implicit association between "mammals" and positivity and "reptiles" and negativity.

While being positive about mammals and negative about reptiles may not be too surprising, imagine what happens when "mammals" and "reptiles" are replaced with names like "Tyler" and "Tyrone" or "Shelly" and "Shameika." Although people would (usually) *never* admit to racial prejudices, it could be the case that they respond more quickly when names associated with a particular race are paired with "positive" or "negative." Participants may not even realize they have these associations, but the IAT theoretically suggests such associations are present based on the response time during the trials.

Before you panic and think that you are secretly racist and don't even know it, you have to understand something about implicit associations and even stereotyping: stereotyping is an *adaptive*, helpful skill that likely has helped our species survive over time. "What?!" you're thinking, "That's a terrible thing to say!" But notice I did *not* say that being racist or ageist or classist was helpful. I said that *stereotyping* was helpful. Let me explain. The process of **stereotyping** essentially involves categorizing incoming information into preexisting bins that we know well. To give you a simple example, imagine two buckets in your brain – one labeled "safe animal" and the other labeled "dangerous animal." Now imagine that you are walking in a tropical jungle somewhere in South America and you come across an animal you've never seen before. The animal is lizard-like, walks with a slithery, sinewy step, has a long tongue like a snake, and what appear to be very, very sharp teeth. Oh, and it's two feet away from you. What do you do? Well, before you can decide to fight or flee, you have to decide whether or not this animal poses any risk to you in the first place. You have seconds, nay, milliseconds in which to do it before this potentially dangerous creature strikes. Fortunately for you, human beings have evolved to make that snap decision very quickly. Within no time at all our brain sees the characteristics of this new creature, associates them with dangerous critters we already know, and then cues enough adrenaline release in our body for us to book it out of the jungle. We throw this novel creature into the "dangerous animal" bucket and flee the scene. Thus, stereotyping is a very useful, adaptive way for human beings to make sense of novel stimuli in an efficient and (most of the time) effective way.

Where stereotyping fails us is when we make unwarranted judgment calls over time even in the face of disconfirming evidence. These are the "if a [insert ethnicity here] person was walking toward you in a dark alley at night, what is the likelihood you would cross the street?" kind of stereotyping that doesn't make much sense, regardless of what ethnicity you put in the blank. Because these "bins" are often products of our cultural experiences, stereotypes are often culturally influenced. This is why one of the best ways to break down stereotypes is to break out of one's cultural confines, to travel, and to experience diversity and evidence that may contradict stereotypes not based on factual data or information.

From a marketing perspective, it is useful to know that humans often process information in this stereotyping/bin manner. If you are attempting to introduce a new product in the market, for example, then you should be aware that customers may make a snap judgment about your new product based on your brand name or its comparison to other already established products in the market. That's just how the human brain works. The savvy marketer can use this to his/her advantage: if I want to introduce a new brand of toilet paper priced at a lower price point than existing brands, I could use a cute, cuddly kitten on the packaging to take advantage of the associations shoppers already have with the cute bears of Charmin or the adorable puppy of Cottonelle. Instead of seeming like a strange new entrant to an established market, I would automatically be pegged as "fitting in" to a particular category of products and increase the shoppers' consideration of my product...all without them even thinking about *why*.

Culture and socioeconomic status are fundamental parts of who we are as people and as consumers. That these core components of our very being are so capable of shaping and colouring our worldviews, our perspectives, and even our behaviors without our realisation of this influence really should give us pause...hopefully the British spelling of two words in that last sentence provided a flavour for just how subtle culture can be.

*   *   *

Michigan Avenue in Chicago, much like Fifth Avenue in New York, is a street popular with tourists and locals alike, with both populated by famous stores and beloved brands. Ten years ago if I were to see someone wearing Abercrombie and Fitch walking down the street I would have not given it a second thought. In fact, *I* might have also been wearing Abercrombie and Fitch! Now, however, when I walk down Michigan Avenue and see someone wearing Abercrombie and Fitch, I immediately assume he/she is European. I may not deliberate on it for very long (if at all), but the assumption is there, and if I were to verify, I bet I would probably be correct.

But beyond knowing the cultural background of the person wearing the Abercrombie and Fitch clothing, I also know something about his/her SES. Abercrombie and Fitch clothing is not cheap; it's not the most expensive clothing on the market, but it's certainly not cheap, either. Whether or not I make the conscious association between, "This person is wearing Abercrombie and Fitch," and, "This person has money," is irrelevant – the association is there and has already affected my evaluation of the person, the history of that person I have concocted in my head, and how my interactions with him/her would likely proceed if we engaged one another.

Earlier in the chapter we described culture as a sort of "how-to" book for existing in a particular country or region, but it turns out that neither political borders nor countries are needed to understand the notion of culture. Indeed, rules for how to behave don't just exist at the national cultural level – there are how-to rules found in *most* groups of people: teenagers, hipsters, rappers, Catholics, retirees, etc. Coincidentally, my grandma is a member of each of those groups. The next chapter is dedicated to these consumer subcultures and the various "how-to" rules found within each.

APPLICATION QUESTIONS

1) A Chinese shoe company, popular in China, is having a difficult time expanding its business abroad. Why might this be the case, and what alternative strategy could the company use to get around the issue?

2) Recently, while at the gym, I noticed that someone was working out in flip flops and blue jeans. Subsequently, when I was on my way out of the gym I didn't engage in my routine purchase of a post-workout protein bar, opting instead to wait to eat one when I got home. Using a concept from the chapter, explain what might have happened.

3) You and your team, people under your direction, have to conduct important meetings with your counterparts in Berlin and Mumbai over the next two weeks. What might you tell your team regarding time commitments, who should be doing the talking, and how important it is to be perceived as a cohesive team or as free, independent workers? Why might this not matter at all?

4) Some large groups of immigrants, such as the Turkish population of Berlin or Chinese populations in large U.S. cities living in Chinatown, operate in their native language and follow their native customs. What kind of challenge does this present to marketing efforts? What opportunities?

5) You work for a major auto company interested in increasing its share of the market among Hispanic consumers in Latin American markets. Your boss tells you to hire someone for the team. When you ask for a list of desired qualifications, he/she replies, "Probably anyone who speaks Spanish will do." Explain why your boss is an idiot. What qualifications would *you* suggest?

6) Give an existing example of a consumer product where it makes sense to pursue a global strategy but not a local strategy. Give another example of a product where it makes sense to pursue a local strategy but not a global strategy. Find a product by you at the moment. How would you attempt to sell that product in Sydney, Australia? How about in Barcelona, Spain? How about in Kigali, Rwanda?

7) Marketers are often tempted to hawk expensive products toward consumers perceived to be wealthier. Why is this assumption that wealthy consumers enjoy spending more money wrought with potential fallacies? Similarly, why might it be wrong for a store selling expensive items to shun consumers of lower SES?

8) You are considering purchasing new glasses and think that you should get a pair of those thick-rimmed glasses that have been in style the past few years. "First impressions matter," you say. Using a concept from this chapter, what do you mean by this?

9) A diversity trainer has come to your office for the day – joy! He/she makes the claim that stereotyping is absolutely no good. You stand up and say, "I agree with what you're trying to say, but it turns out stereotyping can be very useful because..." Finish that thought.

10) Kraft recently launched a commercial for its Zesty Italian dressing featuring an American model with southern European features who was cast in the role of an Italian chef cooking in Tuscany. This is clearly country-of-origin at work. Kraft also makes cheese, steak sauce, and Kool-Aid. How might you use country-of-origin to market those brands if you were a marketing manager at Kraft hoping to emulate the success of the Zesty Italian campaign?

Chapter 9 | Subcultures

Picture it: a room full of middle-aged men ogling and throwing handfuls of cash out for the featured performers of the show – girls named Rarity, Pinkie Pie, and Twilight Sparkle just to name a few. Their wild hair is long and flowing, effortlessly blowing in the wind, and each girl bears a lower-back tattoo of a rainbow, butterflies, or stars and diamonds. The guys in the audience would love nothing more than to take even just one of the girls home with him tonight, and one lucky guy might be able to pay enough to bring *all* of them home.

This gentlemen's club is *truly* a gentlemen's club, but probably not the kind of gentlemen's club you're picturing. This exclusive gathering of men is BronyCon 2013, in which thousands, yes, *thousands* of men traveled to Baltimore, Maryland, to revel in their love of just one thing: *My Little Pony*. Rarity, Pinkie Pie, and Twilight Sparkle are each characters from the television show, each featuring long horse manes and colorful, cartoonish brands on their hind end.

The men of this gentlemen's club, who refer to themselves as "Bronies," come from all walks of life: doctors, retail clerks, self-professed nerds, fathers, sons, brothers, and more. Each year the men fly in from all around the world to participate in the four-day spectacle. Each day's events begin at 9:30 or 10:00am and continue, nonstop, until 2:30am(?!) – that's a lot of *My Little Pony*. An example day at BronyCon includes seminars like "Writing Compelling Pony Novels" and "Life-Size Equestria: An In-Depth Look Into Life Size Plush Making." It turns out that these are not life skills that are easily learned, well, anywhere else.

Now, before you get too bent out of shape thinking that Bronies is only a "boy's club" (as the name probably suggests), you should know that female fans are *also* welcome at BronyCon. What are these female *My Little Pony* lovers called? Pegasisters. Clever, right?

When Hasbro decided to re-launch *My Little Pony* as a show on its Hub television network, the newly revamped version entitled *My Little Pony: Friendship is Magic* was a throwback to the 1980s original animated series.

The premise was essentially the same: magical ponies with colorful hair prancing, frolicking, and galloping their way in and out of trouble and fun in a way that would appeal to little girls. The difference? The show proved to be popular to more than just little girls.

This may not sound like a problem – I mean, who cares if your product appeals to more people than your intended target? It turns out that, in the world of television programming, executives do. Why? Well, imagine going into an ad sales meeting with potential buyers who are looking to attract the eyes of little girls – we're talking doll companies, Mattel selling Barbie, hair and nail polish manufacturers, and the creators of other things little girls love – and showing them the data on who's watching your show indicating that grown men make up a sizeable audience. That's probably not going to get you a lot of ad revenue.

Then consider an alternative strategy. Knowing that a fair bit of your audience consists of middle-aged men, you could approach brands like Axe Body Spray, Gillette razors, and Old Spice deodorant...but now you're isolating the little girls watching the show. Hasbro had an unexpected problem on its hands.

Fortunately, over time, Hasbro has been able to iron out the challenge it faced by having a show that, quite amazingly, managed to appeal to two very, very different segments. Hidden in the show's dialogue are comments and ideas that are generated by and discussed within the Brony community; even the name of one of the characters was inspired by a Brony group. Yet little girls continue to watch the show and enjoy it for the excellent children's cartoon the show is. Unlike some shows that straddle this child/adult line with the inclusion of suggestive humor much to the chagrin of conservative parents, *My Little Pony: Friendship is Magic* keeps a clean, playful tone that is appreciated by kids of all ages.

In fact, in what may be one of the most surprising reasons the Bronies give for their adoration of the show, many echo a similar sentiment that the show's positive focus on friendship and camaraderie is a nice contrast from the typical shows on television today. For that to come from a show in which little girls and grown men can watch and enjoy magical ponies, well, I guess friendship *is* magic.

*   *   *

A famous saying states, "You can choose your friends, but you can't choose your family," and the funny thing about this idea in the context of consumer behavior is that while you may not be able to choose the culture or socio-economic status into which you are born, you *can* choose other important groups to belong to, groups that can influence your choices and behaviors just as much as, if not more than, your culture and SES. These groups and organizations in which we have membership, whether consciously noted or not, are referred to as **subcultures**.

Just like broader cultures, subcultures have their own rules, norms, expectations, symbols, and language. For example, in the world of Bronies, a Pegasister means a woman who shares a love of *My Little Pony*. A play on the words Pegasus and sister, those of us outside of the Brony world who happen to hear the word for the first time may have absolutely *no* idea what is being talked about, while those people "on the inside" know right away.

As this chapter will illustrate, a variety of subcultures exist, groups defined by any number of factors or according to quite diverse dimensions, some that overlap, others that don't. The main point is that we don't just live in a culture or at a particular socio-economic level; we live each day as members of many different groups, and each group can affect our choices and behaviors in ways that we don't always notice.

Geographic Subcultures. In the prior chapter we talked about how our culture can influence how we see the world and affect our consumer decisions. However, it would be quite naïve and inaccurate for us to pretend that *all* Americans are the same or that *all* Germans choose the same way. We don't, of course. Within countries there are regional differences, within regions there are city differences, within cities there are neighborhood differences, within neighborhoods there are household differences, and even within households there are family role differences. However, just as we can make some predictions about how one is likely to think or behave based on his/her culture, we can also make some predictions based on their more defined subculture.

When we consider regions of the United States, there are certain differences for which these regions are known. Southerners, for example, are known for their amazing hospitality. However, on the other hand, some people still associate the South with racial tension and Confederate flags. The Midwest is known for having strong "Midwestern values," which yield both positive outcomes in the form of kind, caring people and less positive outcomes like a reluctance toward alternative or non-traditional lifestyles. The West is known for being super chill, which can be both appealing when you're on vacation and annoying when you're in New York trying to get work done with a colleague in Los Angeles who has prioritized hiking at Runyon canyon before sundown over a late conference call.

The preferences for products can also differ based on regional subcultures. Consider, for example, the difference between seafood preferences along either coast of the U.S. compared to the interior of the U.S. Lobster and clam chowders are far more likely to be found in the Northeast and not so much in the Midwest. Separate healthy menu options tend to appear at restaurants in cities like Los Angeles and Miami more frequently than cities like New Orleans and St. Louis. And need I even attempt to explain how the same beverage – a carbonated soft drink – goes by the name of soda, pop, or even just Coke depending on whether you are in most of the U.S., the north-central region of the country, or the South, respectively. Even in my home state of Illinois there exists a mythical line where, above the line, you say pop, talk with a Chicago-ish accent, and root for the Cubs, while below the line you say soda, have no discernable accent (unless you live in the rural parts), and root for the Cardinals. Even tea differs from north to south, as the northerners tend to assume unsweetened iced tea, while the southerners tend to assume iced tea will be sweet tea.

So even though we are all proud to be an American, an American from Texas can have different needs and motivations than an American from New Hampshire (or really anywhere else in the country…Texas is special like that). This does not mean that we don't share a lot in common, we certainly do, particularly compared on the broader cultural level to another country's people like Zimbabwe. However, along with those similarities come some subcultural, regional differences that can affect our preferences and behaviors.

Race and ethnicity as subcultures. What does it mean to be an African-American? A Hispanic-American? A Caucasian-American? An Asian-American? A Native American? A South Asian-American? A European-American? A Middle Eastern-American? Did I cover everyone? An Antarctic-American? An Australian-American? I think *that's* everyone! …wait, wait…an *Oceanic-American*. That has to be everyone, right?

I joke, a bit, because America consists of *all* kinds of people from a variety of rich ethnicities and backgrounds. We may think of ourselves as Americans, culturally, as Southerners, regionally, but we can also think of ourselves in terms of our ethnicity. I grew up in a household heavily influenced by Hispanic culture given my mother's (Alvarez) side of the family. Hispanics, on average, tend to be very family oriented, more religious than other groups, appreciative of good deals and discounts, and more brand loyal than other ethnic consumer groups. However, as with any generalization of its kind, these trends are precisely that: generalizations. There are plenty of Hispanic-Americans who are not brand loyal or who may not be very close to their families. When we talk about subcultures we must do so with the understanding that the conclusions drawn are based on averages over groups of people. While something may be true, on average, it does not mean that it is always true or prescriptive in every instance.

Still, there are some important considerations when we think about ethnicity and race as they relate to marketing, both in terms of opportunities as well as risks. African-Americans represent roughly 13% of the total U.S. population (with an estimated spending power of $1.1 trillion by 2015), Hispanic-Americans represent nearly 17% of the population (with an estimated spending power of $1.5 trillion by 2015), and both groups have positive growth rates, with the latter group expected to nearly double in the next fifty years while the former group will only increase a few percentage points yet exert a comparable spending power in the market.

What does it mean to marketers that the spending power of these consumer groups will continue to grow? Is it okay for marketers to target these consumers because of these estimates? What does "targeting" a market based on ethnicity even mean?

To consider this point in a real marketing context, let's return to my favorite example – Disney – when it was announced that the company would be adding its first "black princess" to the famous Disney princess club. Tiana, the protagonist in the Disney film *The Princess and the Frog* generated a lot of buzz and positive headlines when Disney seemed to be giving a nod to the importance of making sure its characters were inclusive of all its audience members. Interestingly, this strategy backfired just years later with the introduction of a princess named Sofia on the television show *Sofia the First*. In what became a huge marketing flap for the company, Sofia was first announced to be Hispanic, then wasn't, then was again, then was definitely declared as "not Hispanic." Although any attempt to explain what happened is mere speculation, what seemed to happen was that Disney, thought to be exploiting the Hispanic market with the introduction of a character who was arbitrarily given the distinction of being "Hispanic," backed away from any cultural connection to the character after some consumers protested. Was that Disney's original intent? Who knows, but what we do know is that Sofia exists now and there is no mention of any Hispanic background. That said, I imagine the increasing Hispanic-American market means that we'll probably be seeing a Latina princess in the Disney lineup sooner than later.

Ethnic subcultures are tricky because people tend to be quite sensitive about race and ethnicity, probably for good reason but sometimes to a fault. In 2011, Amy Chua, a professor of law at Yale University, received both acclaim and criticism for her book *Battle Hymn of the Tiger Mother*, which detailed the demanding expectations parents in Chinese and other East-Asian families often put on their children to perform well. Some regarded the book as a lesson in how to rear children to be successful, whereas critics saw the approach as a form of mild child abuse, so rigid and restrictive that any benefits of the tactics were likely outweighed by the emotional and psychological toll on the children. Consider, for example, the tactic in which Chua threatened to burn her children's toys if they did not perform a piano piece perfectly. That's fairly intense to you and me, but maybe it's just not a part of our subculture. And, guess what, not *every* Chinese-American family lives with that kind of upbringing. Still, it is important to know the extent to which your consumers identify with a particular ethnic or racial subculture and how the beliefs and practices of these groups may shape consumer choices.

Age as a subculture. Some of the most commonly used buzzwords in the marketing world refer to the age subculture groups. Whether Traditionalists (born between 1925-1945), Baby Boomers (1946-1964), Generation X (1965-1980), Generation Y (1980-present, a.k.a. Millennials), or even Generation Z or "Nexters" (born after 2000), each of us falls into this age-defined subculture that puts us in a group of people who, allegedly, have a lot in common based on our age alone. So pervasive is this use of age as a subculture that the United Nations, itself, prepared a special HR document on how people from each of the age subcultures work differently so that people could know how to work better with one another.

To illustrate with an example, it is probably rather obvious that people from Generations X, Y, and Z prefer to communicate via email, text messaging, and other digital media whereas people from the Baby Boomers and Traditionalists groups prefer phone calls, in-person meetings, and other traditional forms of communication. From a marketing perspective, we know that attempting to elicit direct sales via a television commercial combined with a call-in telephone number is much more likely to work on an older audience than today's younger generation. Similarly, online retailers and brick-and-mortar stores looking to move online know that it can be difficult to convince older consumers of the security and quality of purchasing products online, whereas young people don't think twice before purchasing online.

These age differences can come at a cost, as well. Younger generations, having only ever lived in a world with 24/7 connectivity, exhibit less patience, in general, compared to older generations who grew up used to waiting days to weeks for product deliveries or service visits. Similarly, the value of providing customers opportunities to customize a product or service may be lost on older generations who, growing up in a very different world from the 3D printing world of today, fail to see the value provided in this greater number of options. Somewhat counterintuitively, selling products with more options and features can actually lead to greater *dissatisfaction* for older consumers who are more likely than younger consumers to suffer from feature fatigue. This is why consumer products with extremely simple features and few add-ons, like the Jitterbug phone, are often targeted for elderly consumers.

Even the understanding and interpretation of marketing communications can vary as a function of age. My doctoral advisor, who does remarkable work researching aging consumers, found that the warnings often blurted out quickly on medicine and health product commercials are actually misinterpreted as endorsements by older consumers who, in their older age, have the mental capacity to take in the information (the first step) but not enough to do the important follow-up step of encoding the message as a warning or as negative. Thus, what was intended to be a warning actually becomes an endorsement of the product or service in question.

Gender and Sexuality subcultures. Beyond ethnicity, race, and age, other demographic variables that can be considered consumer subcultures include gender and sexuality. Despite many similarities, men and women differ in important ways with respect to their consumer needs. Whether this is biological or cultural, there are fundamental differences that are important for marketers to understand.

Consider, for example, the fact that women can give birth while men simply cannot. Although child rearing is a responsibility important to both men and women, women actually undergo physiological changes upon giving birth. Specifically, new moms will see their oxytocin levels vary over the course of their pregnancy and in the period following birth. It turns out that the oxytocin levels expectant mothers have in their first trimester of birth are the most predictive of how much affection they provide to their child upon delivery. From a prosocial consumer marketing or policymaking perspective, it seems like this kind of information should inform the kind of resources we provide to mothers particularly in the first trimester of their pregnancy.

Culturally, at least in American culture, women are also expected to play a nurturing role both with children and in general. Whether or not this is fair or correct is not the issue; the point is that this association among women, motherhood, and nurturing is prevalent. There is a reason that women do a disproportionate amount of the shopping in American households and a reason that women are often the intended target of marketing messages.

However, men certainly take on important roles based on gender. In fact, it could be argued that advertising portrayals of men as masculine, strong, secure, brave, and stable create just as much of an expectation for men as advertisements featuring nurturing and caring roles do for women. In addition, the increasing use of a sexualized male figure has had a profound impact on male body image in a way that the use of sexual female imagery has impacted female body image. Consider, for example, the marketing of Axe Body Spray and other products from the Axe brand. In each commercial regular men are shown using an Axe product which then makes women flock to them like flies to honey. This idea that the man should be a sex object for women reinforces ideas that are then transformed into real life expecations about gender roles.

Moving beyond gender roles as influences on subculture, another related idea is that of sexual identity. Often, people may refer to the "gay market," which doesn't make much sense – is this a market who has sexual feelings for other markets of the same sex? A better term to use is probably the LGBT market, as this market includes more than just gay men; it also includes lesbian women, bisexual men and bisexual women, transgendered and transsexual men and women and others who prefer non-traditional sexual identifiers (or sometimes prefer no sexual identifiers). The estimated spending power of the LGBT market is estimated to be about $790 billion. Interestingly, roughly a quarter of those who identify as LGBT are more likely to switch products to a company that has publicly indicated support for the LGBT community and LGBT-related causes even if the product or service is more expensive than alternative products. But like any of the subcultures listed here, these preferences do not apply to every person who identifies as LGBT. Certainly, while some gay men have higher-than-average disposable incomes or vacation in popular gay-friendly destinations, other gay men have lower-than-average disposable incomes or don't even know what a gay-friendly destination is. The important thing to keep in mind about subcultures is that these generalizations are exactly that: generalizations that should be treated with the appropriate degree of caution and not broadly applied in every instance.

Religious subcultures. Another subculture based on demographic information is that of the religious subculture. Religion can actually tell marketers a lot about a consumer's likely preferences and/or behaviors. Did you know that Protestants tend to be much more conservative than their liberal Catholic counterparts and the even more liberal Jewish community? Jews and Catholics also tend to report a higher than average income than Protestants who report a higher than average income relative to Baptists.

Of course, our religion can obviously influence the kind of products and services we purchase. As a Catholic, my fish consumption increases exponentially during Lent, particularly on Fridays. There's a reason McDonald's advertises its Fish Filet more during this time of year than any other time of year. Similarly, my Jewish friends who keep kosher are very careful about the food they purchase at the grocery store and are quite knowledgeable about the way their food is prepared. My Muslim and my Jewish friends are also much more aware of food containing pork than I will ever be because they grew up following cultural traditions that forbid eating pork whereas I did not.

Even our engagement in social activities can differ as a function of religion. For example, on Friday nights when I am not ordering Italian for two and watching *Dateline* by myself, I enjoy going out to dinner with friends or out for a night on the town. However, my observant Jewish friends spend Friday nights enjoying a Shabbat dinner and enjoying family and friends, which is to last (traditionally) until Saturday evening. I make the distinction of "observant" here to reiterate an important point I've made throughout on the various subcultures – ethnic, gender, sexuality, etc. Not *every* member who identifies as an adherent of a particular faith follows the same beliefs in the same way all the time. I have many Jewish friends who do not observe Shabbat, just as I have many Catholic friends who don't regularly attend church on Sundays, and Muslim friends who are a bit more liberal with respect to the faith's view on alcohol consumption. This is okay – without sounding too *Sesame Street* on you, these differences are what make the world go 'round. As marketers we just need to be aware of how these important subcultures *can* affect our choices and behaviors, particularly with respect to anchoring our thoughts and preferences, and understand that they are not perfectly prescriptive of how people will always behave in every situation.

Self-Selected and Consumption subcultures. Beyond those subcultures rooted in demographic differences there exist subcultures to which people belong because they *choose* to and/or because their consumption behaviors lump them into a group with others who also have engaged in similar consumption patterns.

An example of a self-selected consumer subculture in recent times is our skinny-jeans, rimmed-glasses wearing Hipster friends. Hipsters, who (almost by definition) try to seem just a bit removed from mainstream culture, have become such a sizeable, trendy group that they, themselves, are actually influencing mainstream culture likely in ways that they had never hoped or anticipated. Skinny jeans became popular with the masses for a while, as have old-fashioned glasses, and Bon Iver. Yet Hipsters keep moving the boundaries further, exploring new trends and territories that modern mass culture can only ever hope to catch up to. In an episode entitled "Dawn of the Dave" from the now-cancelled ABC show *Happy Endings*, one of the characters, Penny, begins dating a Hipster named Toby only to find that it is exhausting trying to keep up with the pace at which her Hipster boyfriend and his friends keep changing what they like to avoid seeming "mainstream." As one of her friends puts it, "He's a Hipster, Penny. All those things you like, he likes them ironically." Consider this clever dialogue in which Toby introduces Penny to fellow Hipster friends:

> Toby: Oh, hey, meet my friends, Iony, and Atticus. (Gestures toward Iony) She has a blog about zines and he (gestures toward Atticus) won the mustache contest three years in a row.

Atticus: (Dismissive) Like I care.

Toby: (Gesturing to a guy playing a guitar) Hey, see that guy? He's right-handed but he refuses to play with his dominant hand; it's too commercial.

Tony: He's huge on the abandoned gas station circuit

Atticus: (To Penny) What do you think?

Penny: (Startled) Oh, uh (remembers the rules of Hipsterdom) Over it.

All: (Agreeing) Totally. Yeah, super over it. Why are we even here?

An older version of a self-selected subculture is that of the 2000-era "Goths." These dark-clothing wearing, angst-ridden youth rebelled from mainstream society in a slightly darker way than Hipsters. In both cases, though, the individuals belonging to the group chose to belong to the group. Membership in the group is likely to lead members to perform in socially-expected ways. Therefore, as marketers, we might gather that making salient one's Hipster or Goth identity in the moment of purchasing might lead them to deliberately prefer non-mainstream choices or products. In the context of Amazon.com, this might be one instance in which the star rating system or "Other people purchased…" features may not come in so handy.

Beyond these self-selected, opt-in subcultures, there are also subcultures in which membership is gained via product or service purchasing. The most commonly cited example of this is the Harley-Davidson consumer group known as HOG (Harley Owners Group). Although sponsored by the company, HOG is a subculture of people who not only share a love of the brand and its products but who also participate in social events (e.g., HOG member-only rides) and even charitable events. Another fascinating group who share a subculture based on their consumer behavior is LARPers. LARP, which stands for live action role-playing game, brings together people from all around the world, who tend to be heavy gamers particularly of massively multiplayer online games (or MMOGs), for the purpose of reenacting many of the games they play online in real life. These events consist of elaborate costumes, extensive sets of rules, battles involving magic and fake weapons, and other social activities outside of the game context. One of my favorite consumption-oriented subcultures, however, is that of the Furries. After never having heard the term "Furry" before in my life, you can imagine my surprise when a friend, telling me about his brother (who, it turns out, is a Furry), revealed that there existed a consumer subculture of men and women who enjoy dressing in very elaborate and professional anthropomorphic animal costumes, meeting at hotels and convention centers around the world, and, in some cases, engaging in sexual activities while in costume. Although that's never something I would do, this guy isn't one to pass judgment. Still, I mention Furries to show that there can be any kind of consumer subculture, each featuring its own traditions, practices, language, and even preferences…skinny jeans and fox costumes alike.

Other consumption-based subcultures, from fitness buffs to foodies, all possess distinct characteristics, goals, and preferences that set them apart from other consumer subcultures and affect how they engage in various consumption behaviors. While a consumer's subculture membership may not influence his/her behavior all the time in every product or service category, knowledge of these subcultures can be useful for the purpose of predicting what a consumer is likely to value or how best to position a marketing message in a way that a consumer may be more receptive to hearing based on values espoused and encouraged by his/her subculture membership.

Degree of Identification and Situated Identity. Each of us is likely a member of *several* subcultures, and researchers of self and identity are well aware of the fact that our identities are not static. Instead, our identities are often a function of our situation or context. The identity that is salient to us at any given moment is likely a function of both external cues, as well as internal drives (i.e., how we perceive ourselves or what we want to signal to others in the moment).

To give you an example of how this can change our behaviors, consider a study in which Asian-American women were given a math test. In one condition, the participants' ethnic identity was made salient via priming. In a different condition, participants' gender identity was made salient. Both groups were given the same math test. Which group do you think performed better on the math test?

If you said the Asian-American group primed with ethnic Asian cues, you would be correct. Pulling from the same population of Asian-American females we should expect there to be no difference, yet participants whose ethnic identity was made more salient performed better while participants whose gender identity was made more salient performed worse. This idea, a concept known as **stereotype threat**, refers to situations in which beliefs about our identify and how those possessing our identity are expected to perform affect our actual performance. In American culture, Asians are perceived to be better at math while women are perceived to be worse (in spite of the fact that this is certainly not at all always true). Just as we discussed in the chapter on Personality, Attitude, and Persuasion, although we may share certain traits with others, whether or not we express those traits in our choices and behaviors is a function of many things, including situation and context. So, too, as we share our ethnic, gender, sexual, consumer, or other identity with groups of people, the degree to which our identity is made salient can produce radically different choices and behaviors.

*   *   *

The idea that grown men from all walks of life have bonded over toys originally intended for young girls may seem…odd. However, as the Brony subculture has shown, marketers cannot always predict how their products and services will be received and evolve once they hit the market. Fortunately for the producers of *My Little Pony: Friendship is Magic*, they have figured out a way to appeal to multiple and very different audiences in such a way that no particular audience feels left out, alienated, or isolated, which is no easy task. Yet, in some great and poetic way, Hasbro has successfully shown that a show encouraging friendship among mythical creatures has a way of bringing even the most seemingly disparate groups of people together. That is optimistic, indeed.

Consumer subcultures are of interest to marketers not just because of the ability to better predict choices and behaviors based on the shared characteristics of a subculture's members but also because of the purchasing power these subcultures possess, power that, almost by definition of the subculture, is already targeted toward particular interests and experiences (e.g., toy ponies in the case of Bronies, Urban Outfitters and vintage shops in the case of Hipsters).

However, I mentioned throughout this chapter that we, as members of many groups and subcultures, may vary in the degree to which we express any one of those identities or let a particular identity influence our choices and behaviors at any given moment. Part of whether or not a particular identity is salient involves our Self motivations and goals, but another factor affecting which identity of ours is salient has to do with our surroundings. As the next chapter will discuss, it is often the case that our context, environment, and situation can affect our consumer behavior in profound ways even though we are not consciously aware of this influence.

APPLICATION QUESTIONS

1) Think about university alumni and sports fans. Are these groups subcultures? Why or why not? What rituals, norms, and/or symbols are shared among members of these groups?

2) Think of different regions you've traveled to in the U.S. Did you notice anything different about the culture of those places? How was it different from your own culture? If you were given an insane amount of money to start a business based on this cultural difference, how could you monetize this cultural difference?

3) Recently, while applying lotion, I read the back of a lotion bottle for a brand of lotion I had been using for a long time. The copy on the bottle talked about how, "She loves her skin, so she buys the best," and so on. I clearly had bought a lady's lotion despite nothing suggesting it was, in fact, intended for a lady (i.e., not in a women-only section, not an effeminate bottle or brand name). Why might companies choose to position its product toward men or women despite the fact that the product could serve the needs of both?

4) Most of us span several subcultures – ethnicity, race, gender, age, etc. – how, as a marketer, would you decide when to appeal to a particular part of someone's identity?

5) Although it is important to be sensitive and respectful of the religious differences of customers, how might a market use knowledge about religions, religious holidays, and religious practices to better serve the needs of his/her consumers?

6) Why might the creation of a product/service users community be a good investment for a company?

7) Targeting consumers based on characteristics like race, ethnicity, sexual orientation, and gender can be seen as discriminatory to many. How can you justify the use of these variables in marketing?

Chapter 10 | Context, Environment, & Situation

DisneyWorld's Magic Kingdom is a magical place.

From princesses and princes, to enchanted castles and fairytale attractions, Disney has cornered the market in bringing out the child in all of us. But beyond the costumed characters and the cheerful music providing a familiar soundtrack as we travel through the theme park, subtler cues loom around the House of Mouse, most of which you are likely completely unaware [...insert mysterious "ooooh" here].

This subtle influence actually begins *before* you even get to the park. You see, in Walt Disney's original vision, the Magic Kingdom was to play out as a movie. This is the reason all employees are referred to as "cast members" and also the reason that, up until 2013 with the expansion of Fantasyland and the French beer and wine served at the Be Our Guest restaurant, no alcohol was served in the park, as Walt feared a drunk visitor might "disrupt the movie."

Now, any movie worth watching is likely to have a movie trailer that serves as a sampling or preview of what is to come, and the Magic Kingdom "movie" is no different. The theme park consists of several lands: Main Street, U.S.A., Adventureland, Frontierland, Liberty Square, Fantasyland, and Tomorrowland. What you may not have realized, even if you have been to the Magic Kingdom many times, is that the Disney resorts located near the Magic Kingdom are essentially the "movie trailers" for the specific lands in the park. The Contemporary Resort, with its futuristic and modern design, is a preview of Tomorrowland. The Polynesian Resort, with its tribal designs and palm trees, is a preview of Adventureland. The Fort Wilderness Resort and Campground, with its rugged, Old West design, is a preview of Frontierland. The Grand Floridian pulls double duty relying on its Victorian architecture to preview the similar charm of Main Street, U.S.A. and Liberty Square. Perhaps the only themed land not currently advertised by a "movie trailer" is Fantasyland...but I imagine that's just a matter of time.

Once eager visitors get through the gates, they have a beautiful view of...what? Cinderella's castle? Not yet. No, instead, what greets visitors is a train station with a famous flower patch. The symbolism here is that the train passing by is meant to be analogous to the curtain opening on an old-fashioned cinema stage before the movie begins. Just as any good movie has a preview movie trailer, a movie poster also accompanies most films. The Magic Kingdom movie is no exception: featured in the archways of the train station, through which all visitors must pass, are movie posters that advertise the rides and attractions in each of the themed lands in the style of classic movie posters. The Imagineers clearly thought this through.

The next sight guests to the park see is the postcard picture view of Cinderella's castle positioned perfectly at the end of Main Street, U.S.A. However, before strolling down the street while dancing to the music of the live marching band likely playing nearby, visitors might first notice a statue of a very important man and a very important cartoon character. Can you guess the man and the character?

If you said Walt Disney and Mickey Mouse you would be…wrong. Dead wrong. Sorry. Glad we don't have any money on these guesses! No, the first statue in the park is actually Roy Disney, Walt's brother, seated with another famous cartoon mouse: Minnie Mouse. There *is* a statue of Walt and Mickey (so if you can picture one in your mind, you're not going crazy), but that statue is not at the entrance of Main Street, U.S.A. Instead, the famous Walt and Mickey statue known formally as *Partners* and informally as "the hub statue" (as it is located at the hub of the park's hub and spoke layout) comes at the *end* of Main Street, U.S.A.

Why would this be the case? After all, Walt was the creative genius behind the Disney empire and Mickey its beloved icon. Shouldn't they be front and center?

Remember: the Magic Kingdom is a movie. The opening credits of a movie have a very specific order that you may have never noticed unless, of course, you work in film or television. It turns out that in the order of opening credits, the producer (a.k.a. the person who paid for the film) comes *first*. Roy, the bankroller and finance guy of the Disney empire's early days, must come first. The final name to appear in a movie's opening credits is the creative genius behind the film, the director. That's Walt. We can only assume that Mickey and Minnie's placement was more contingent on the brothers' respective placement, but I like to pretend she was the financier of Mickey's wild antics.

You may be thinking, "But Jim! Credits consist of more than just the producer and the director! Why aren't there other statues or names in the Magic Kingdom's credits?" Ah, apt pupil, it turns out that there *are* other names that appear between Roy's statue at the beginning and Walt's statue at the end. Next time you walk down Main Street, U.S.A., take a look at the windows, both on the main level and on the upstairs windows. Prominently featured on the windows along the street are the names of *real* people who were instrumental to the creation of the Magic Kingdom. If you have been to the Magic Kingdom many times before and have never noticed this, you might be freaking out a bit right now. This is an almost *scary* level of detail…but we're just getting started.

For example, did you know that the ground between the themed lands within the park often feature a slight incline? Park designers did this so that your body would *physically* feel an experience of change to accompany the psychological change from transitioning from Main Street, U.S.A., to Adventureland or Fantasyland to Tomorrowland. The inclines aren't the only trick. If you listen to the music as you travel between lands you'll hear it change *very* subtly so that the sounds match the location. After all, it would be strange to hear futuristic music in Frontierland. Another thing to check out: the plant life. The foliage changes as gradually as the ground and the music between lands to make the transition feel seamless. And ever notice how tall Cinderella's castle seems? The castle, at 190 feet, feels much taller thanks to a design trick known as "forced perspective." The "blocks" at the bottom of the castle are designed to look bigger than the same "blocks" at the top of the castle; essentially the scale of the castle gets smaller as you from bottom to top, making the castle *seem* much taller than it actually is. This technique is used throughout the theme park to fool our eyes into thinking attractions are much taller (or much smaller) than they actually are.

Perhaps the most famous "hidden" stimuli found throughout the Magic Kingdom (and actually *all* of Disney's theme parks and resorts) involve what die-hard Disney fans refer to as "Hidden Mickeys." A "Hidden Mickey" is any design element found within Disney's many properties that emulates the familiar silhouette of Mickey Mouse's head. Some Hidden Mickeys aren't so "hidden" (e.g., floor tile featuring the famous shape). Other Hidden Mickeys are deceptively difficult to find (e.g., the light projected onto a wall from a wall lamp through strategically placed holes in the holder that leads the beams to form a Mickey head). Still other Hidden Mickeys come and go so that you might see them at some times but not others. A great example of this is a technically "unofficial" Hidden Mickey found in the Magic Kingdom's iconic ride "The Haunted Mansion." During the ride there is a famous scene in which it appears that the 999 "happy haunts" (with room for one more) are dancing and frolicking in a dining room where the table has been formally set. Rumor has it that the cast members working at the attraction occasionally place two small saucer plates at the top-left and top-right of a dinner plate, thereby creating a "Hidden Mickey." Imagineers, who never intended for this to be a Hidden Mickey, are known for removing the saucer plates when conducting ride inspections. Even with this Hidden Mickey removed, chances are you are encountering the familiar mouse head shape countless times throughout your Disney experiences all without your conscious awareness.

So while it may or may not be true that you can see the word "sex" in the dust that flies up in the air when an adult Simba lies down in *The Lion King* (that is not *really* true), or that if you look carefully during a crowd scene in *The Hunchback of Notre Dame* you can see Belle from *Beauty and the Beast* (that *is* true), what is certain is that Imagineers have deliberately designed the Magic Kingdom and many of Disney's attractions with your brain and body in mind knowing that, even though you may not see all the details, you will certainly *feel* the magic.

* * *

The world is a rich and dynamic place and, quite fortunately, we are designed to hear the songs of birds, to see the light of the sun and the glow of the moon, and to smell the sweet smells of flowers growing in a garden. Ahh, life! …If only we had the time! I imagine there will be some day in the future, maybe during retirement, where the only item on my "to-do" list will be to go sit on a park bench and listen to chirping birds. In the meantime, I barely have time to breathe and my mind is constantly aflutter with the millions of other things I need to be doing. I'm sure you can relate?

So while the world *is* certainly a rich and dynamic place, we are often too busy, too distracted, or even too tired to pay much attention to *everything* that's happening around us. But this raises an important question: if the birds are singing their songs but I'm too busy or distracted to pay attention, am I still *hearing* the birds? Whoa. This is some profound stuff here.

To bring it back to the context of consumer behavior, if I, as a marketer, go through great pains to design my store a *certain* way, to paint the walls a *certain* color, to make sure songs of a *certain* sound and tempo are playing, to make sure my employees all have a *certain* look, etc., but consumers do not consciously think about these features of my store, will all my hard work actually have any affect on my customers' choices or behaviors?

The good news is that the answer to this question is a resounding, "Yes!" which means your work and life have value and you don't have to cry yourself to sleep in the fetal position tonight asking, "What am I doing with my life?" The tricky part, however, is these environmental cues may not operate exactly as you *think* they do and may not be affecting choice and behavior *all* the time. But before you start tearing up again, let me ask you this: does a television commercial always have the effect a company *thinks* it is going to have? Does it *always* lead to the same behavior from viewers? Of course not.

This chapter is dedicated to the subtle ways our context, environment, and situation can influence our choices and behaviors. From sensory experiences to the physical design of retail environments, many of the peripheral stimuli around us at any given moment are affecting our thinking, our feeling, and our doing regardless of whether or not we realize such influence is taking place.

Atmospherics & Ambiance. Anyone who has ever moved furniture knows that careful planning goes into the placement of couches, sofas, wall hangings, and even rugs. You don't want to block a walking path, you want to draw someone's eyes to a particular area of the room, you want to keep enough white space so that the room doesn't feel cluttered, etc. It's funny that we often give so much thought to our own room design when we are decorating, yet we rarely pay attention to the design of retail stores or companies.

It turns out, of course, that the design of a store matters. Sure, very attractive stores (e.g., Apple's super simple, cleanly designed retail stores) or very interesting stores (e.g., the highly interactive Build-a-Bear Workshop stores) may catch our attention, but the physical design of stores and placement of products are actually so involved that people's *entire jobs* are dedicated to these very functions. Have you ever noticed the great efficiency with which you can get in and out of a Subway restaurant? There's a reason the sandwiches are made in front of you: you proceed down the counter and create a people flow that keeps traffic moving. The classic example involves why grocery stores put things like milk and bread in the back of the store despite people having to buy those items the most. Why? Well, it's precisely *because* people have to buy those items the most that they are placed in the back of the store with the hope that shoppers will pick up more items on the trip to the milk and bread and back.

Researchers have also explored things like ceiling height, aisle width, height of product placement, and overall perceived size of store on consumer behavior. Although it may seem fairly obvious, products placed on store shelves at eye level tend to sell a lot better than products placed above or below eye level. What is less obvious is the finding that a tall store ceiling promotes free, abstract, and relational thinking whereas lower ceilings promote direct, specific, and focused thinking. This may be one reason why you buy chips *and* salsa when at your huge, tall-ceilinged neighborhood Costco but only chips when you are purchasing from your much smaller neighborhood convenience store.

Another interesting finding involves how empty shelf space affects our perceptions of a product. Let me pose a hypothetical situation to you: let's say you are a huge fan of Red Bull and you know that others are, too. You go to your local market to buy a can and, when you arrive, you discover that the shelf is bare! The horrors! What is your first thought about the empty shelf? Well, if you're like most people you probably thought, "I guess the store has sold out of Red Bull because it's so popular!'"

Now, consider a different scenario: let's say you happen to be at your local market and just so happen to notice that a shelf is bare. This time it's a product you've never heard of called Perk!Energy. What do you think? Well, you may think that this must be a popular product because that's what you just thought in the prior Red Bull example. However, what people *actually* wind up thinking is that the store has done a terrible job stocking or that the product isn't popular and, as such, has been discontinued. Their perceptions about the product suffer as a result. So let's recap: you experienced the same situation in both stories, the shelf space was bare, but based on your perceived knowledge about the demand for either product your interpretation of the *same* situation was different.

The best way to demonstrate how situational factors can influence our behavior without our knowledge is to give you some specific examples:

- **If Music Be the Food of Love:** Just about every retail store known to mankind has a music track playing in the background. Human beings like many things but apparently awkward silence is not one of those things. So imagine how delighted researchers were to find out that the kind of wine shoppers purchased could be influenced by the kind of music playing in the store. Researchers had two conditions, one in which French music was playing quietly in the background in a wine store and a different condition in which German music was playing. As predicted, shoppers purchased more French wine when French music was playing and more German wine when German music was playing *without even being aware they heard music.* Other stores use music to set the pace of consumption or to subtly attract some swarms of shoppers while repelling others. For example, one study found that playing fast tempo music led diners to eat and leave much more quickly than slow tempo music. Abercrombie, Hollister, and American Eagle are thought to play fast tempo, louder music to attract younger audiences and to keep older ones out.

- **Smells Like Clean Spirit:** In one of my favorite studies on how ambient odors can affect our behavior without our conscious realization, researchers secretly piped in citrus aromas – like lemons and limes – and found that participants were much more likely to clean up their seating area than a condition in which no smells or smells not associated with cleaning products were piped into the room. One company that puts this into practice in an extremely subtle but super effective way is my favorite: Disney. I'm not sure if anyone else has ever noticed, but the Grand Floridian, one of the fanciest, most expensive resorts at Walt Disney World featuring a classic, Victorian theme, has a particular store *right at the entrance* from where visitors arrive from the famous Monorail system. Keep in mind, many Disney visitors staying at other properties make a special trip to the Grand Floridian just to revel in its majesty and beauty, hopping off the Monorail to go inside and see the splendor of this beautiful hotel, so this particular entrance is quite busy. So what's the store located conveniently between this entrance and the center of the hotel where one can take in a few of the gorgeous lobby? It's a candles, soaps, and bath scents shop named Basin White – you literally *smell* the crisp cleanliness of the Grand Floridian's Victorian designs and white purity thanks to the very smart placement of the Basin White shop. Better yet, if you buy one of the scented products from the store, you'll likely take those memories of your majestic Grand Floridian visit with you well into the future. Job well done, Disney; job...well...done.

- **Are The Lights Dimmer Or Are You Just Happy To See Me:** We have all heard of the concept "mood lighting." You know, you dim the lights a little bit, turn on some soft rock music, lower your voice to a deep Barry White bass level. But why does mood lighting work? What does it even do beyond making someone easier to look at who may not have everything working for them in better lighting (...just being honest here)? Well, one theory has to do with pupil dilation. Did you know that your pupils tend to dilate automatically when you are sexually aroused? Well, not just *you* specifically but human beings in general. It's true. You know when else our pupils dilate? When a room gets darker. Why? Because when our pupils dilate, our eyes let in more light so we can see better. See where I'm going with this? It is believed that pupil dilation *actually* caused by dim lighting will be misread as thinking the person sitting across from you is all about you...mmhmm...that's right. So next time you're out at dinner and a restaurant dims the lights, do make sure you're with a special someone and not with, I don't know, your grandma or else things could get awkward. Another example of how visual cues can influence our behavior and cognition is the cultural fluency example from the chapter on Culture and Socio-Cultural Differences. Being subtly exposed to a wedding photo in which a bride is wearing a green dress and a groom is wearing a purple tuxedo may seem innocuous but can actually affect your subsequent behavior and thinking.

- **Roomy Memory Encoding and Retrieval:** My freshman year at WashU I took the required introductory psychology course that served as a prerequisite to just about every other psychology course. During that class we learned about studies of memory suggesting that students tended to perform better on examinations if they took the exams in the same room in which they first learned the information. "Amazing," I thought, but you can imagine my horror when I found out that our class, because it was a huge introductory course of 200+ students, would be split into different rooms to take the midterms and final for the course. If memory serves me correctly, I believe the professors deliberately rotated us so that we all had an opportunity to take only one examination in our main lecture hall...perhaps this was to keep things fair. However, I do remember dreading taking the exam in the non-lecture hall rooms thinking to myself, "I'll never be able to recall what I learned!" It turns out I did okay, but if I ever give you an exam, I promise to do my best to make sure it's in the same room where I teach you because I care.

Temperature, Weight, and Embodied Cognition. Let's do a simple study. Let's say I give you a fairly large book to hold. The name of the book is entitled *Critical Knowledge That Every Man and Woman Should Know*. The book is rather thick and is quite heavy. Then I ask you one simple question, "How profound do you think the content of this book is likely to be on a scale from 1, not at all profound, to 10, extremely profound?" I *know* what they say about not judging a book by its cover, but do you ever wonder if we judge a book by its *weight?*

According to a colleague at MIT, we do. Josh Ackerman conducted a study comparable to the hypothetical one above in which he handed some students a book and a different group of students the *same* book with a heavy weight secretly hidden inside so that the book felt much heavier. When asked to rate the perceived importance of the book, the group holding the heavier book rated it to be of much greater importance than the group holding an identical book that weighed less. In a different study in the same paper, Ackerman and his colleagues found that people say that a person evaluation task is much more difficult or "rougher" when they are simultaneously touching rougher as opposed to smoother sandpaper. Nuts, right? Other studies have been done to show that people act differently on warmer days or when touching something warm than when making the same choices on colder days or when touching something cold. In one of my own labs when I was a student at the University of Michigan, I proposed seating students in a shaky chair to elicit a sense of greater uncertainty in the world for one of my colleagues, and the manipulation worked!

These techniques are often referred to as **embodied cognition**, which is the phenomenon in which we cross wires of our cognitive ways of thinking about particular stimuli and our physical experiences. That is, people may rate the design of your product as being "cold" and "unfriendly" if you crank up the air conditioning in a room. Conversely, a spokesperson may be seen as being "warm" and "friendly" if you have the thermostat set to a cozy, warm temperature or have a gentle fireplace burning and crackling nearby. In what amounts to yet another example of misattribution, the processes within embodied cognition seem to include another component: a symbolic or metaphorical link between concepts (e.g., a *rough* texture and a *rough* task). In order for these effects to manifest, it is likely that these associations must be well established. So I imagine that, say, in French culture where a "warm or hot person" (Il/elle est chaud(e)) means something *very different* (and very sexual) than the same language in America, you may not get comparable effects. Still, each culture has its own interesting metaphors that could potentially produce comparable results.

Time: Mysterious Minutes and Sneaky Seconds. Recently, upon leaving Ann Arbor to move to Chicago, I had to pay a visit to the United States Postal Service's website to have my mail forwarded to my new address. As I proceeded through each step, the USPS took every opportunity it could to try to sell subscriptions and partner company deals to me (which, unfortunately for the USPS, I did not accept). Then, in what seemed like a somewhat tricky but equally clever maneuver, I was taken to a page where a 5:00 minute clock started counting down...4:49, 4:48, 4:47. "You only have five minutes for these deals!" read the caption. Nowhere on the page were the words, "Congratulations, your mail forwarding is now complete!" in big bold letters (instead they appeared in fairly small, barely noticeable letters). The time counting down, however, was a bright bold red and very large so that your eye was immediately drawn to the countdown. Despite paying absolutely no attention to the products being hawked at me up to this point, I found myself looking at the deals offered on this page. I also felt the urgency to hurry, as I thought my address forwarding was not yet complete (I didn't notice the small confirmation). And, of course, the marketer in me was equally annoyed and impressed by this clever tactic by the USPS.

Now, the experience I had was not at all subtle: I noticed the countdown, I noticed the advertisements, and I knew what the site was *trying* to do. However, imagine a situation in which you are pressed for time. Say, for example, that instead of the USPS site dictating my timing that I had my own time limit. Maybe I had only five minutes to finish my mail forwarding before going on a hot date (can't be late for that!). Somewhat cognizant of my need to rush, I may have placed the *same* time pressures on myself that the USPS forced on me, and perhaps, just maybe, I would have actually purchased or agreed to some of those offers in my haste to just be done with the mail forwarding process maybe *thinking* I'd like one of the deals more than I actually did because of the arousal from my time constraint.

Time, like culture, is one of those things we tend to take for granted. Aside from that period of time in our formative years in which we are learning how to tell time, we don't really spend a lot of time thinking about "time" other than when we realize we never seem to have enough of it (…time is quite like money in this regard). However, what we *do* know about time is that all of us are operating on a fairly similar biological schedule based on a 24-hour cycle known as our **circadian rhythm**. Humans are not the only creatures to have such a schedule. Plants, trees, and other animals also operate on these 24-hour cycles, and the crazy thing is that these 24-hour cycles continue *even in the absence of sunlight or light*, in general. Although exposure to light or dark can affect the rhythms, the body naturally restores itself to the 24 cycle in time. Indeed, it would seem that our brains and bodies are hardwired to operate on this 24-hour schedule after years and years of evolution made it so.

Now, because this schedule happens independently of context, it truly is more of a Self factor than a Situation idea, but what makes the circadian rhythm relevant in the Situation chapter is the idea that at any given moment in time, in any given context, we are at *some* point in our circadian rhythm. Scientists can actually *measure* melatonin levels and identify where a person is during his circadian schedule. So you may wonder, then, whether or not a customer is more or less likely to engage in deep levels of thought and elaboration from 9:00pm onward, when the body's natural circadian rhythm is winding things down for the day. Maybe extremely early or extremely late advertisements would be better if they appealed to consumers peripherally, with good music, bright colors, and movement as opposed to a lot of details and facts?

Health researchers have shown that disruptions to the natural circadian rhythm, due to lack of sleep, prolonged exposure to light or darkness that is inconsistent with normal light/dark exposure, or traveling across several time zones can have effects on a person's weight, mood (e.g., Seasonal

Affective Disorder), and even biological processes. One can imagine, then, how disruptions to an individual's circadian rhythm might affect his/her sensitivity to his context.

A savvy marketer might exploit the use of the circadian rhythm to time specific marketing executions or to craft the messages in a particular way. Although untested, it would be interesting for car advertisers to launch spots talking about having a "hunger for speed" or a "deliciously fun ride" during the middle of the day and the evening. Similarly, companies that pay good money to advertise at airports and even on planes would be wise to consider how differences in circadian rhythms could facilitate or deter their marketing efforts to flying customers.

Beyond urgency and circadian rhythms, another way that time exerts influence on consumer behavior is through seasonality. Now, anyone who has taken an introductory business course or maybe an accounting course has likely come across the idea of seasonality when looking at a chart of product sales or financial statements for a particular time of the year for products like backpacks (hint: Back-to-School happens one time a year). The notion of **seasonality** is that there exist specific, distinct durations of time or time periods that, by nature of distinguishing attributes and repetition, reappear reliably. The most basic example of this is our four seasons: winter, spring, summer, and fall. We know, each year, that spring will take place between March and June and will be full of showers and flowers. Similarly, winter rears its head between December and March and is full of snow, snow, and more snow (...*winter is coming*). But so, too, do fashion seasons come and go, hunting seasons come and go, Girl Scout Cookie seasons come and go, and fitness/diet plan seasons come and go (typically after New Years, right around May before beach season, and in the few weeks after Girl Scout Cookie season...those sneaky girls and their addictive devil cookies!).

Although we may not realize it, we are extremely sensitive to our seasons, diverse as they may be. We have busy seasons at work (v. downtime), stockpiling seasons for food (particularly in winter, when frequent, short trips to the grocery store become a pain), and even new clothes season (which typically correlate with the weather seasons) where we tend to purchase *a lot* more clothing than we normally would during a shopping trip. Seasons can even affect our taste perceptions: why does cinnamon taste so much better in winter? Why does pumpkin taste so much better in the fall? Why is lemonade so much more refreshing in the summer compared to the fall, even if the outdoor temperature is exactly the same?

As the circadian rhythm and season examples both suggest, our bodies like routines and schedules. Even the perception of how quickly time passes can vary as a function of our situation and ourselves. For example, time seems to move at a painstakingly slow pace when something boring is taking place, even more so when you have to pee during it and can't excuse yourself. And, as the saying goes, time "flies" when you are having fun or enjoying yourself, which can be dangerous when you have work to get done! Although we may not notice these subtle effects of time, they are there, quietly ticking away.

Online v. offline shopping. In today's constantly connected, ecommerce world we often close our laptops at night only to hop in bed and get on our smart phones to surf the net, check Facebook, and do pretty much the exact same thing we were just doing on our computers. Consumer behavior has evolved from visiting brick-and-mortar stores to a hybrid in-person, online, and virtual purchasing process. The reason I call this to your attention at this point of the book is to remind you, dear marketer, that even your most carefully planned interior design, your cleverly worded in-store advertisement copy, your emotion-laden point-of-purchase priming display all mean *nothing* to the consumer who is shopping for your product or service from the comfort of his/her home.

If this is upsetting news to you, don't worry. A lot of the peripheral cues and situational effects described herein translate to an online context, as well. Work by my very own Consumer Behavior professor, the great Amar Cheema, showed that using a bright red background in the context of an online auction site increased competition and the dollar-amount of bids compared to a no color condition and to alternative color (e.g., blue, grey) conditions. If you think about websites as their own contexts, environments, or even as their own *experiences* for multimedia-laden sites, you can likely recreate the contextual effects found in the real world and perhaps even uncover some virtual-specific situational effects. Even in-app purchases for products and services may be influenced by such peripheral factors like phone ease-of-use, user interface design, comfort of the hand/body while using the mobile device, and other, seemingly irrelevant situational factors. As consumerism continues to expand within this hybrid online/offline world, I imagine we will start learning more about how these incidental cues affect consumer behavior.

The Role of Misattribution. We've been together for a long time thus far in the book (so many memories made!), but if you can try to think back to our earlier chapter on Affect, Mood, and Emotion, then you may be able to recall our discussion on misattribution of arousal. In that discussion we talked about how the rapid heartbeat and sweaty palms we get from a risky or dangerous situation, such as crossing a rope bridge over a huge chasm, can be misattributed to another source, such as the pretty young research assistant standing at the front of the bridge. Well, it turns out that misattribution also plays an important role in the way that our context, environment, and situation affect our choices and behaviors.

Just as the shaky bridge might not have affected our love for the woman if we attributed the source of our arousal as the bridge or how the eyes in the coffee break room would not have led to greater pro-social donating behavior if we thought, "Hey! I bet those eyes are there for a reason!" so, too, do these ambient effects of environment rely on our tendency to misattribute the source of our thoughts, feelings, and behaviors as products of our *own* devices and not to the context from which they actually came. To give you an example of what I mean, if we were shopping in a wine store (or a cheese store if you're less than 21) and *noticed* the French music playing, then we might think, "Ah, yes, French music. I wonder if there's a connection between the French music and the French wine?" At that point in time any subtle potential influence that the music *could* have had on our behavior is done-zo. Might we still buy a French wine because of the French music? Maybe, but we might also exhibit what psychologists refer to as reactance: doing the exact *opposite* of something in some strange attempt to reassert our self-control. "You want me to buy French wine with this music? Hah! I'll show you – German wine it is!"

This raises an important point: too often practitioners hear about the subtle ways in which consumers make decisions and think, "Oooh, good! I'll start flashing subliminal messages in my television commercials to make them buy more of my product and to make them hate my competitors!" It doesn't work like that. At all, really. Although it *is* true that human beings can and do process subliminal and supraliminal cues, any consequences of these effects can be short lived. And, it turns out, people are differentially sensitive in their susceptibility to cues at various points in times. In research I have with my advisor, we show that the *same* cues are more effective for people in a conflicted state of mind than those who are in a compatible (non-conflicted) state of mind. Our guess is that the processing of subtle cues is adaptive: when you are experiencing conflict, stress, or some other arousal, you may turn to cues in your context, even nonconsciously, to help reduce, mitigate, or eliminate that arousal to get back to some steady state.

And then we have yet *another* caveat: steady states are not, in fact, stable. That is, a steady state is situational. To give you an example, imagine a scale from 1 = completely dull to 10 = completely energized. My normal operating level might be a 5. However, if I am playing soccer or working out, my steady state probably needs to be higher, say a 7. If I am in church or a quiet movie theatre where a serious movie is playing, my steady state probably needs to be more at a 3. We refer to this differential, dynamic steady state as "allostasis," which is often contrasted with "homeostasis."

I drone on a bit here to make one simple point: just because you incorporate strategic environmental or situational cues into a marketing context does not mean the cues will work each and every single time a customer comes into contact with them. Whether or not a cue is likely to have an effect is a function of the customer's state, the misattribution process, and even what the target intentions of the customer are in the first place (e.g., to search for information, to purchase, to peruse).

*   *   *

In what has to be one of the best Disney films of all time, Belle of *Beauty and the Beast* fame, ponders about how her feelings toward the Beast have changed despite not understanding quite how or why her feelings have changed. She sings, "There's something sweet / and almost kind / but he was mean and he was coarse and unrefined / but now he's dear / and so unsure / I wonder why I didn't see it there before." In reality, Belle was probably suffering from the psychological phenomenon known as Stockholm Syndrome, in which a captive or hostage strangely begins to have positive feelings for his/her captor, but for the sake of the children, we'll pretend they really fell in love.

Perhaps it was the romantic castle gardens? Maybe it was the misattribution of the anthropomorphic furniture surrounding her that primed Belle to seek out deeper relationships? Or, my personal favorite, maybe it was the dim lighting at dinner, compliments of the seductive candelabra, Lumière, that led to some misattributed pupil dilation on behalf of Beauty and her Beast. Regardless, just as *Beauty and the Beast* creates a certain ambiance, a certain feel-good feeling, a certain, "Je ne sais quoi?" so, too, does the Magic Kingdom, Walt Disney World, and the Disney company's many theme parks and properties. Through careful planning, attention to detail, and clever placement of stimuli that stimulate the senses, Disney continues to ensure that the "Happiest Place on Earth" still feels happy, whether you know *how* they do it or not.

APPLICATION QUESTIONS

1) After reading this chapter, your boss says he/she wants to subtly whisper the word "buy" on repeat on the store's sound system. Explain to your boss why he/she needs to re-read the chapter.

2) An important factor in the efficacy of incidental cue influence is the concept of misattribution. Explain what misattribution is in this

context, and describe reasons why it might be hard for a consumer to attribute the true source of information even if he/she wanted to.

3) Why might experiences of arousal make us more susceptible to the influence of contextual cues and stimuli? What purpose might this heightened sensitivity serve?

4) In order for an incidental cue or prime to influence our thinking and/or behavior, it is first required that we have an established association or goal in our mind. How might seeing party favors or hearing a song like "Happy Birthday" affect our drive to socialize?

5) The growth of real-time data collection, both online and through wearable items like Jawbone's UP band and Nike's Fuelband (and the rumored Apple iWatch), means that marketers will have more real time information about a shopper's context and situation. Be creative with how you might use this information as a marketer. What would you do?

6) Walgreens and CVS have noticed that their stores see spikes in traffic at the emergence of the first snow and the first blossom of spring, yet summer and fall see much less foot traffic. What might explain this? What could Walgreens and/or CVS do, relying on the same underlying reason for its spikes, to get more customers in the store in fall and summer?

7) Most consultants working in the realm of atmospherics and store design/layout specialize in tangible, brick-and-mortar store applications of their work. However, with the ever increasing volume of online and mobile shopping, how could you incorporate some of the ideas in this chapter to those consumer contexts? What would the research and executions look like?

8) Just as emotions can be difficult, if not impossible, for customers to report accurately, so, too, is it nearly impossible for customers to tell you how their context or environment influenced their choices or behaviors. How can you conduct in-store field research to see if efforts taken to influence consumer choice/behavior via context have been effective?

PART III:

THE SOLUTION

Urges must be dealt with, whether that means taking action to fill some need or deliberately not taking action in order to save resources for a future point in time, an urge needs resolution lest it drive us crazy. The prior chapters addressed how our Self and our Situation affect our interpretation of information and feed into our urges. The following chapters address how these factors interact to affect our decision-making. In particular, the following chapters discuss value and valuation, or how we ascribe a quantifiable judgment to a product or service, as well as decision-making and how different decision-making strategies can lead to different product/service choices. Sometimes the solution involves taking no action, other times the solution involves taking drastic action, but no matter which option is pursued, the different methods available to us for the purpose of satisfying our urges can, themselves, influence our choices and behaviors — this section explores the many ways said urges are often addressed.

Chapter 11 | Value and Valuation

"O, be some other name!
What's in a name? That which we call a rose
By any other name would smell as sweet;
So Romeo would, were he no Romeo call'd,
Retain that dear perfection which he owes
Without that title."

-Romeo and Juliet, Act II, Scene II

In the famous balcony scene from William Shakespeare's classic *Romeo and Juliet*, the star-crossed lovers lament that because Romeo is a Montague and Juliet is a Capulet, their love is forbidden by their quarreling families. Juliet points out that if a rose were called something else, like a schlerpopple or a billyboop, it would still smell as sweet as a rose. So why, oh why, couldn't Romeo just forsake his name and go by a new name, like John McGillicuddy or Bubba St. Clair? His kindness and good looks would remain the same – only his name would change, and they could run off into the Verona sunset, holding hands and frolicking safely in their love.

Unfortunately, our world is not so simple. Any marketer knows that a rose by any other name does *not* smell as sweet. A white Diesel v-neck t-shirt retails at Nordstrom for $55. A white Hanes v-neck t-shirt retails at Dollar General for $9...*for three shirts*, so that's $3 per shirt. Just so you don't have to do the math, the Diesel v-neck shirt is 18.333 times more expensive than the Hanes v-neck, despite both shirts being 100% cotton, all-white t-shirts. See the difference a brand makes?

Tiffany & Co., the jewelry company famous for its trademarked iconic robin egg-blue color, knows the value of brand all too well. In early 2013, Tiffany & Co. filed a lawsuit against wholesaler Costco claiming that the buy-in-bulk store infringed on its trademark name by selling rings featuring a "Tiffany cut." The setting, which refers to a diamond placed on a thin silver band and held in place by six silver prongs surrounding the diamond, is advertised as being created "over a century ago" on Tiffany & Co.'s website, so the jewelry giant is claiming that Costco is benefitting unfairly by likening its products to the famous Tiffany brand and, in doing so, is tarnishing the value of Tiffany & Co.'s brand and products.

Now, the funny thing about this quarrel is that, as of summer 2013, Tiffany & Co.'s "Tiffany setting" engagement rings start at $11,000 for 1 carat and max out (at least on the website) at the $53,000 2.5-carat model. In comparison, Costco has a 1.2-carat ring featuring a "Tiffany-like setting" (see what I did there? That's called "avoiding a lawsuit") retailing for $11,999.99 and a 2.5-carat version priced at $47,999.99. Costco even has a 3.02-carat ring currently retailing for $98,999.99. So when it comes to actual *dollar* amount, it would seem that the rings are fairly comparable.

Even worse for Tiffany & Co., a 2005 study by *Good Morning America*, in which the show had jewelry experts appraise diamonds from both Tiffany & Co. and Costco, found that the appraised Tiffany & Co. ring was valued at 37% less than its asking price whereas the Costco ring was valued at just 17% less than its asking price, suggesting consumers could get both good quality and "more for their money" (a.k.a. better value) at Costco.

In spite of this, you would be hard-pressed to find consumers who would prefer a ring from Costco instead of the same ring from Tiffany & Co. If you don't believe me, try proposing to someone, telling them you bought the ring at Costco instead of Tiffany & Co., and see what happens. Why is this the case? Because there's something about that familiar robin egg blue and brand name that just makes the jewelry seem *better*...even if it technically isn't much different. Of course, part of the value stems from being able to tell your friends where your diamond came from or conveniently leaving the iconic packaging out in your home when they come over to visit. "Oh!? Did I leave this Tiffany & Co. box on my table in plain sight for everyone to see?! How silly of me!"

Although the Tiffany & Co. v. Costco litigation is ongoing as of this book's publication, there is a recent update to the controversy, this time involving the luxury designer Michael Kors. Kors, the famous fashion designer, has a line of "highly sought-after luxury handbags" (according to the company) and, as such, was annoyed upon seeing a Mother's Day Costco advertisement featuring Michael Kors-branded products despite Costco not being an authorized retailer of Michael Kors products. Costco may soon discover that not everything is better in bulk...especially lawsuits.

While Tiffany & Co. and Michael Kors duke it out with CostCo to preserve the value of their respective brands, sometimes a company's loss of brand equity happens for reasons *no one* sees coming.

Consider the case of the once-indestructible Paula Deen brand. In 2013, Deen, the famous white-haired, Southern-accented chef, admitted during court proceedings that she had once used a racial slur when describing an episode in which she was held up at gunpoint. Almost overnight the Paula Deen name went from being a brand that commanded *premium* prices for cooking and kitchenware to a brand that everyone wanted to avoid. As I strolled through a Target store that same week, I noticed that Paula Deen-branded products had found themselves on a deeply-discounted shelf in a remote corner of the store. Target was practically *giving away* Deen-branded products to get her inventory out of their stores without suffering too much of a loss. The Deen empire collapsed in days.

Whether diamond rings and luxury handbags or buttery southern food and cookware, how we value a product depends largely on intangible qualities like a brand. Although Juliet Capulet might not have believed in the value of a brand's name, she also died a tragic death at the end of the play. Moral of the story: never take advice from characters who die tragic deaths after they follow their own advice.

*　　*　　*

Calculating value in the consumer world is tricky: what you may *love*, I may only *like*; what only slightly irks me may drive you crazy. Not only do our preferences differ from one another, our own preferences can vary as a function of our Self and Situational influences as described up to this point in the book. For some people, a diamond ring is a diamond ring, regardless of brand, so a ring from Tiffany & Co. is going to be worth as much to these people as the same carat ring from Costco.

If you have ever studied Economics, then chances are you've learned about quantifying or calculating this notion of "value." To calculate value in an economist's world, we must first calculate "utility," which is this sort of abstract representation of how much satisfaction, happiness, or fulfillment something brings us. Technically, utility is measured in "utils," which is yet another abstract concept like a "currency" measuring our satisfaction, happiness, or fulfillment. Confused yet?

Basically, economists say that we try to "maximize" our **Total Utility** (TU in the equation below), which is really just a sum of the **Marginal Utility** (MU) we receive for consuming each additional unit of a product or service. In other words, our "total amount of happiness/fulfillment" is merely a sum of the "individual amounts of happiness/fulfillment" each unit of a product/service provides. The equation looks a little something like this...

$$TU_i = \sum MU_i$$

So, using this idea, if we said that eating a piece of candy brought us 3 utils of happiness/fulfillment, then eating 4 pieces of that candy would bring us a total utility of 12 utils (TU = 3 + 3 + 3 + 3 = 12).

However, marginal utility isn't so straightforward. For example, when you go to a parade, the first piece of candy you catch feels *amazing* – let's say worth 100 utils. You treasure it, cherish it, and maybe even hold off on eating it just in case you don't get any more candy. Then a second piece of candy finds its way at your feet. This piece is pretty amazing, too, but maybe doesn't feel as good as 100 utils like that first piece did, but, instead, more like 80 utils. Onward comes piece three, piece four, until finally you have over *twenty* pieces of candy. However, unlike the first few pieces of candy you had the fortune of getting, the last few pieces probably feel less special. In fact, you might not have valued those final pieces very much at all, say 1 or 2 utils each. This, friends, is the concept of **Diminishing Marginal Utility**, an idea that suggests that we tend to value things *more* when we have less of it and *less* when we begin accruing or consuming more of it.

Still with me? If your eyes just glazed over for the past two paragraphs and you cried a little bit on the inside while reading the confusing words on the page, worry no more: this is **NOT** an Econ book. So let us abandon the Econ world of "utils," and return to the Marketing World (a.k.a. the REAL world)! Hurrah!

God bless those economists and all their hard work, but the fact of the matter is that the real world just *does not* operate according to the rules of Econ. Sure, sometimes the value of an additional piece of candy diminishes over time…but, in the aforementioned parade candy example, what if the 20th candy is my *favorite* flavor of that particular candy? Or what if the person throwing it was super hot (because *that* happens at parades)? Or what if 20 is my lucky number? Or what if I had bad gas up until that moment that has suddenly (and mysteriously) disappeared upon receiving this miraculous twentieth piece of candy? Or what if it stopped raining at precisely that moment? The very reason the discussion of value and valuation is not in either the Self or the Situation sections of this book is because value *changes* as a function of self and situation. The traditional econ model does not account for Self or Situational factors that could be influencing how much I value each piece of candy or the candy collection in total.

So then how *do* we value products and services if not through the pretty, fancy economics models? This chapter will explore several ideas pertaining to value and valuation or, in other words, how we mentally calculate how much a particular product or service is worth to us.

Brainy Banking. The best place to start trying to understand how our brain assesses value in consumer contexts is probably the brain. Dr. Brian Knutson of Stanford University, a friend of my Ph.D. advisor (and a truly nice guy), worked with a team of collaborators to explore the idea that observing brain behavior could *predict* purchasing. The researchers based their hypotheses on prior findings showing that particular brain areas tended to activate when humans thought about rewards and gains (e.g., the nucleus accumbens or NAcc) while other areas of the brain, such as the insula, tended to correlate with physical pain, anticipated pain, and loss prediction. Using fMRI, Brian and his team found that they were able to predict participants' actual purchases *better than self-report measures.* To put it differently, the scientists knew that the participants were more likely to purchase specific products better than the participants knew for themselves. Crazy, right?

So how did it work? Well, in the context of Brian's study, the researchers could "see" the activation of the NAcc correlated with product preferences, while the presentation of extremely high price points led to greater activation of the insula (an area implicated in pain processing) and a deactivation of the mesial Prefrontal Cortex (mPFC), which is an area typically involved in decision-making and coordinating ones thoughts and behaviors. To put the findings more plainly, basically participants' brains were quickly asking and answering the questions, "How much do I prefer this product?," "Does this price seem fair for this product?," and "Does my pain of paying outweigh my anticipated benefit of acquiring and using this product?"

This may seem intuitive. After all, every day when we make purchases we might ask ourselves those very same questions: how much do I want this smoothie? Am I willing to pay $8.00 for it? But the beautiful thing about Brian's research is that the researchers demonstrated that this process has neural correlates, areas of the brain that activate when these specific kinds of questions are being asked and answered, perhaps without us consciously engaging in these calculations. The fact that the areas of the brain are parts of distinct neural circuits is also an important finding, as it suggests the gain and loss components that go into evaluation are not one and the same but rather two, distinct processes that, when combined, lead to a decision.

So if you have ever studied business, you know that the classic equation for profit looks something like this:

$$\pi = TR - TC$$

Pi (π) in this equation symbolizes profit, whereas TR and TC represent the total revenue and the total cost, respectively. In the business world, we add up all the money we bring in, subtract all the costs that we spent doing business, and whatever is left over is profit. The brain, it seems, is constantly engaging in a comparable, profit-maximizing (or at least profit-detecting) process in which the brain seems to ask, "Are we breaking even or coming out on top? If so, let's buy!" This is certainly an oversimplification of what is a very complex process, but it gives you an idea of how to think about valuation.

But this is where things get a little complicated because we don't live in a world that simply consists of product preferences, a pain from payment, and an appraisal of profit. No, we live in a world of credit cards, borrowing, loans, warranties, sales, discounts, limited time offers, layaway, loyalty rewards, mistaken or inflated preferences, overpromising, misidentification or misunderstanding of a product's attributes, and many, many other messy variables. So even though the brain is likely still engaging in its beautiful, parsimonious equation of "how much good stuff" minus "how much bad stuff," the information going *into* the equation isn't always the best.

Furthermore, the preference and highs of anticipated gains for one person can differ drastically from those of another. Similarly, the pain of paying is *much more* painful for some of us than it is for others. This obviously presents *some* challenges when it comes to trying to determine how your consumers value your products. However, there are also opportunities to be had.

For example, if you can encourage your customers to focus on the gains of what consuming a product or service may bring and distract them away from thinking about any potential costs or losses, chances are they will be more likely to purchase your wares. Similarly, in the world of competitive advertising, a smart strategy would be to focus marketing messages purely on the pain associated with purchasing and consuming a competitor's product or mitigating the perceived anticipatory gains associated with such a product. This may seem foolishly straightforward (e.g., a "Get more for less money!" kind of argument), but the research suggests that's exactly the kind of calculation of our brains are doing each and every time we consider making a purchase.

Breaking down the value calculation. If we want to know how consumers arrive at a valuation, then the equations and neural findings above suggest it might be worthwhile to delineate the positive, anticipated gain factors and the negative, painful loss factors.

One proprietary method of understanding the values of consumers that has circulated around the business world over the years is the VALS approach, which segments consumers based on their level of resources and their primary motivations (ideals, achievement, or experience-oriented). I only mention this approach because it sometimes comes up at companies and in discussions on developing user segments based on their "values." If you're interested, you can Google that approach, but I think a different way of thinking about values that is more relevant to this book and our urge approach is to think waaaaaaay back to the beginning chapter on Needs, Wants, and Motivation. In that chapter we discussed theories of innate needs that drive us – from Maslow's hierarchy to McClelland's Trio of Needs – learning how our most basic needs for food, shelter, and security, as well as our more advanced needs for self-expression and creativity, can motivate behavior.

It's no different here. When we assess the positive gains that a product might provide, we are essentially asking ourselves, "Okay, what fundamental need does this product serve and how well does it fulfill that need?" So if I'm starving, for example, an apple looks really, really good to me, but if I'm stuffed after eating a large meal, that very same apple may only be *slightly* appealing if it's even appealing to me at all.

Similarly, even the same product or service can take on different *kinds* of value depending on my needs at the time. Sites like Facebook and Tumblr provide both an opportunity to fulfill social and affiliation needs, as well as the opportunity to fulfill more creative, self-actualization needs in which one can create or produce content. My engagement with the site may differ depending on how the site would be more valuable to me in any given moment. If I were recently excluded from an important social event, I might hop on Facebook to restore my social connections with others. If I just got back from a fun night out with friends, I may go on Facebook to write a funny post or capture the evening in tagged photos and clever captions.

As a marketer, it is useful to know what core need(s) is being thought about when your customers are thinking about your product. The customers may not be thinking about your products and services on such a fundamental, philosophical level. For example, the dude that buys Maxim or the lady who buys Cosmopolitan may not realize that the suggestive imagery and racy stories are addressing their innate needs for sex, but it could very well be the case that this is an underlying motivation for their purchase. Similarly, a kid who thinks creating a pair of customized Nike shoes at a NikeTown store is just a cool thing to do may not realize that he/she may be fulfilling needs related to self-esteem and self-actualization. So how can we understand what is driving a consumer's value if our customers can't even articulate it themselves?

Value Laddering Method. A very useful way to elicit the underlying values behind consumer motivation is a technique known as laddering or the Value Laddering Model. The **Value Laddering Model (VLM)** is a technique based on psychoanalytic approaches designed to abstract from specific, concrete attributes (A) of a product or service to consequences (C) of using that product and then to the underlying core values (V) that are truly motivating behavior, comparable to climbing up rungs of a ladder. The procedures for laddering vary slightly from researcher to researcher, but essentially you, as a marketer, get to pretend to be celebrating your terrible twos again, constantly asking the question, "Why?"

To help illustrate the Value Laddering Method with a vivid example, let's take the case of Burberry scarves. Burberry, a popular yet pricey British brand, is known for its line of scarves and its popular tan, red, black, and white plaid "Burberry check" design. Say I purchased a few Burberry scarves and articles of clothing. A marketer wanting to understand why I purchase Burberry might engage me in a laddering technique like this:

Marketer: So tell me what attributes about your Burberry scarves are most important to you?

Customer: I like the way they feel and the way they look.

Marketer: Why do you like they feel?

Customer: The fabric is soft and it keeps me warm.

Marketer: Why do you like feeling soft and warm?

Customer: Because I hate being physically cold and my scarves remind me of home.

Marketer: Why do your scarves remind you of home?

Customer: I remember building snowmen with my siblings outside while wearing full winter garb including scarves; it evokes many happy memories.

From this (somewhat cheesy) example, we can see that simply asking, "Why?" like a two-year old child does and diving as far deep as possible at each step along the path led us to an underlying core value related to familial connection and acceptance. If we can tap into this core value, then we know a lot about how to position our product toward this particular consumer. What's even better is when consumers of a particular segment ladder back up to a similar or shared value. You could even segment your market according to these underlying values for consuming your product.

But the laddering approach need not be limited to the positive side of valuation. You could equally ask about consumers' concerns regarding your product or service. When they list some reasons for their concern you simply prod them with the, "Why?" question until you get to a more abstract value. Let's continue our example:

Marketer: So tell me what attributes about Burberry scarves give you concern or hesitation?

Customer: I think they are nice, but they are so expensive. I wonder why they are so costly.

Marketer: Why do you worry about how expensive/costly they are?

Customer: I have a limited budget. I feel like I shouldn't waste money on myself.

Marketer: Why do you feel like you shouldn't waste money on yourself?

Customer: I have other responsibilities and costs; my appearance is not a top priority.

Marketer: Why is your appearance not a top priority?

Customer: I am no model. I probably don't look as good as other people wearing Burberry.

Hmm, sounds like somebody has some self-esteem issues that could be holding him back from nice things? If I were a marketing manager at Burberry equipped with this information, I might be motivated to design a campaign that focused on incorporating these findings. Picture it: a wintery, snowy day in London; a mediocre-looking man seems stressed at his office. He looks at the time in a meeting seeming to wonder if the meeting will ever end. We see him filing through his papers, alone, in a cold, secluded office where everyone seems to be separated from each other. But then, it's time: 5:00pm on a Friday. The man's demeanor suddenly changes. He grabs his coat, briefcase, and (importantly) his Burberry scarf. Upon exiting the door of the office, the world around him is no longer a dreary, snowy mess but, instead, a magical snowy wonderland. He walks through the streets of London where street performers perform, carolers sing, and warm fires burn. Finally, he gets to a flat where friends greet him and welcome him inside. An upscale party is already underway. A beautiful woman across the room catches his eye, and she looks back. He mouths the word, "Hi," – she returns the, "Hi," and adds, "Nice scarf," which the man has left around his neck. The narrator is heard, "Burberry brings people together, because you've *earned* happiness." Bam.

Just like that we have managed to drive home the value of Burberry as a social facilitator while mitigating the cost of feeling like one is not worthy of the scarf. We did not subject the luxury brand to a discount "any layman's scarf" positioning – our protagonist clearly has a good job and makes a decent salary even if he is not David Beckham attractive. We could probably come up with several other creative executions, but I think you get the point of how we can use laddering to uncover these underlying motivations and subsequently translate those motives to actual marketing executions.

In the marketing and ad agency world, you'll often hear the buzzword "customer insight" or "critical consumer insight." In fact, entire divisions of "consumer insights" have emerged over time. The goal these groups share is that they are trying to undercover the *true*, deep, underlying motivation for why consumers behave as they do. Laddering is one way to get to these insights, but laddering is just *one* tool. Too often marketers get hung up on one method, but the best approach is an integrative one that includes a combination of the ideas we have discussed from the sections pertaining to the Self, the Situation, and now the Solution. Later, I'll present an outline of these key concepts that will provide a better, more comprehensive approach to eliciting these consumer insights.

Consumer Numeracy and Miscalibrations. Another reason the laddering approach is so useful is that consumers are pretty terrible at calculating value. If you have ever gone out to eat with a group of people and split the bill, you know what I'm talking about. For whatever reason sometimes the simplest math is extremely difficult to us. Apart from splitting the bill, diners often have a tough time figuring out tips in spite of the fact that this simply requires calculating 10% (one decimal point to the left) and doubling that number (if giving 20%) or adding half that number (if giving 15%). If we can't do these things easily, then what chance do we stand in mentally calculating how much benefit something is likely to bring us and how much it is likely to cost?

This concept of having fluency with numbers and calculations is referred to as **numeracy**. Perhaps the best way to understand numeracy is to first discuss the word equivalent of numeracy: literacy. Literacy refers to the ability to write, read, and think about verbal and/or written words. Consider that, with respect to literacy, 40% of American adults operate at *basic* proficiency or lower. Medicine manufacturers and other companies are actually advised to write their directions at a junior high reading level (maximum) lest people not understand the directions. Numeracy scores in the U.S. tend to be worse than literacy scores. In a recent International Adult Literacy and Lifeskills (ALL) Survey, the U.S. was significantly outperformed by Norway, Canada, Bermuda, and Switzerland (to name a few) on numeracy in which the U.S. scored a 269…out of 500 total possible points. At least we beat Italy? In a somewhat alarming pattern, Caucasians outperformed Hispanic- and African-Americans on numeracy, but there was no significant difference between the numeracy scores of Hispanic- and African-Americans. Part of the big STEM (science, technology, engineering, and mathematics) curriculum push by the U.S. Department of Education is to improve upon the nation's numeracy.

Another challenge with actually trying to determine value is the fact that we are prone to innate biases when it comes to numbers and pricing. Consider, for example, the **final-number effect**, which suggests that rather than actually doing the rounding we are taught how to do as a child (i.e., anything ending in 5 or greater gets rounded up, anything lower than 5 gets rounded down), we see prices like $5.99 to be *significantly* less than $6.00, despite the actual difference being just $.01. If you go to a store, any store, and look at the prices, odds are you will find more products priced ending in .99 than any other ending. And it's not just the final number that trips us up. There's another effect, the **left-number effect**, that comes into play when we are comparing two or more prices. In the left-number effect, we tend to overvalue the left number in a relative comparison, so that $1.99 v. $3.00 feels more like a $2 difference (i.e., 3 − 1 = 2), as opposed to a $1 dollar difference (i.e., 3.00 − 1.99 = 1.01). This may seem so small that it's negligible, but if you are moving 500,000 units of a product weekly, you could *make* consumers think they're getting $2 off when, in reality, they're just getting half of that. Similarly, from a buying side, you may *think* you're getting a really good deal, but, in reality, your perceived value is actually better than the actual value.

Aside from the costs associated with the fundamental needs addressed above, there are also some very common cost considerations that often factor into our valuation process. The first cost, of course, is money. In fact, when you ask a consumer, any consumer, to figure out the cost of acquiring a product, he/she is probably most likely to think of the financial cost first. This makes sense, of course, as the associations between the word "cost" and "money" are likely pretty strong in our brain. That said, however, you can often fool someone into thinking they are getting a better deal if you tell them they can "buy two shirts and get a third shirt half off" compared to telling them they can "spend $25 on three shirts instead of $30." This is the exact same deal, of course, but the first positioning *feels* like a better deal to a lot of people, maybe folks for whom seeing numbers feels threatening or scary.

Beyond financial costs, however, there are some other very common "costs" that we don't always think of right away but certainly factor into our valuation. Consider, for example, time as a cost. Now more than ever we live in a busy world where our increased accessibility has led to greater impatience for things like news, shipments, email replies, and more. We often think of ourselves on the receiving end of this (i.e., we are impatient when we don't hear back from others), but this is a two-way street: others are likely often frustrated by our lack of a quick reply or decision. Thus, with respect to valuation, products or services that are going to take some time may *seem* or *feel* like they actually "cost" more. Similarly, providing services to others that need to be done sooner than later are likely to seem costlier in our minds, as time focused on the immediate task at hand means less time to dedicate to other responsibilities. So, it seems like our old saying has some truth to it: time *is* money.

Finally, another potential cost is that of effort. The classic example here involves telling people that they can purchase deodorant or some other consumer product at their local store for $5.00, but that they can walk a bit further to get the exact same deodorant for $3.00. That $2.00 difference is fairly significant (40% off), yet some people would still rather spend the $5.00. Financially speaking, you would be an idiot not to go for the $3.00

product, but remember: cost involves more than the financial cost of something. In this case, walking the extra couple of blocks likely involves more time and definitely involves more effort, and these things add up. And, like all things in consumer world, these costs are *conditional*. Case in point: I am happy to walk to the local city grocery chain two blocks away from me to buy groceries in summer, but in the middle of January, I will gladly pay more money for my food and shop at the pricier grocery store connected to my building so I can avoid the cost of trudging out in the Chicago winter.

Cost miscalibration is just one part of the equation, however. Consumers are equally bad at guessing how much value they are going to get from something. We all have made a purchase *thinking* a product was going to be great only to be sorely disappointed when we're actually consuming it. For example, last year I purchased a laptop fan to keep my computer cool while working in processing-heavy programs like Adobe Photoshop and Illustrator. I found a cooling fan system that even had this cool blue light powered by my computer's very own USB port. I was so happy when the device arrived that I immediately plugged it in expecting to feel an Arctic chill that would keep my Macbook from overheating. The result? Nada. Nothing. Me blowing on my computer would have been more effective than this $50 contraption. When it comes to our expectations about how well a product will fulfill our needs, we can often be pretty far off. As marketers, setting expectations is part of the game; the phrase "under-promise and over-deliver" comes to mind.

The benefits we get from a product can also extend beyond the actual need or service the product fulfills. Thomas Foolery, a restaurant in D.C., serves food and drinks like *any* restaurant, but the restaurant is famous for encouraging its patrons to do funny tasks or challenges for discounts, like performing (and singing) the "Cups" song from the movie *Pitch Perfect* for $1 off a cocktail kit, tying a cherry stem into a knot to score a $1 cherry soda (it's free if you can do it in 10 seconds), or doing the limbo "below your thigh midpoint" to get free candy from Tom's Candy Store. Other companies incorporate social value into their products and services. Although you'll never meet the person receiving a pair of Tom's Shoes when you purchase your pair, the feel-good feeling you get from knowing someone else will now get a brand new pair of shoes may affect your valuation of the shoes you are purchasing.

Aside from the actual value derived from the product, however, consumers also miscalibrate information about *themselves*. Consider, for example, the fact that there tends to be a disconnect between one's *perceived* age and one's *actual* age. We all know people like this. Cougars, for sure, but also Sugar Daddies (yep, you just read about Cougars and Sugar Daddies in this book – I told you we'd be going places). The preference for dating younger partners is not something we'll concern ourselves with here – I mean, who cares, really? – but what *is* interesting is whether or not these people tend to see themselves as younger or, alternatively, if there's a contrast effect and they see themselves as even older because they are constantly surrounded by younger people? A friend in Italy, Cesare Amatulli, researches this very idea looking at how this difference between a consumer's real and imagined age can affect the kinds of products they purchase (youthful products v. mature products). This works the other direction, too, of course. Tweens and teens often like to see themselves as being *older* than they truly are, so they may place undue value on products that reinforce this perceived older age rather than products that seem younger or more youth oriented.

Other examples of these miscalibrations can be seen in the disconnect between fitness/body image, wealth, and other important consumer variables. The concept of vanity sizing, in which retail clothing stores will deliberately affix smaller size tags to clothing that is actually larger (e.g., calling what is normally a Large size a Medium size), is one example of playing to consumers' miscalibrations. Similarly, perceptions about one's wealth are equally relative. Cruise ships are a fine example of this: most cruises have a formal night in which guests are encouraged to wear suits, tuxedos, evening gowns, and other formalwear as they come and dine in the chandeliered, fancy dining room of the ship…even if the cruise was only $200 for 5 days and not $10,000 for the same period of time. There is no doubt that consumers feel a lot fancier and maybe even *wealthier* in that context compared to the dining nights they are in board shorts and tank tops at the buffet line. A smart cruise line would take advantage of this to sell the duty-free products and photo packages for that sailing, which many cleverly do.

Value as a Relative Construct. Up to this point you probably noticed a pervasive theme: value is not fixed. In my dissertation, I showed that people's willingness to pay for an ice-cold bottle of water varied not only as a function of thirst (of course one's willingness to pay for a bottle of water increases with thirst) but also as a function of context. Merely stating the question differently led consumers to indicate a willingness to pay twice as much for the same bottle of water. The difference? "Say you are in Miami and you are thirsty…" and "Say you are in Seattle and you are thirsty…" Just mentally placing people in a context was enough to get them to say they would spend *twice* as much money on the same product. Crazy. I guess that's why you should never shop on an empty stomach.

In 1999, Coca-Cola attempted to take advantage of this "relativity of value" idea when it tested vending machines that changed the price of a can of Coke depending on the temperature outside. On colder days, a can of

Coke would be cheaper, and on hotter days, the same can of ice-cold Coke would be more expensive. Coca-Cola reasoned this was simple supply and demand, as the beverage maker noticed that patrons attending summer sporting events were willing to pay outrageously higher prices to street vendors who, on a whim, were able to change the prices for their bottles of water depending, literally, on the changing weather. Just as gas stations change gas prices and airlines change flight prices based on market demand, Coca-Cola's implementation of the new technology would have allowed it to let the demand for Coke dictate the price *in the moment*. Consumers, however, were not pleased and Coke scrapped the plans shortly thereafter.

Perhaps the most famous academic study that forever changed the way we look at value is Kahneman and Tversky's Prospect Theory. **Prospect Theory** refers to the idea that losses loom larger than gains and that most valuations stem from a subjective reference point. In the context of our discussion on value and valuation, most of us establish some anchor in our minds of how much something is worth or valued to us. Greater value than this anchor point is perceived as a gain whereas any value lower than this anchor point would be construed as a loss. Now, the silly and perhaps irrational thing about human behavior is that we tend to weigh losses much more heavily than gains. This violates the rational world of economists in which $20 is $20, as in the real world a gain of $20 is fundamentally different from a loss of $20. For whatever reason, that $20 in a loss framing feels a *lot* worse, as if we lost $100, whereas the gain framing doesn't have that effect.

To give you a more consumer friendly example of this, consider what is referred to as the Endowment Effect. In the **Endowment Effect** people tend to value a product *much* more once they are in possession of it as opposed to when they are considering the product for purchase. For example, if you ask people how much they are willing to pay for a wall hanging, they may quote a price, say $200. But if you ask people how much they would charge to sell that same painting, the price is almost *always* higher. "People may be looking to make some money, right?" you're thinking. Maybe. But let's reconsider this from the perspective of Prospect Theory. The acquisition of the paining is a gain. The loss of the painting is a loss. Thus, from a gain framing, we see the value of the painting as much smaller relative to the value of the painting when thinking about it from a loss framing, which may be one explanation for why we command a higher price for selling than we are willing to pay for buying. To apply this to a marketing context, imagine the amazing things you could do via product sampling and trial ownership using the properties of Endowment Effect.

To give you another example of how relativity affects valuation, consider an effect known as the **Compromise Effect** in which we tend to prefer an option that seems like a compromise between two extremes even if the calculated value of that option is not, in fact, a better value. Think of gas prices. Almost every gas station you drive by features three prices: a low, a medium, and a premium price. More often than not, consumers will opt for the middle-of-the-road option because humans have a bias against choosing at the extremes. So if you are originally selling gas at $4 or $3 a gallon, introducing a third premium option at $5 a gallon might actually increase sales of the $4/gallon option. The value here is not as much "financial" as it is "psychological," believing you are making a better decision.

Taking this relative concept of value one step further, some researchers believe that consumers don't really assess the value of a product or service independently at all but, instead, engage in comparative valuation of alternatives. The theory, **Comparison Theory of Value**, suggests that as consumers narrow down their options from an evoked set to a consideration set to a final purchase that value is constructed not in a vacuum but rather relative to the other alternative products in that moment of consideration. This, of course, is one reason that in-store price promotions and point-of-purchase coupons are extremely effective, as the value for a product relative to its competing products is suddenly *that* much better at a critical point in the purchasing process.

So again, as our concepts from the book continue to merge together, remember from our earlier chapter on Perception and Attention that it is not *reality* that matters in the world of consumer behavior but rather *perceptions*. The real or objective benefit and cost of a product or service is merely more information we add to the mix, but our true decisions are actually a function of our relative comparisons, our contexts, our *perceived* benefits and costs, and even our internal state at the moment of valuation.

Risk and Value. Not only is value relative, it is also often *conditional*, not guaranteed but rather based on probability. That is, like many things in life, sometimes there is a *chance* of something happening; the world is *not* a certain place. Say, for example, you have a 50% chance of winning $40 in a lottery drawing. Rational economists would calculate what they call the **Expected Value** of that gamble, which is simply the outcome of the event multiplied by the likelihood of that event actually happening (e.g., EV = ($40) x (.50) = $20), so the expected value of that gamble is $20.

The once-famous game show *Deal or No Deal* was simply a game of expected value. If you never saw the game show, *Deal or No Deal* involved a contestant opening a series of briefcases, one at a time, while being propositioned with offers from a mysterious banker to accept the banker's offer of money and to leave the game. The smart strategy (based on economics) is to *take* the banker's deal if he offers more money than the expected value of the remaining suitcases of money and to *reject* the banker's deal if he offers less than the expected value of the remaining suitcases. Of course, contestants on game shows are not rational economists and, as such, did *not* follow this strategy. This meant a lot of stupid decisions were made, which is what makes for good television in modern time (see: Maury Povich).

So, according to economists, if I were to offer you the gamble of a 50% chance of winning $40 (and an 50% chance of winning nothing), you would be smart to *take* the gamble if the only other choice I gave you was a 100% chance of winning $19, but you should *reject* the gamble if the only other choice I gave you was a 100% chance of winning $21. See how that works in Econ world?

But what happens in the real world? Consider the following example:

A vicious disease is killing the cat population of Ancient Egypt. Cleopatra has to make a choice; her best doctors have created a cure, but the cure is not perfect. The leading doctor comes to her and gives her one of two options:

Option A1: 1,000 cats will be saved for sure
Option B1: ¼ chance of saving 4,000 cats, ¾ chance of saving no cats

If you were Cleopatra, which option would you choose? Have you picked one? Okay, now say the leading doctor comes back to Cleopatra after reformulating the cure and gives her two different options:

Option A2: 3,000 cats die for sure
Option B2: ¼ chance of zero cats dying, ¾ chance of 4,000 cats dying

Which of these two options would you choose? Got it?

So if you are like most people (and like me; despite my disdain for felines, I'd still save them) chances are that, when presented with the first two options above (i.e., A1 and B1), you chose option A1. Am I right? And then, when you were presented with the second set of options (i.e., A2 and B2), you probably chose option B2. Did I read your mind?

If I correctly guessed the options you chose, don't worry; I'm not *actually* reading your mind. Most people presented with these kinds of questions choose these particular responses. The secret has to do with human preferences. The first set of options, presented in a **gain framing**, focuses on *saving* the cats. It turns out that humans tend to prefer *certainty* when gambles are framed as a gain. The second set of options, presented in a **loss framing**, focuses on *losing* the cats. It turns out that humans tend to prefer taking risks when gambles are framed as a loss. Because of this innate preference, it's likely that you chose the certain option in the gain framing and the risky option in the loss framing. So how we value depends on our framing of a situation *as well as* the likelihood of a particular outcome actually taking place.

Utilitarian v. Hedonic Value. One final point I want to make before moving on to a discussion about decision-making involves the different perspectives we often take regarding value. Sometimes we tend to focus on the **utilitarian value** of a product, or its ability to serve a functional role, to serve as a utility. Other times we tend to emphasize the **hedonic value** of a product, which refers to its ability to fulfill pleasure-oriented needs. To give you a consumer example, a fancy Maserati is *probably* not the most cost-efficient way to drive from home to school or to work; however, it looks really, *really* nice and is likely to attract a lot of attention to you (focus on hedonic value). A Prius, on the other hand, may not be the sexiest of cars, aesthetically speaking, but the gas mileage of the car is among the best in the market (focus on utilitarian value). Any product or service on the market is likely to cater both to utilitarian and hedonic needs, but which one is emphasized is likely a function of one's self and situation at any given moment throwing yet *another* wrench into our consideration of value.

By now, you should understand the main point of this chapter: value is as difficult for the consumer to articulate as it is for the marketer to measure. How we value an object is a function of many moving pieces, interactions among those pieces, and Self and Situational factors that are often changing. Thus, I think one of the best ways of thinking about value is that it is "dynamically constructed" in the moment – that is, we honestly don't know how much we value something until we *think* about it, and even then we're pretty poor at quantifying and subsequently articulating how much we *feel* we value something.

Where does that leave us? Well, as neuroscientists continue to observe the brain as it thinks about value and we better understand the underlying processes involved in assessing and calculating value, perhaps our ability to quantify value will improve. In the meantime, we'll just focus on bolstering perceived benefits, mitigating perceived costs, and knowing as much about our consumers' internal and situational states as possible so that we can clearly communicate just how valuable our products and services are…or at least are perceived to be.

*   *   *

As the Tiffany & Co. v. Costco case rages on, academic researchers continue to uncover interesting findings about human beings, value, and luxury. For example, did you know that money *can* buy happiness, but that the marginal happiness that one additional dollar can buy you tapers off after around the 75,000th dollar (other research claims a higher cutoff, but the point is the same: at some point, the marginal utility of an additional dollar with respect to happiness diminishes).

Also, although we began with a conversation about how many consumers attribute value to the brands they purchase and/or wear, recent research by colleagues at the University of Southern California have found that the *truly* wealthy actually prefer to wear unbranded clothing products and to consume unbranded products as opposed to flashy or showy brands as a way to signal their true value to others "in the know." This finding supports the saying my parents used to tell me, "People who *really* have money don't brag about it."

Marketers now use individualized valuation to their advantage – websites like Kickstarter allow people to pay whatever they want to get a product, service, or even a movie off the ground. Auction sites like eBay facilitate auctions between those who have and those who want. A new personal favorite of mine, PledgeMusic.com, allows fans to contribute as much money as they want to an artist to help the musician or band cover the costs of creating a new album. There's a certain elegance and efficiency to cutting out the middlemen – the producers, the agents, the behind-the-scenes spinners, and, as much as it pains me to say it, the marketers – so that producers and consumers can engage in market transactions that maximize value for both.

However, that said, even in the most efficient markets buyers and sellers bring their subjective biases to the table, biases not resulting from any nefarious production campaigns but from simple daily life. In fact, humans are seemingly hardwired with biases that can affect choices and decision-making. The following chapter is dedicated to these biases and decision-making as we, friends, reach the final point in the consumer behavior process.

APPLICATION QUESTIONS

1) Because you like torture, you agree to go on a date with an economist. He/she takes you to a lovely Mexican restaurant that serves delicious chips and salsa. "You know," he/she says, "After your first few chips, each subsequent chip tastes less delicious?" What reasoning is the economist using? Give an example of how he/she could be incorrect.

2) You land a sweet job working for a game show production

company in Los Angeles. Your first assignment is to develop a game show that exploits people's irrationality (e.g., expected value misunderstanding; the tendency to overemphasize losses and underemphasize gains). What would your game show look like?'

3) Now you're a marketing manager at a company that sells household cleaners, laundry detergents, and air fresheners. Using Prospect Theory, how might you go about boosting the value of gains and mitigating any potential losses or negatives consumers might have about one of your products?

4) A marketing researcher asks a group of teenagers why they think a certain musician is "cool." One teen responds, "He's just really sweet," while another says, "He just seems funny and, like, cool and stuff." Hating your life at this point, what can you do to elicit deeper, more meaningful responses from the teens? Aside from gaining more information, why is getting to these root reasons so helpful?

5) You're working as a salesperson for a national diet program that sells sets of meals to customers for weeks at a time. Your national manager is upset that your region has yet to reach its volume goals for the year for the 30-day, $300 option. What one *small* change might you make that could boost volume without hurting revenues too much?

6) Peapod, a company that delivers groceries straight to your door, is popular in some larger cities. Explain, using cost ideas, why some people are willing to pay higher prices for this service? Can you think of another product or service missing out on an opportunity like the one Peapod has seized?

7) Many "As Seen on TV" products offer to mail you a product to "try out for 30 days," and then, if you are unsatisfied, allow you to "ship it back at no cost to you!" Aside from knowing people are lazy, why else might this tactic be a smart marketing move with respect to value?

8) Say you're in the middle of a negotiation with a retail partner on how many units of your product they plan to carry. You would prefer they take roughly 10,000, but they only want to do 7,000. What would a savvy marketer do in this instance? Why might their plan work?

9) Companies often compete for shelf space in retail environments

and pay for premium locations. According to how some theorists believe people determine the value of a product, why might separating your products away from its competition be a bad thing? Explain this same idea in the context of Ron Johnson's new vision of JCPenney's layout.

10) What's the difference between utilitarian value and hedonic value? Below is a list of products and services – see if you can figure out the utilitarian value and hedonic value each provides:
-Apartment or house
-Meal at a restaurant
-Laptop computer
-All-inclusive resort
-Airplane flight
-Community park
-Mobile phone

11) Think of a consumer product or service that screams hedonic value but not utilitarian value. Got one? Now come up with a marketing plan that emphasizes the utilitarian value the selected product/service provides. Whom would you target? What would the marketing communications say and how would they look? How would you communicate the message? Now do the same thing for a consumer product or service that screams utilitarian value but not hedonic value.

12) The concept of value is all about increasing perceived gains and benefits while mitigating or eliminating perceived costs. Using some of the concepts from previous chapters – emotions, attitude theories, social influence, cultural trends, etc. – give some suggestions on how a marketer might boost value and mitigate costs in simple, efficient, effective, and non-costly ways via consumer psychology.

Chapter 12 | Decision Making

How do you vote?

I don't mean to pry, so I don't mean for you to indicate whether you are a Democrat or a Republican, a Libertarian or an Independent. What I want to know is when you have to make up your mind to cast your ballot for *one* person or either yes *or* no on an important initiative, how do you decide?

Now, some voters certainly vote according to what is referred to as "party lines." If I am a Democrat, I will just vote according to what seems to be in favor with the Democratic Party. If I am a Republican, I will do the same but with whatever the Republican Party endorses.

We also have what we refer to as "single-issue voters." These are the folks who focus on *one* issue – abortion, tax reform, welfare rights, gay marriage, etc. – and cast their vote for the party whose view is in line with their view on this single issue. They may disagree with the party on every other issue, but the single issue is all that matters. Abortion, quite a contentious issue, often sees pro-life voters endorsing conservative candidates and pro-choice voters endorsing liberal candidates.

Still, there are those of us who vote neither by party line nor by single-issue beliefs but who, instead, actually do a line-by-line review of major issues and ideas, compare candidates' positions on these many issues, and then ultimately make a decision.

Let me ask you another question: which approach is the best?

That's a trick question, of course, because it is difficult to say that one voting strategy is better than any other. But what *is* true is that even if one is given the same set of products, the same attribute information, and the same ratings on those different attributes, different decision-making strategies can lead to drastically different results.

You might be wondering why we are talking about voting and politics in a book about marketing, but here's the beautiful thing: elections *are* markets. You have products (i.e., politicians, causes, laws, mandates, etc.), consumers (i.e., you, me, voters everywhere), and the market in which these products and consumers interact (i.e., the ballot box, the real world). In fact, many people credit Barack Obama's historic presidential win and reelection to smart marketing – knowing the needs of the constituents and focusing on appealing to these important segments to gain a critical number of supporters (and, by proxy, electoral college votes) necessary to win the election.

Let's return to our example of the different kinds of voters. To avoid the uneasiness of talking about our real politics, let's imagine we live in the fictitious world of Oz. The Wizard of Oz, Glinda the Good Witch, and the Wicked Witch of the West are all running for public office. Hopefully you don't have strong feelings about these people.   According to the inhabitants of Oz, there are four major issues: Safety from Flying Monkey Attacks, Equal taxation of Munchkinland and the Emerald City, Reduction in drug-related violence (I mean, they did have an entire field of opium producing poppies), and Immigration control (particularly for immigrants who have a nasty habit of dropping houses on current inhabitants).

The independent Oz Daily Newspaper has conducted a detailed poll with voters to get a sense of how important the issues are relative to one another (i.e., issue importance weight), how passionate each candidate is perceived as being about a particular issue of importance (ratings for each candidate for each issue), and a determination of the minimum acceptable cutoff of passion voters feel each candidate should have regarding each of the issues (i.e., cutoff). The newspaper then summarized these findings in a handy-dandy chart for the voters of Oz:

Issues	Issue Importance Weight	Minimum Cutoff	Glinda	Wicked Witch	Wizard of Oz
Monkey Safety	0.05	3	9	1	8
Taxation	0.15	5	3	8	4
Drug Violence	0.3	6	9	2	4
Immigration	0.5	8	2	10	5

So, to be clear, the products (i.e., the candidates), the attributes (i.e., the issues), and the ratings (i.e., the perceived level of passion for each candidate on each issue) *are the exact same for everyone.* However, let's say we have three different voters: the Scarecrow – a single-issues voter (he lacks the brain capacity to do much else), the Tin-Man – a holistic voter who seeks to find the best overall candidate (likes to oil the creaks of the interconnected parts), and the Cowardly Lion – a party-line voter who lacks the courage to make decisions for himself. The Scarecrow, most concerned about safety from monkey attacks after an unfortunate incident with the creatures, should vote for Glinda for whom Monkey Safety is a top priority, as he is a single-issue voter. The Tin Man, focused on the best overall candidate, decides to create a score for each candidate based on the total sum of each issue's importance weighting times each candidate's score for each rating. After doing this, he finds that the Wicked Witch actually has the highest overall score (6.85/10) compared to Glinda (4.6/10) and the Wizard (4.7/10). Finally, the Cowardly Lion, a member of the Wizards and Wild Beasts Party, opts to go with the Wizard because that's whom his party endorses. Just like that we arrive at three different votes based not on differences in importance or evaluations but, instead, due to which decision rule was used.

Although this may seem like a silly example, I hope you realize the importance of the main point: *how* we make a choice can actually influence the choice itself. That is, over and above our preferences, the *way* we choose can trump our preferences, our perceived benefits and costs, and even our value and valuation. That should be surprising, alarming, and maybe even scary. Think about all the people who vote for *real* leaders in this country and have no idea that *how* they choose their preferred candidate may have very little to do with their actual beliefs. Scary, right? To think about it on a more positive note, consider how even though we may vote for different candidates or different directions on initiatives, perhaps our actual preferences aren't so different at all, it's just *how* we went about deciding that ultimately led us down different paths. Isn't that a nice warm and fuzzy thought?

This chapter is dedicated to the science and art of decision-making: part science because of the logic and rules we often employ, and part art for the biases and heuristics that creep into just about every decision we make. Decision-making is rarely an exact science, but it is an important one; and knowing how your consumers make their decisions can drastically change the strategies and tactics you pursue as a marketer.

*   *   *

We spend the majority of our lives making decisions. Some decisions are big – like where to go to school for college or whom to marry or whether to marry in the first place. Other decisions are small – like how much toothpaste to use on your toothbrush or whether you want to set the alarm for 6:00am or 6:15am. Yet rarely a day goes by in which we are not making some decision. Even the path we choose to walk or the clothes we choose to wear each day are examples of daily decision-making.

Given that we have so much experience making decisions, one might expect that decision-making gets easier over time. Try asking your grandparents or parents about that or a judge or a trauma doctor or nurse. Many decisions never get any *easier* to make. Granted, these people may make *better* decisions with experience over time, but just because the decisions are better does not mean they are any easier.

So why is decision-making so difficult if we do it so frequently? Well, part of the problem is that rare is it the case that any two problems are ever *exactly* the same. We know this by now because we know that there are myriad Self factors and Situation factors changing dynamically at any given point in time. We do not live in a static world and, consequently, we do not make decisions in a static, predictable world.

Furthermore, despite the beauty of the human brain's abilities and its speedy efficiency, it isn't perfect. Sometimes the very shortcuts the brain employs in its attempt to make our lives easier on cruise control actually lead to some pretty terrible decisions.

The remainder of this chapter is dedicated to the various decision-making strategies that we often employ, as well as the decision-making biases we often cannot prevent ourselves from having.

Dual Process Models of Decision-Making. Earlier in the book in our discussion on the Self, we discussed how our perceptions, cognitions, and emotions influence consumer behavior. However, as you know from your own life experiences, it's rare that we are *only* using emotions or *only* using cognitions (i.e., rational thought processes) or even simply relying on our implicit perceptions to make decisions. In reality, we make decisions using a blend of these fundamental tools, but the primary method leading that blend of tools is often contingent on the Situation in which we find ourselves. Now that we have discussed both Self and Situation, we can integrate the two to understand how we *actually* go about making decisions.

Current views on decision-making tend to take on a very similar, two-pronged approach. Although the names of those two prongs differ among the competing (but related) theories, the basic idea is the same: one prong involves more automatic, reflexive, and associative processing (a.k.a. System 1) while the other prong involves more deliberative, analytic, and systematic processing (a.k.a. System 2). To put it in plain language, the first system involves going with one's gut and intuition while the latter system involves relying on logic and thinking.

It turns out that this two-pronged approach shouldn't be much of a surprise. Conscious thought is most commonly associated with the neocortical region of the brain. Neo means "new," and it is no mistake that the *neo*cortex bears this name, as this part of the brain evolved much more recently than the rest of the brain. The older areas of the brain (e.g., the limbic system) are often recruited in basic, automatic processing of emotions, motivation, motor skills, and fundamental survival abilities (e.g., fight or flight). This division of the brain is a *bit* of an oversimplification of how the brain *actually* works, but for now think of it as an easy way to think about the physiology underlying this idea of how the brain can process information more automatically or more deliberatively.

Let me give you an example. Here's a simple math problem for you:

Johnny wants to go fishing. In order to go fishing, Johnny needs to buy a new fishing rod and bait. Together, the fishing rod and the bait cost $11. If the fishing rod costs $10 more than the bait, how much does the bait cost?

Have your answer? $1 right? Let's check. We know that the total cost of fishing rod *and* the bait equals $11 and that the fishing rod costs $10 more than the bait. So if we let x = "cost of the bait," and x + 10 = "cost of the fishing rod," then we know x + (x + 10) = $11, which is 2x + 10 = 11, then 2x = 1, x = $.50. But wait? I thought we said the bait cost $1? What gives?

This mathematic example illustrates the difference between the two systems of processing. When you first read the math problem, your gut instinct was to think, "Oh, simple! $10 plus *what* equals $11? One, $1 is the answer!" But the math problem is more complicated than that: the fishing rod does not cost $10, it costs "$10 *more than*" the bait. So unless you stopped and deliberated for a second, you were probably unlikely to catch this detail and, relying on your gut instinct, gave the intuitive (but incorrect) answer of $1.

It is rarely the case that we are completely engaged in one type of processing and not the other (i.e., purely automatic v. purely deliberative), but it is usually the case that one type of processing is slightly more dominant at any given point in time. What factors influence the system with which we are processing information? It turns out there are several. First, we have our friends **motivation, opportunity**, and **ability**. If a decision is highly engaging and stimulating, then it may be the case that we are more motivated to process information carefully (System 2). An example of this in a consumer setting would be paying close attention to the environmentally-friendly specs of a car in a car commercial if you are a tree hugger. Sometimes, however, we lack the opportunity to process at a higher level. Say you are that same tree-hugger in a crowded room, a room so loud that you cannot hear the environmentally-friendly points being made about the car but, instead, can just see pretty pictures and hear the commercial's music. So even though you are motivated to pay attention, you don't have the opportunity to do so. Finally, let's say the same commercial comes on in an empty room with just you, so you have the motivation and the opportunity to hear the environmentally-friendly messages in the commercial, but your mind is thinking about an important meeting you have at work tomorrow. Because your brain is so taxed in the moment, you simply do not have the ability to process the information at a deep level.

This last point leads us to a conversation on cognitive load. **Cognitive load** is based on a theory that humans have a finite pool of mental resources that can be expended at any given time. A classic example of a cognitive load manipulation in the lab involves creating two groups, a control condition and an experimental condition, both of which will be completing simple math problems. Both groups are presented with a string of numbers – 1832388724822 – except the experimental group is told they must memorize these numbers as they may be asked questions about them later. They are not permitted to write anything down. So, go ahead: memorize the numbers above and proceed to solve the following math problems without looking back at any information in this paragraph:

3 x 23 = ??	147/3 = ??	1,482 – 871 = ??
87 + 46 = ??	201 – 17 = ?	96/4 = ??

Now, without looking back at the string of numbers in the previous paragraph, write down as many of those numbers (in the correct order) that you can recall. Hard, right? Even doing the math problems was likely more difficult. That's the idea of cognitive load: when your mind is so taxed doing other things and dedicating so many resources from your finite pool of resources to other needs, you simply don't have the mental capacity to deliberate about anything else. Thus, when cognitive load is high or heavy, people tend to rely on System 1 processing (the intuitive, less effortful kind). However, when cognitive load is low or light, people can rely on System 2 (rational, deliberate) if they desire, but they may not (e.g., if I'm carefree and in a good mood I *could* spend time debating myself about the show I want to watch on TV, but chances are I won't).

Another factor that affects our tendency to rely on either System 1 or System 2 slightly more is that of processing fluency. **Processing Fluency** refers to the ease with which we are able to engage in the cognitive processing of incoming information. When something feels fluent, we tend to process less actively, relying on System 1. When something feels disfluent, we tend to engage in more active processing, relying on System 2. Now, we talked about the related concept of cultural fluency in the chapter on Culture and Socio-Cultural Differences, but to give you an idea of what fluency means in this context consider the following two paragraphs:

<u>Paragraph 1:</u>

Alvamour Resorts and Hotels is an exclusive, upscale global resort company with properties in over 20 major cities around the globe! Featuring world-class dining options, state-of-the-art fitness centers, and freshly-baked European pastries delivered to guests' rooms each morning, Alvamour specializes in bringing the relaxation back to vacation. Our custom-designed pools and free spa services help revive and rejuvenate our valued guests as they escape from life for awhile. For more information, or to book a room today, call us at 1-800-555-TRIP.

Paragraph 2:

Alvamour Resorts and Hotels is an exclusive, upscale global resort company with properties in over 20 major cities around the globe! Featuring world-class dining options, state-of-the-art fitness centers, and freshly-baked European pastries delivered to guests' rooms each morning, Alvamour specializes in bringing the relaxation back to vacation. Our custom-designed pools and free spa services help revive and rejuvenate our valued guests as they escape from life for awhile . For more information, or to book a room today, call us at 1-800-555-TRIP.

As you probably realized by now, the two paragraphs say *exactly* the same thing: they are both brief descriptions of the hotel company Alvamour. However, you probably noticed that the first paragraph, although readable, was *much more difficult* to read compared to the second paragraph. The typeface (i.e., font) used for the first paragraph fit the luxury branding of the hotel chain, but the difficulty of reading the passage made it feel *disfluent*, whereas the second paragraph seemed *fluent*. Research has shown that experiencing disfluency tends to kick us into a more deliberative, System 2 processing style while fluency keeps at an associative, System 1 level. As an example, the math question I gave you a few minutes ago about a fishing rod and bait is one *most* people tend to get wrong as they give the intuitive, yet incorrect, answer of $1. However, writing out the same math problem in a difficult-to-read font may actually *increase* his/her chances of getting the correct answer of $.50, as he/she is more likely to engage in a more deliberative, System 2 level of processing.

So from a marketing standpoint, it might be useful to use fluency as a tool to get people to process your product or service at a more heuristic level (focusing on the emotional appeal, stimulation through music, design, etc.) and disfluency as a way to make people pay more attention to reasons and logic in the persuasive messages you are communicating about your product or service.

Our tendency to engage in System 1 or System 2 processing due to various reasons including cognitive load, processing fluency, and other factors has the potential to influence several different components of our shopping experience: how much time we spend making a decision, engaging in information search about a product or service, purchasing an item, and even consuming the item we purchase. For example, if I have the ability to engage in more effortful, deliberative processing, I may spend more time searching for information prior to making purchases or more time *thinking* about how much I enjoy or do not enjoy a product as I am using it (e.g., "This shampoo makes my hair feel like sunshine on a spring day in Paris. I bet it's because of ingredients X, Y, and Z. I think the price for this shampoo was a good value because...etc."). If I am under time constraints, cognitive load constraints, or engaged in an extremely fluent consumer context, I may spend very little time searching for information and perhaps only pay scant attention to thoughts about my consumption experience (e.g., "This is the shampoo I always buy. I buy again. Shampoo smells minty. Good stuff."...apparently I also think like a caveman when I am processing at a System 1 level).

I discussed, at great length, the influence of situation and context in the chapter on Context, Environment, and Situation, because this kind of automatic influence is adaptive and extremely helpful in directing our choices and behavior. However, what follows next is a discussion of the more deliberative processes in which we engage when making a decision followed by a discussion of biases that are relatively more automatic and that affect our choices even when we are attempting to be deliberative.

Decision-Making rules and strategies. We all, at some point in time, have made use of a pro/con list to help us make a tough decision. Even this simplest of tasks is an exercise in strategic decision-making. By imposing a very simple rule – positive valence → pro, negative valence → con – we develop a list and, either by counting (quantity) or comparing (quality) the lists, we make a choice.

You may not realize it, but there are many other, more complex decision-making strategies that we use daily. As I describe several of these strategies below you may realize that you have incorporated them in your decision-making without ever realizing that they actually have fancy names and decades of research behind them.

Before we dive into specific strategies, it is first useful to talk about the two broad classes of decision-making strategies: **Compensatory** and **Noncompensatory Strategies**. Any decision-making strategy has to do with attributes and our evaluations of those attributes. If a strategy is a compensatory strategy we consider *all* the attributes of a product or service and how those attributes can compensate or interact with one another. If a strategy is a noncompensatory strategy we do *not* consider all the information and do *not* consider potential tradeoffs among attributes. The difference between the two types of strategies should become clearer with the specific examples that follow.

Conjunctive Decision Rule. An example of a noncompensatory strategy, the Conjunctive Decision Rule involves establishing minimum acceptable cutoffs for each attribute of a product or service and then eliminating *any* product/service if even one attribute of that product/service fails to surpass the minimum acceptable cutoff. This is clearly noncompensatory in that the product/service's attributes could meet or exceed the minimum acceptable cutoffs for *all but one* of the attributes, but that one deficient attribute is enough to have the option thrown out.

Disjunctive Decision Rule. Another example of a noncompensatory strategy, the Disjunctive Decision Rule is the mirror image of the Conjunctive Decision Rule. The Disjunctive Decision Rule again involves establishing minimum cutoffs for each attribute of a product/service, but this time brands can stay in the consideration set as long as at least *one* of the attributes exceeds the minimum acceptable cutoff. The reason this is not a "compensatory" rule is that we don't care that the other attributes are lacking; we pay no attention to whether some exceed the cutoff and some do not – we are just looking to see if any one attribute meets or exceeds its cutoff.

It is worth pausing here to give you a helpful reminder for keeping the Conjunctive Decision Rule and the Disjunctive Decision Rule clear in your head. The way to think about it is that Conjunctive is looking to "throw out" options while Disjunctive is looking for what to "include." If *any* attribute scores *below* its minimum acceptable cutoff, it will be *excluded* according to the Conjunctive Decision Rule. If any attribute scores *above* its minimum acceptable cutoff, it will be *included* according to the Disjunctive Decision Rule. It's tricky, but together we can manage.

Lexicographic Decision Rule. Another noncompensatory rule, the Lexicographic Decision Rule involves *first* ranking the attributes in order of their importance and then selecting the product/service with the highest rating on the most important attribute. If there is a tie for the most important attribute, only those products/services that are tied are included and attention shifts to the *second*-most important attribute. The product/service with the highest rating on this *second* attribute is selected. If there is still a tie, the *third*-most important attribute it looked at (and so on) until a decision is made.

Elimination-by-Aspects (EBA) Decision Rule. Slightly related to the Lexicographic Decision Rule, the Elimination-by-Aspects Decision Rule incorporates *both* 1) attribute importance, and 2) minimum acceptable cutoffs. First, one prioritizes the importance of the product/service attributes. Then, minimum acceptable cutoffs are established for each attribute. Then, starting with the most important attribute, options failing to meet the minimum established cutoff for that attribute are eliminated. The products/services that survived the first cut are then subjected to the second-most important attribute. Only those products/services whose attribute meets/exceeds the minimum acceptable cutoff are allowed to remain (and so on) until only one product/service remains. This approach is also a noncompensatory strategy.

Compensatory Decision Rule. The final decision rule, the Compensatory Decision Rule, is…well…compensatory, and involves developing a "score" for each product/service that is a function of 1) each of the option's attributes multiplied by 2) the importance of that attribute to a consumer. First, consumers weight the importance of a product/service's many attributes, similar to the EBA rule. Then the consumer rates the product/service on each of those attributes. Each attribute rating is *multiplied by* the weighted importance of that attribute, and these totals are summed together across a product/service's attributes to give one, overall score for the product/service. The product/service with the highest "score" is then selected.

Got it all? Just kidding. I know that's a lot to digest, so the next section is going to provide an example to show you how it all works.

Different decision rules, different outcomes. So that was a lot of text to explain the decision rules, but it is important to me that you understand how these different decisions rules can lead to different outcomes. To do this, I created a chart featuring some Chicago-area restaurants in my neighborhood, ratings on attributes I consider important when considering restaurants, and weights on how important those attributes are to me. The chart is pictured below:

Attributes	Attribute Importance Weight	Minimum Cutoff	Bistrot Margot	The Refinery	Declan's Pub	Pour Haus
Food Quality	0.3	5	8	9	7	6
Price	0.22	5	5	2	8	6
Location	0.18	8	5	9	9	5
Ambiance	0.05	8	6	8	6	8
Social Scene	0.15	7	7	9	5	7
Comfort	0.1	7	6	4	9	5

Before we jump into applying the decision rules, it's first useful to wrap our heads around the chart itself. There is a lot of information here. First, on the left-hand side, we have a list of the attributes I considered important: Food Quality, Price, Location, Ambiance, Social Scene, and Comfort. Next to this column is another column in which I have identified *how important* each attribute is to me as a weight. Food Quality is the most important (.3), while Ambiance appears to be the least important (.05). The weightings add to 1, suggesting the % importance each attribute has in my overall decision. The next column contains my minimum acceptable cutoffs for each of the attributes. You'll notice I like places with a strong social scene but also a high level of comfort. Finally, we have our options – in this case four restaurants that are located in the Old Town area of Chicago: Bistrot Margot, The Refinery, Declan's Pub, and Pour Haus. For each restaurant I have rated, on a scale from 1 (terrible) to 10 (amazing) each of the attributes as they apply to that particular restaurant.

Now, here's where the fun part comes in. Depending on *which* decision rule we apply, the final decision on where to go may differ. I will walk you through each of the decision rules below in the context of this restaurant example.

Conjunctive Rule. If we apply the Conjunctive Decision Rule, we first look at the minimum acceptable cutoff for each of the attributes and throw out any option if even *one* of its ratings fails to meet or exceed the minimum cutoff for any of the attributes. We can start wherever we want, as we will go through *all* the attributes. Starting with Food Quality, we see that all our options surpass the minimum cutoff (5). No one gets the boot. Moving to Price, we see that The Refinery, with its rating of 2 (it's kinda pricey) fails to meet the minimum cutoff for that attribute (5). The Refinery gets tossed. We move on to Location next, with its minimum cutoff of 8. Unfortunately, Bistrot Margot (with a rating of 5) and Pour Haus (also with a rating of 5) fail to meet the minimum acceptable cutoff. They get tossed. We don't stop here, though; we still have to check the other attributes. The order we're proceeding in is totally random – we could have started at the bottom of the attribute list and worked our way up. Moving along we get to Ambiance and see that Declan's Pub, our last remaining option, has an Ambiance rating of 6, which fails to meet or surpass the minimum cutoff of 8. The result: NONE of the restaurant options is worth choosing. Looks like we need to look elsewhere.

Disjunctive Rule. If we apply the Disjunctive Rule, we first look at the minimum acceptable cutoff for each of the attributes and include any option if even *one* of its ratings meets or exceeds the minimum cutoff for any of the attributes. We can start wherever we want, as we will go through all the attributes. Starting with Food Quality, we should notice right away that all four of the restaurants' food quality rating exceeds the minimum acceptable cutoff. We can stop there. The result: ALL the restaurant options remain in our consideration set. We'll have to employ some other decision rules if we want to narrow down our options.

Lexicographic Rule. If we apply the Lexicographic Rule, we first look at the order of importance of our attributes. Food Quality dominates as the most important attribute under consideration (.30 weighting). We then look at the restaurant options to see which restaurant dominates on this, our most important option. The Refinery has the highest Food Quality rating (9) of the four choices, and there is no tie. The result: We choose to go to The Refinery.

Elimination-by-Aspects Rule. If we apply the Elimination by Aspects

Rule, we must pay attention to the attribute importance *and* the minimum acceptable cutoff for each attribute. Starting with the most important attribute, Food Quality (.30), we see that all four restaurant options meet or exceed the minimum acceptable cutoff of 5. We then look at the second-most important attribute, Price (.22). At this stage, The Refinery gets booted because its rating of 2 does not surpass the minimum acceptable cutoff of 5. We then go to the third-most important attribute, Location (.18). At this stage, both Bistrot Margot and the Pour Haus are booted because their respective ratings (both 5) do not meet or exceed the minimum acceptable cutoff of 8 for this attribute. That leaves us with our final option, Declan's Pub. The result: We dine at Declan's Pub.

Compensatory Rule. This is my favorite decision rule because I am all about compromise. If we apply the Compensatory Rule we need to multiply each restaurant's rating for each attribute by the importance weighting of that particular attribute. To walk you through this, let's consider Bistrot Margot. To come up with the Compensatory Rule "score" for Bistrot Margot we would perform the following calculation: (8 x .30) + (5 x .22) + (5 x .18) + (6 x .05) + (7 x .15) + (6 x .1) = 6.35. To break it down, the (8 x .30) refers to the 8 rating for Bistrot Margo's Food Quality times the weighted importance of the Food Quality attribute of .3. The (5 x .22) refers to Bistrot Margot's 5 rating for Price times the weighted importance of the Price attribute of .22…and so on. The sum of all these products gives us the Compensatory Rule "score" of 6.35 for Bistrot Margot. If we were to perform the calculations for each of the remaining restaurants, we find that The Refinery gets an overall score of 6.91, Declan's Pub receives an overall score of 7.43, and Pour Haus receives an overall score of 5.97. The result: Declan's Pub, with the highest overall score of 7.43, is our dining destination. This is a good illustration of how the Compensatory Rule is "compensatory," as even though Declan's Pub scored 3rd on the most important attribute of Food Quality, it scored higher on other attributes. The weighted average scoring approach evened out the highs and lows.

So, there you have it: we can take the *same* product choices and the *same* attribute evaluations for those options and still arrive at *different* choices depending entirely on which decision rule we use. When you think about how factors pertaining to the Self or the Situation can encourage us to use one decision-making rule over another, you can begin to understand a bit more how these components work together to influence our choices and behaviors. For example, whereas some of the rules are relatively simple (e.g., Conjunctive, Disjunctive, Lexicographic rules), others are more complex (e.g., Elimination-by-Aspects, Compensatory). If we know our consumers are under high cognitive load or experiencing strong affect, both Self factors, we might expect they would be more likely to rely on the easier decision rules. Similarly, if our customers find themselves in a highly crowded retail setting or a noisy, fast-paced environment, both Situation factors, we might expect the same. The idea that we, as marketers, might be able to control which decision rules our consumers use is exciting, but equally as important is the notion that we, as consumers, may be making decisions using rules influenced by our Self and our Situation…without even realizing it!

Although it is super helpful to have decision-making rules and logical strategies for the purpose of making important choices, the world simply isn't this rational. The rest of the chapter is dedicated to discussing how our brains often throw a wrench into our decision-making process.

Decision-Making Heuristics and Biases. Remember that the human brain, like the rest of the human body, evolved over time in ways that were adaptive or helpful to survival. The easiest way to think about this is how/why sex is pleasurable. If sex feels good, people are going to do it. And people who have sex are considerably more likely to have offspring compared to those who do not have sex. Having offspring passes on those genes for people who derive pleasure from sexual intercourse and, before you know it, sex is fun for everyone…well, almost everyone. It really depends on the people.

However, sex being pleasurable is not without its downsides. Some people become addicted to sex, others commit acts of sexual crime, and some cheat on their partners in the pursuit of sexual gratification. The adaptive role of pleasurable sex from an evolutionary standpoint had no way of knowing that it might lead to some of these potential problems, but that's the nature of evolution – it is *not* perfect.

Just as some of our physical and physiological characteristics have evolved primarily for good but with some side effects, so, too, have many of our decision-making approaches. In the paragraphs that follow, I'll elaborate on several of these biases in alphabetical order, mentioning both when and how they are helpful, as well as how they can lead us down a suboptimal path.

First, consider the **Above Average Effect**. The Above Average Effect refers to the idea that when asked to subjectively rate ourselves and our abilities, we all tend to rate ourselves as being above the statistical average. I often use this phenomenon as sort of a parlor trick during public speaking engagements because it works 100% of the time. I ask the audience to close their eyes and to rate themselves on a scale from 1-10 by raising their hands on questions like, "On average, how good of a worker are you?", "On average, how smart are you?", and, my personal favorite, "On average, how good are you in bed?" Always, *always*, the majority of the room rates themselves as being above average (particularly on the last question), but this is statistically impossible – we cannot all be better than average! So how is this mental miscalculation helpful? Well, imagine the opposite. Imagine walking around thinking that you are *below* average. These people exist. They're called depressed. In fact, some researchers have shown that when doing an exercise like the one I do with audiences those people who qualify as "depressed" are more accurate in assessing their relative position. So while it may be helpful for us to get through our day by seeing ourselves as "above average," it can be dangerous when it comes to our confidence and abilities in areas in which we are actually not above average or, worse, quite below average. In consumer contexts, imagine how this affects our accuracy when we *think* we know a lot about a purchase we are making. Chances are we may know less than we think.

The next heuristic, known as the **Affect Heuristic**, is fairly familiar and straightforward. Essentially, any time you rely on your emotions instead of thinking through information you are applying the affect heuristic. This is fight or flight, going with your gut instinct, going with the flow or "what feels right," and avoiding "what feels wrong." In a consumer context this could involve creating a retail environment with a lot of excitement and positivity so that consumers think less and just *do*. Casinos are a good example.

Anyone who has ever participated in negotiation should know the following mind trick: Anchoring and Adjustment. **Anchoring and adjustment** refers to how our minds tend to get wrapped around an initially-proposed number or starting point from which it subsequently makes adjustments. In the context of salary negotiation, for example, it is wise to quote a salary up front that is higher than what you intend to get and then to give concessions to the person hiring you until you get to the dollar amount you had hoped for all along. The "anchor" is the initial starting point and the "adjustment" is the wiggling that takes place thereafter. Consider the alternative: if you *don't* quote an anchor starting point, your prospective employer has the liberty to begin negotiations *anywhere* he/she wants, which is unlikely to work in your favor. Set the anchor and go from there or, if the second-mover in an anchoring and adjustment situation, call your negotiation partner out on setting an anchor bias so that you can shift it.

The next heuristic explains why we think we are going to die every time we get on a flight or why we believe we are going to win the lottery despite the odds being one in 175 million. The **Availability Heuristic** refers to thinking that the likelihood of something happening is *much greater* than it actually is because it is extremely easy to recall examples of the event happening. Plane crashes are featured prominently in the news (the thousands of safe flights that occur daily are not). Lottery winners are paraded across TV screens, as well. Because we can think of such salient examples of these events we come to believe that they happen much more frequently than they actually do. From a marketer's perspective, the availability heuristic is particularly useful when trying to sell insurance or warranties if you can somehow make salient a car accident or laptop crash. These events are probably a lot less common than we think, but if consumers can think of a salient example of these events, they are likely to believe the events occur a lot more often than they actually do.

The next heuristic, the **Backfire Effect**, seems to rear its head during election years. The Backfire Effect occurs when an individual is presented with information conflicting with his/her current beliefs and, instead of realigning or adjusting his/her beliefs to be more neutral, the person actually shifts even *further* in support of his/her initial beliefs. This is what happened, for example, when die-hard Sarah Palin supporters, when presented with evidence regarding the Vice Presidential candidate's lack of a basic understanding of tax policy, political news sources, and even world geography, actually shifted their support to be even stronger for the former Alaskan governor. Before you think I'm picking on the Republicans, understand that this effect works both ways. In consumer contexts, consumers who may be loyal to a particular brand or company may become even *more* loyal even when you, a competing company, present them with information on how you are better. Thus, it is often useful to assess for these loyalties early on before potentially wasting time with some consumers who are unlikely to abandon their original ship.

Anyone who has worked in a group has likely experienced the **Bandwagon Effect** (a.k.a. **Groupthink**). Our need for affiliation and belonging is always operating, so in group settings this tends to lead us to cooperate with others, which includes everyone embracing the same ideas for the purpose of promoting group cohesion. Research in this area shows that colleagues placed into teams or groups earlier in the ideation process tend to be less creative and produce fewer ideas than those teams that were first allowed to work as individuals and come together later in the process. Although social cohesion is certainly good in general, it can come at a cost of creativity and independent thinking. In a consumer context, this is one reason you have to be careful when conducting research in groups of people, like focus groups. One dominant view or opinion can taint the rest of the group's willingness or ability to think as an individual and to provide feedback that could be useful for your decision-making.

The next bias, the **Base Rate Fallacy**, is also known as the "false alarm" bias. The Base Rate Fallacy refers to situations in which actual "base rate" or objective statistical information is available yet we rely on case-specific information to make a decision. For example, an investor may know that a particular stock delivers solid returns about 50% of the time. However, he may have recently read a story about the company or had a positive experience with the company that leads him to believe that this stock will outperform this 50% number based on actual data. This disregard for actual data and preference for situation- or case-specific information is the base rate fallacy: ignoring the base rate for extraneous, often non-diagnostic, information.

The next term, cognitive dissonance, came up in our discussion of attitudes earlier in the Self section. **Cognitive Dissonance** refers to the conflict between our thoughts/beliefs and our actual behaviors, a conflict that produces internal tension that requires us to either adjust our beliefs or change our behaviors to bring them into alignment with each other. To apply this in a consumer domain consider the case of young smokers. Ever since I was a child, anti-smoking messages have been drilled into the minds of young people. Yet, despite all the health warnings, many young people still smoke cigarettes. If you *ask* these people, they will tell you that they *know* it is dangerous...yet they still smoke. What you find then is that these people update their beliefs and say things like, "I know it's dangerous, but my grandmother smoked for years and hasn't suffered any adverse health effects." Other times people will update their behaviors to be in line with their thinking. Consider, for example, the market for electronic cigarettes. Many of these consumers, long-time smokers, *know* that smoking is unhealthy and, as such, update their behaviors by switching to non-tobacco products that allow them to have the sensation of smoking without the negative health effects. Cognitive dissonance can be a *very* useful persuasion tactic in the context of marketing. "You know your family's health and safety are the most important things to you in the world, but you are driving a dangerous car. Vovlo has the safest rating each year. You should be driving a Volvo." How could you say no?

Somewhat related to the Backfire Effect previously described, **Cognitive Inertia** refers to the sluggish pace or inability to update one's knowledge or beliefs in light of new information. Unlike the Backfire Effect in which individuals become even further entrenched in their initial beliefs, Cognitive Inertia is *less* about becoming further entrenched and more about staying put. In other words, to hearken back to the previous example on Sarah Palin, a supporter who learns that his VP-of-choice is geographically-challenged won't become an even *stronger* supporter as in the Backfire Effect but, instead, would stay put at his level of support or even edge a bit away from the candidate. The idea here is that it's often difficult to shift people's preferences because it's just so easy for them to stay put.

Confirmation Bias refers to situations in which we tend to seek out only that information that supports a belief we already have. I refer to this as the "Fox News" bias. Fox News is known for being a source of politically conservative perspectives. Thus, it is unsurprising that my conservative friends tend to watch Fox News, as nearly everything the correspondents say align with their preexisting views. In a consumer domain, shoppers often "conveniently disregard" negative reviews in online forums and, instead, focus on the positive comments in support of the product that they are already keen on purchasing. So subtle is this tendency to heed only the information that corroborates our initial opinion that we rarely realize we are doing it, so it is often important to seek out disconfirming information when making major purchases.

The **Decoy Effect** (aka **Asymmetric Dominance**) is a technique often employed by marketers particularly in a competitive marketplace. The effect refers to the introduction of a market "decoy" that, because of its introduction, increases the appeal or demand for an intended target product or service. Let's say we are working in real estate and are trying to move two apartments in a building. Apartment #1 is 1,000 sq. ft. and costs $700/mo. Apartment #2 is 800 sq. ft. and costs $560/mo. Clearly, some customers will prefer Apartment #1 for its size whereas other customers will prefer Apartment #2 for its price. Let's say we want to get Apartment #1 rented as soon as possible. Perhaps there is a third apartment available, Apartment #3, which is 900 sq. ft., and we decide to price it at $800. Suddenly, Apartment #1 looks like a steal! The "asymmetric dominance" comes in because Apartment #1 is better than Apartment #3 both in size and price but Apartment #2 is only better than Apartment #3 in price. You may have never realized it until just now, but *many* product categories include varieties of sizes, colors, and options *not necessarily* because the assortment meets various consumer demands but, instead, because including these alternatives as decoys increases the demand for some intended target product.

If you have ever watched any of the television shows about hoarding, you may immediately understand how this next bias applied. The **Endowment Effect**, which we discussed in the previous chapter on Value and Valuation, refers to how our valuation of a product increases once we are in possession of the object. That is, if you ask people how much they are willing to pay for a product, say a coffee mug, they will state a certain price (e.g. $5.00). However, if you give people the coffee mug and ask them how much they are willing to sell that mug for, the price is almost always higher (e.g., $10) than how much the group paying for it says they are willing to pay to acquire it. With respect to marketing implications, this may support the use of "trial periods" for products, as consumers tend to see products as being more valuable once they are in possession of them.

Have you ever taken a vote on something *thinking* you had enough support only to find out you came up short? If so, then you have fallen victim to the **False Consensus Effect**, a bias in which we tend to overestimate the degree to which others agree with our opinion. We like to think we are always right, but that's just not how the world works. For marketers this is a serious problem. Novices to marketing often mistakenly believe that consumers will prefer the *same* products that the marketer him/herself also prefers. This usually can't be further from the truth – the majority of people are *nothing like* the marketer, almost by definition. Thus, learning to create objective measures and to analyze findings as far-removed from the data as possible is a strategy marketers must learn early on.

The next heuristic is one of my favorites because it's one we fall for all the time and one that is usually funny. The **Fundamental Attribution Error** refers to how we tend to attribute everything good and positive (i.e., every win, every success) to ourselves and to our genius while we attribute everything bad and negative (i.e., every loss, every failure) to our context, to others, and really just everything other than to ourselves. Like the Above Average Effect, this is adaptive; we tend to get upset when we attribute failures to ourselves. Yet this is the sort of bias that gets Wall Street execs in trouble – only wanting fame and glory for their wins and shirking responsibility and blame for when they ruin people's lives or crash the economy. "It was bound to happen as part of a natural market correction," they say. Not true. Consumers are just as likely to internalize the good deals they get at your store as being due to their "hard work," so it's worth reminding them of your company's role in saving them money. Similarly, consumers are quick to blame a company for their own mistakes – the Fundamental Attribution Error at play.

One heuristic you may have actually heard of, the **Halo Effect**, refers to situations in which we let information in one particular domain affect our assessments or evaluations in other, unrelated domains. For example, we have all met those amazing people who have super charismatic personalities, good looks, nice white and straight teeth, and fashionable clothing. Because of this generally positive outward appearance we *assume* they must also be fairly smart. But nay, once we start speaking to them we realize they are dumber than a box of rocks. Politicians aside (see how I did that), there are other examples of the halo effect in consumer domains. For example, television manufacturers recently started lobbing 3D technology at consumers, which, for some shoppers, was enough for them to think the rest of the television must be just as technologically advanced. In reality, however, there exists a great variety of TVs incorporating 3D technology with respect to other tech specifications. Some consumers let the excitement for the 3D technology create a "halo" of positivity around the televisions' other attributes…cue the Beyoncé song here.

As a Type A, borderline OCD control freak, I can definitely relate to the next bias. The **Illusion of Control** refers to exactly that: believing that we have greater control of a situation than we actually do. Investors and gamblers often *truly* believe they can call the shots in a world that, despite their very strong beliefs otherwise, includes a lot of randomness. Marketers like to believe they have control over how a product will be received in the market (they don't); consumers like to believe they have control over how a shopping experience will go (they also don't). Sure, there are certain aspects of any interaction of which we have *some* control, but the bias here refers to how we tend to *overestimate* that of which we have control. Sometimes, when we accept this, our experiences in the market are much more refreshing.

If I asked you to recite the "Golden Rule," you would likely say something like, "Do unto others as you wish others to do unto you." Or, in modern English, treat people the way you want to be treated. There is this idea out there that the universe is balanced, that good things happen to good people and bad people have misfortunes coming their way. Known as the **Just-World Hypothesis**, many of us live in a version of the world where people get what's coming to them. However, we all *know* this is not the way the world actually works. The jerk that we went to college with who skipped class and generally sucked at life now has a corner office in Manhattan thanks to his parents' connections. The kid who came from nothing, worked hard to put him/herself through school, and graduated at the top of his/her class still struggles to find a decent job. Sometimes the world seems like a cruel, cruel jerk. Yet, in our own idealized, Hollywood-esque script unfolding in our heads, we tend to default to this "just world" belief. Consumers who spend a lot of time doing information search for a product feel like they will wind up with a better product than people who did no background research…even if it is the *exact same* product.

Mentioned in the previous chapter on Value and Valuation, **Prospect Theory** refers to the idea that losses loom larger than gains and that most valuations stem from a subjective reference point. That is, despite economists believing that a gain of a determined amount should feel the same amount of good as a loss of the same amount should feel bad, this is not how the real world works. If you checked your couch cushions right now and found a $100 bill, you'd feel pretty great. However, if you had a $100 bill in your pocket all day and then, when you arrived home, realized that the $100 bill must have fallen out at some point during the day, chances are you would feel like crap…major crap. The feeling of losing is much worse than the feeling of gaining. In consumer contexts this finding leads to an interesting strategy: gains should be separated while losses should be combined. So if you are giving your consumer discounts, you should emphasize each discount as being distinct and separate to maximize the positive feelings likely to be elicited from the customer. If you have to charge a consumer for various services, you're better off lumping the services into one lump sum so the customer can swallow it all at once instead of parsing it out. Case in point: I just realized my local grocery store delineates all the many taxes it charges *and* even separates out the charge for using a debit card. While there are likely legal requirements for making each of these costs a separate line, I would feel a lot better if they just totaled my cost into one line item. Instead, I will just complain about over-taxation like every other American.

If you were to ask someone the likelihood of a natural disaster or terror attack taking place, he/she is significantly more likely to say that such an event will occur much sooner if a natural disaster or terror attack *recently took place*. The **Recency Bias** refers to overestimating the likelihood of a particular event as a result of that event having happened in the recent past. Gamblers are more likely to think they will win if they have won in the recent past. Shoppers are more likely to think they will get a "good deal" if they got a good deal on a recent shopping trip. The odds of these events do not actually change, of course, but we fool ourselves into thinking the events are much more likely to occur again because they happened recently.

The next bias helps explain why companies continue to invest so much money in banner advertisements in spite of the fact that neither you nor I have likely ever clicked on a banner ad (although some people certainly do). The **Repetition Bias** describes how we tend to evaluate stimuli to which we have been repeatedly exposed more positively over time. That is, flashing the same logo in the corner of your computer screen each time you go to Yahoo!'s website actually leads to more positive affect for a company. Sounds crazy, right? A related idea, the concept of **mere exposure**, suggests that "merely exposing" a person to a stimulus increases his/her affect toward the stimulus. The underlying reason behind this effect has to do with familiarity; we tend to like that which is familiar. So even subtle exposure to a stimulus, even one to which we do not pay conscious attention, is enough to increase our positive affect toward the stimulus and its associated extensions. From a consumer behavior perspective this certainly explains why companies will spend millions to get their products placed during television shows or to have their logos featured prominently on NASCAR vehicles.

Addressed a bit earlier in the context of social influence, **Source Credibility Bias** refers to our automatic tendency to believe (or to disbelieve) information based on the credibility of the source providing that information. Thus, even the best-intentioned car salesman is facing an uphill battle when he is trying to provide a customer with information because the customer is likely (and reasonably) skeptical of the salesman's motives. This is one of the reasons PR is such a popular form of communication for marketers, as readers of newspapers and other, *seemingly* objective sources are less likely to question or to counterargue what they are reading. This can be dangerous from a consumer's perspective, which is why companies are often required to label sections of their magazine as "Special Advertising Sections" or to identify an article that appears to be a news story as a "Paid Advertisement." In spite of this, many consumers don't realize that a lot of the information they are perceiving as "objective" is actually coming straight from the mouths of companies.

One final fallacy is that of the **Sunk Cost**, which describes a tendency for humans to include an investment of time, money, energy, or resources that they have already made (and typically have no way of recovering) into their decision-making. An earlier example in the book talked about purchasing concert tickets, terrible weather on the day of the concert, and the feeling of obligation to venture out into the terrible weather because the tickets were so expensive. Another common hiccup for consumers regards the investment of time. Consider, for example, a shopper who has spent months researching vacation options in the Caribbean. He or she may come across appealing trips to the Mediterranean but, because s/he doesn't want to think of all that time and energy researching Caribbean trips as being "wasted," may refuse to consider the European options. It seems silly, yes, but we factor sunk costs into our decision-making *all the time*.

Phew. That was a long list, and that's not even all the cool heuristics and biases that we know of! Still, now you have a really nice overview of the crazy tricks and mind games we play on ourselves all in our automatic attempt to be more efficient decision-makers. However, there's still *one* bias left…

The final bias is one I deliberately saved for last. Known as the **Bias Blind Spot**, this bias refers to the tendency to believe that others are *more* affected by biases than you are yourself. So if you were reading through the list of heuristics and biases just now thinking, "Well, I can see how *other* people can fall for this stuff, but I'm much smarter than those people!" it turns out that this, too, is a common bias.

But don't feel sad. Remember, our heuristics and even our biases are actually helpful a fair bit of the time. It's just that sometimes, when we apply a heuristic or bias in the wrong context, these shortcuts are counterproductive to our decision-making.

Avoiding the side effects of heuristics and biases. Just as many medicines designed to help us come with nasty, unhelpful, and potentially harmful side effects, so, too, do our mental shortcuts. While it can be difficult to know when we are employing such shortcuts (that's kind of the point of having them – we recruit them automatically and expend fewer cognitive resources as a result), half the battle is simply *knowing* they exist. Think about it: you now know a lot more about the tricks our brains play, tricks that your friends, family, and colleagues have absolutely no knowledge of (…until you recommend this book to them, which you totally should, by the way). So just *knowing* about the biases and heuristics is helpful, as you can now ask yourself, "Okay, [insert your name here], you're making a big decision here. Is all or part of this decision being influenced by one of these heuristics or biases? If so, do you need to reconsider your choices more deliberately?"

Another really helpful approach to making more objective decisions is to project the core question or problem you are attempting to solve as if it were *someone else* making the decision. That is, part of the reason we have these automatic heuristics and biases is to protect ourselves and to minimize the effort required for ourselves to make decisions. The same is *not* true for making decisions for others. We also remove ourselves a bit from the arousal and emotions that are automatically activated when we make decisions for ourselves. Indeed, decision researchers often show differences in the way we decide for ourselves compared to the way we decide the same decisions for our friends or for strangers. We have all lived this in the context of advice giving. If our friend is dating a total lame-o, we are the first to tell him/her to break things off. Easy decision. Yet, if we find ourselves in the same situation, making a choice is significantly more difficult. The same applies for career advice, purchasing decisions, and other daily problems; it's just a lot easier to make decisions for other people than it is to make decisions for ourselves. So, to get around this complicated decision making process wrought with heuristics, biases, and so many moving pieces, it is often useful to externalize the decision-making process to the best of your ability. Sure, it is a bit of a mind game, but if you can make a better decision as a result, then why not?

Similarly, from a marketer's perspective, it is often useful knowing that *how* you position a problem facing a consumer can lead them to recruit these heuristics and biases or not. If a customer is considering a major purchase, say a fancy new flat screen television, there's a difference between addressing your customer with, "You need…" or, "You probably want…" and, "Most consumers need…" or, "People who buy this TV probably want…" Suddenly, the decision is less about my situation, my risks, and my benefits and, instead, about the product, the risks, and the benefits more generally.

Specific heuristics or biases can be addressed with approaches tailored to the specific heuristic or bias, as well. Consider, for example, how helping consumers visualize their place in a market may help them to understand how much (or how little) they *actually* know compared to the "average consumer." Customers in the market for a new car, for example, may suffer from an above average bias in how much they *believe* they know, but if a savvy salesperson who read this book is smart, he may casually work in that the average car purchaser spends eight months researching potential new cars and makes five visits, on average, to dealerships before making a purchase. The overconfident customer may then readjust his/her initial position and, in addition, may be more easily persuaded upon feeling less certain about his/her confidence.

*   *   *

In spite of our best intentions to make thoughtful, rational decisions, our brains are designed to rely on shortcuts, tricks, and heuristics intended to make our lives easier. A lot of times, these tricks are super helpful, leading us to good outcomes while requiring us to make a lot less effort to get there. Other times, these shortcuts are not so good, leading us to suboptimal solutions when a bit more careful thought or planning would have led us to a better outcome.

As the voting example illustrated at the beginning of this chapter, consumer behavior is about a lot more than which restaurant to go to for dinner or which movie to go see. Our decision to commit a crime or not, to make a risky bet or not, to partake in illegal drug use or not, to engage in risky sexual behavior or not, and even to vote or not in the first place are all examples of *consumer* behavior because whatever choice we make, whatever the decision, and whatever the context we have to *consume* the consequences of our actions. Here's to hoping you continue to make wise choices and maybe even make *wiser* choices by applying the concepts from this book.

APPLICATION QUESTIONS

1) Academics are fairly good at eliciting a more associative level (System 1) or a more deliberative level (System 2) of processing from participants in controlled laboratory environments. How might you as a marketer attempt to encourage your customers to be more associative or more deliberative at various points in the purchasing process? When might you prefer they engage in more of one type of processing than the other? Why?

2) There is, undoubtedly, a relationship between our System 1 and System 2 processing styles and MAO (motivation, ability, and opportunity). Compare online shopping with in-store shopping. Which factors online might affect MAO, which then, in turn, affects processing style? What about in-store?

3) Meditation is thought to have beneficial brain effects. Indeed, some fMRI research shows that experienced meditators demonstrate differences in brain regions implicated in attention and nervous system control. How might helping your customers clear their mind change the way they go about learning about, choosing, and consuming your product?

4) Lorne Michaels, the famous producer of *Saturday Night Live*, is working with the show's writing team trying to figure out which sketches to keep for the final show. Lorne proposes making the decision based on a minimum cutoff of audience reaction (based on a laugh-o-meter…it's a thing. Google it.). He says any sketch that exceeds that threshold should be considered. Seth Meyers, the current head writer, likes Lorne's idea but suggests that instead of including sketches that pass the threshold, they should throw out sketches that fail to meet it. What kind of decision rule is Lorne proposing? Seth?

5) As a marketing manager for a major theme park and resort destination, you are obsessed with both quality research about your customers and developing the most effective, creative marketing campaigns. Say your research reveals that your customers *do not* engage in compensatory decision rules when considering a vacation destination. How might this affect how you allocate your marketing spend? Conversely, say you find your research reveals that vacationers *do* engage in compensatory decision-making. How might this information affect your budgeting decisions?

6) Match.com is thinking about offering two new services. In the first, users can rank the attributes that are "most important" to them in a potential date. From there, the person with the highest score on the most important attribute that pops up is your ideal match. In the second, attributes are again ranked, but this time users also use a slider to indicate a minimum cutoff of how a prospective date needs to perform on that aspect. Anyone failing to make the cutoff gets taken out of the results. Which decision rules do these two approaches involve?

7) You approach your boss about incorporating decision-making into the research you do on your customers (and non-customers). He/she replies, "What? That's a waste of time and money. I don't care *how* people decide; I care about *what* they decide." Give a compelling example showing that *how* people decide can be critically important to

what they decide, justifying the change to your research practices.

8) Your customer service representatives continue to echo the same problem: callers always blame the company for their own mistakes. From misusing a product to not following instructions properly, they estimate that over half their calls are from customers who broke their product. What bias do these customers seem to have?

9) Lucy is afraid to upgrade her flip phone to a smart phone because she has heard stories about smart phones exploding, people being tracked via GPS technology, and even identity theft occurring as a result of a stolen or hacked mobile phone. In reality, these crimes are fairly rare. What seems to be Lucy's bias?

10) You are working as a marketing manager for a major clothing brand. The store currently offers two major lines: Salinger, which is not as stylish but carries an affordable (good) price, and Fitzgerald, which is more stylish but also perceived as too pricey. What would you propose to the designers so that you could increase sales of the Fitzgerald line?

11) When out with a group of friends trying to decide on a place to go eat, you suggest going to a delicious pizza place called Pi. "Bleh, no way," says your friend, "I just went there last week and the service was terrible." However, you know this friend has been to Pi many times over the years and never complained. What's going on?

12) You've just spent the past few days, weeks, or months reading a book by this weird, quirky, ethnically-ambiguous-looking fellow who seems to know a thing or two about marketing and consumer behavior. Aside from the joy you'll get *knowing* that applying the concepts from the book will help you make better decisions in your work life and in your *own* life, as well as bring more satisfaction to you and the people affected by your work, why else might you feel compelled to try out the approaches herein? That is, what bias may also compel you to action? ☺

EPILOGUE:

RATE & REPEAT

Wow! You made it…well, almost. This is the end of the book. You should pat yourself on the back for learning more than you knew about Consumer Behavior when you started, but it's not over just yet! The credits haven't rolled! Consumer Behavior is dynamic – the Self, the Situation, and even the Solution are always changing. This last section briefly touches on the idea that Consumer Behavior is a cycle: you will ultimately make better, more informed decisions using the Self, Situation, and Solution approach, but now you have to measure that progress, see what worked and what did not, and then revisit the Self, the Situation, and the Solution to bolster what worked, tweak what did not, and then measure and do it all over again. I told you I was going to forever change the way you saw the world, and I meant it – you'll never be able to get out of the Self, Situation, and Solution cycle ever again (mwahahaha!)…but it's okay; you are going to be a better, more successful, and happier person as a result. I promise.

Epilogue | Rate and Repeat

Congratulations! You have made it to the end of the book! You never thought you'd get here, did you? Hopefully the trip wasn't *too* painful. I know it was *a lot* of information, but just think about how much smarter you are now?! Think of all the many stimulating conversations we can have about marketing and business and all the weird stuff people do the next time we hang out!

Before I leave you, there is just *one* brief matter we must discuss: evaluation. That is, in order to know that you have put the Self, Situation, and Solution approach to good use, you need to have some sort of metric to capture changes in consumer preferences, behavioral intentions, or actual behavior/purchasing so you can be aware of what worked and what did not. Just like how your shampoo bottle instructs you to "rinse and repeat" after an initial application, I am telling you to *Rate* and *Repeat*: rate the effectiveness of your marketing efforts based on the 3S (i.e., Self, Situation, and Solution) approach, and then start the process over.

The good news and bad news is that there is no one right way to go about doing this. That is, I cannot simply give you an evaluation form for your specific consumers in your specific industry buying your specific products. What I can and will do, however, is provide you with some pointers on things you should remember to include and, even better, provide you with an outline of the major ideas from this book detailing **The URG3S Model of Consumer Behavior**. With a title like **URG3S**, you can never forget the 3 S's to keep in mind – Self, Situation, and Solution – as well as the core purpose of the approach: to identify, to elicit, and to create consumer *urges*.

It is my hope that keeping this handy document nearby will help you, your colleagues, and your company improve your business. And, as an added bonus, the icing on the cake, the cherry on top, it is my hope that *your life* will see increasing happiness, greater satisfaction, and more value as you apply these concepts in your day-to-day living.

*   *   *

One of the most frequent mistakes people make when they are trying to make important changes in their life is failing to measure progress. This is the reason dieters who keep track of their calories and gym visits tend to do better than those who don't and why weightlifters who keep workout journals or diaries tend to gain more muscle than those who do not. In a similar way, we should be keeping track of how the changes we make in the context of our marketing strategies affect key variables like purchase intentions and brand awareness.

Now, if you work in marketing, then chances are your company already has several metrics in place to measure key variables. That's smart. However, unless you're some huge multinational company with countless resources at your disposal, chances are you have very little information on the key consumer insights discussed in this book. Usually this is cost prohibitive at companies because collecting, storing, and analyzing that kind of data is simply too expensive given the resources, both in terms of money and time, available to a company. It's much easier to go to consumer insights companies and pay for this service than to do it yourself.

Here's the problem: a lot of those insights companies *aren't very good.* It's not that they are inherently bad people or even bad researchers, but needs vary as a function of industry, product, consumer segment, and other factors. If you can find a consumer insights company that is an expert in *exactly* what you do all the time and that addresses your research questions perfectly, then you really should consider acquiring them because that, friends, is extremely rare.

I am not advocating that you fire or stop using these consumer insight companies – they can be useful, for sure – but you should consider devoting at least some of your resources to tapping into the pulse of your consumers continuously so that, at any given point in time, you know precisely your consumers' Self, Situation, and Solution strategies. If you're really good you can automate this process so that your system reaches out to your consumers, collects data, and populates your database in real time. However you do it, the point is that you *should* be doing it lest you get left in the dust by your competitors who have managed to secure this real-time data collecting with friends like Google who specialize in this up-to-the-minute, dynamic data collection. Just recently, two of the world's largest advertising companies, Omnicom and Publicis, announced a merger to stem competition from companies like Google and Facebook that signaled the direction the world is going: Big Data. But here's the secret – that big data can be useless outside of an abstract level; if you want to be on top in your market and get down to the nitty-gritty, concrete details, you need to be collecting data the way the big kids like Google do it, but you need to be doing it with three key audiences in mind: your consumers, your would-be consumers, and your non-consumers.

First, for your consumers, you need to keep tabs on how your better understanding of their Self, Situation, and Solution strategies is improving their experience with you and your products. Knowing, for example, that Self-related factors are significantly improving their satisfaction with you but their Situation variables are not, you would know that you need to tweak their Situational experiences which may involve changing the context in which they are purchasing your product, their perceptions about what others think of your products, or maybe cultural perceptions regarding your product or industry. Until that situation is resolved, however, this data also suggests how marketing spend should be allocated: every dollar should be spent on something that is working well.

Second, for your would-be consumers, consumers who have your company and its products or services in their consideration set but who don't wind up choosing you, it is worth taking the time to figure out where the consumption process breaks down. Is it something to do with the Self? Something to do with the Solution strategies? Remember that *how* potential customers choose can affect their actual choices, so if you find it is the case that your would-be consumers are like your actual consumers on Self and Situation factors but differ with respect to how they go about making decisions, you might want to consider a campaign designed to change the decision-making strategies your would-be consumers use or mitigating the biases to which they succumb.

Finally, for your non-consumers, it is not always clear that spending money on people who aren't even giving you the time of day makes any sense. It is useful, however, to know who these consumers are so that you don't waste your time or resources continuing to go after them like so many companies tend to do. My very first marketing professor put it very well when her brother-in-law told her that he didn't like a commercial she worked on for Nestlé Purina pet food. She said, and I quote, "I don't give a $#!* what you think, Barry. You're not in my target market." She wasted no time nor worry on her brother-in-law because there was no way he would ever purchase her product. Her time, energy, and resources would be better spent elsewhere.

The key takeaway, however, is ABCD: always be collecting data. As you implement changes based on your insights regarding your consumers' and would-be consumers' Self, Situation, and Solution strategies, things will change. The world is a dynamic place, and you need to keep up with it. The better you are able to do this, the better you will be able to meet and surpass the needs of your consumers; you will be rewarded handsomely.

What follows next is an outline of **The URG3S Model of Consumer Behavior**, which summarizes the key ideas from this book. The hope is that you will be able to use this model as you make decisions in your position as a marketer. The outline is intended for your easy access of the tools and ideas from this book, but the good news is that if you ever need more detail or depth about the ideas, the book is here for your reference, and I am always an email away (Urge@jimmourey.com) to talk through any ideas or concerns you may have; *that* is how much I care about you. With no further ado, here's the outline:

- THE URG3S MODEL -
(Self, Situation, Solution)

Objective: To seek "urge opportunities," or instances in which you can create, elicit, or discover an urge, based on factors pertaining to the Self, to the Situation, and/or to the Solution strategies of consumers.

SELF

- **Needs, Wants, Motivation**
    1) What core need(s) does the product/service address?
        Physiological – Safety – Love/Belonging/Affiliation – Esteem/ – Self-Actualization/
        Power   Achievement
    2) How do consumers see current self v. ideal self?
    3) Do consumers have clear goals? Are they explicitly aware of goals?
    4) Are consumers positively/negatively motivated to your product/service?
    5) How arousing is your product/service to consumers on each dimension:
        Physiological – Safety – Love/Belonging/Affiliation – Esteem – Self-Actualization

- **Perception and Attention**
    1) How does the product/service stimulate each of the following:
        Vision/Sight – Smell/Odor – Taste – Sound – Touch/Haptics
    2) How well do consumer perceptions align with marketing intent?
    3) How attentive are consumers to your product/service and its attributes?
    4) Which tools do you use to capture attention and how effective are they:
        Intensity of Stimuli – Contrast – Movement – Surprise – Size - Involvement
    5) Which attributes do consumers in your category find most important?
        Where is your company relative to others on a Perceptual Map of these
        attributes?
    6) Looking at a Preference Map of consumer preferences in the market, how
        well positioned is your product to serve a cluster's needs? Is there a need
        to influence perceptions about your product to better align with consumer
        preferences? Are there sizable clusters whose needs are not yet being
        met?

- **Learning and Memory**
    1) When consumers think of your product/service, what do they *know*?
    2) What potential inertia might you face trying to teach new information?
    3) Do you have systems in place that reinforce desired consumer behaviors
        and punish unwanted consumer behaviors with respect to your
        product/service? Are you modeling the desired behavior of consumers?
    4) Where and how do consumers *learn* new information about your
        product/service?
    5) How do you reinforce the memory of your core information messages?
    6) What consumption scripts/schemas are in place for your product/service or
        within your product/service category? Are you using these scripts to your
        advantage or are you doing anything that might violate these scripts?
    7) Have you maximized consumer *involvement* with your product/service
        (i.e., developed engaging, fun, clever, and memorable interactions)?
    8) Is there a metric in place to measure consumer learning of information?

- **Affect, Mood, and Emotion**
  1) What level of arousal does your product/service evoke in consumers? (Also, when thinking of the need served by the product/service, what level of arousal and valence is evoked?)
  2) What thoughts mediate the arousal → emotion link in your consumers? That is, how do your consumers explain their arousal and translate their arousal experience into an *emotional* experience?
  3) How can you change or alter these thoughts to help consumers reinterpret their arousal experience or an event experience?
  4) What, if any, of the following appraisals may be affecting cognitive mediation of arousal/events:
     Agency – Anticipation – Equity – Outcome
  5) Is misattribution of arousal taking place? That is, might consumers be misattributing contextual arousal to the product/service or arousal from the product/service to external, unrelated sources?
  6) Are the emotional components of your marketing strategy effective at generating recall, recognition, and business objectives (e.g., sales) as opposed to simply evoking the intended emotion?
  7) Are there metrics in place, self-report and/or autonomic, to capture data on consumer arousal and emotion?

- **Personality, Attitude, and Persuasion**
  1) What is the personality profile of your target consumer segment(s)?
  2) What shopper traits are present/absent in your target segment(s)?
  3) Compared to your objective measures of your consumers, how does your consumer's self-image compare? How can this be used to your advantage?
  4) Is you brand perceived to have a personality? If so, do all your marketing executions reflect that personality consistently?
  5) When assessing consumer attitudes about your product, service, and/or company, are you missing any opportunities to:
     a. Highlight new or additional attributes
     b. Underplay or remove undesirable attributes
     c. Change beliefs about the extent to which the product (service, etc.) possesses an attribute
     d. Change the evaluations consumers have regarding a particular attribute
     e. Change a consumer's attitude toward engaging in a particular behavior
     f. Change a consumer's perceptions about *others'* attitudes about engaging in a behavior
     g. Shift the weight applied to a consumer's own attitudes v. the perceived attitudes of others
     h. Do any/all of the above for competing products, services, and/or companies
  6) For an attitude consumers identify, is the functional motivation(s) of the attitude rooted in one or more of the following:
     Utilitarian – Knowledge – Value-Expressive – Ego-Defensive
  7) Are your marketing executions aligned with the order of effects in a Hierarchy of Effects model based on your consumers' involvement?
     -Low-Involvement: Cognition (Think) → Behavior (Do) → Affect (Feel)
     -High-Involvement: Cognition (Think) → Affect (Feel) → Behavior (Do)
     -Experiential: Affect (Feel) → Behavior (Do) → Cognition (Think)
     -Behavioral Influence: Behavior (Do) → Cognition (Think) → Affect (Feel)
  8) Does your marketing strategy include components designed to persuade via the central route *as well as* components designed to persuade via the peripheral route in the Elaboration Likelihood approach? To which components does your target market(s) respond most favorably? And does this change depending on the particular touch point?
  9) Are all the components of your communication chain (Sender, Message, Medium, Receiver, Feedback) functioning as intended?

SITUATION

- ## Social Influence

    1) How social do consumers perceive the purchasing and consuming of your product or service to be?

    2) Which groups do your target consumer segment(s) consider to be normative reference groups and which groups are perceived to be comparative reference groups? Do these comparisons align with your marketing strategy or provide ideas for updating that strategy?

    3) To what degree do each of the following reference groups play a role in the minds of your consumers and how is your marketing strategy designed to incorporate and use this information:

    > Friendship Groups – Shopping Groups – Work Groups – Virtual Groups
    > Consumer-Action Groups – Indirect Reference Groups

    4) To what extent do your consumers prefer appeals from people like themselves or people they may aspire to be?

    5) Traditionally, what role(s) has your consumer played in the context of family decision making and how might that be influencing his/her choices now?

    6) With respect to the Family Life Cycle (FLC), at which stage is your target consumer? Is this objective placement the same as their subjective idea?

    7) How empowered do your consumers feel in general, in the context of purchasing your product/service, and when consuming your product?

    8) How do your consumers respond to the following power appeals and how might you use that sensitivity in your marketing strategy:

    > Referent Power – Legitimate Power – Expert Power – Reward Power – Coercive Power

    9) Where do your target consumer segment(s) fall on a self-monitoring scale? Is your strategy designed to account for differences in social sensitivity?

    10) Does your strategy contain viral components for word-of-mouth & buzz marketing?

    11) Do you know where your target consumer segment(s) fall on the adoption curve? Are marketing messages designed to appeal to the appropriate consumers along the curve, as well as between groups so that early adopters can influence innovators and so on?

    12) Are any social components malfunctioning (e.g., social loafing, diffusion of responsibility, poorly moderated user forums/communities)?

- ## Culture & Socio-Cultural Differences

    1) Where do your target consumer segment(s) fall on the following Dimensions of Culture and how might these affect your strategy:

    > Individualism/Collectivism – Indulgence/Restraint – Long-Term/Short-Term Orientation
    > Masculinity/Femininity – Power Distance – Uncertainty Avoidance

    2) What cultural associations, if any, do consumers have with your product?

    3) What are the core cultural values of your target consumer segment(s) and does your product, service, or company fulfill those core values?

    4) Do you have a strong understanding of the norms, values, and traditions of the target consumer segment(s), and does any part of your information gathering, purchasing, and consumption process violate any cultural norms, traditions, or expectations (even subtly)?

    5) Is it possible to make use of established culturally-specific language, symbols, myths/rituals/stories, or other markers of culture in your marketing communications strategy to encourage consideration and/or understanding via familiarity?

6) Does it make sense to pursue a global or local strategy for your product, service, or company? Would regionalizing/rebranding make more sense?

7) What is the SES breakdown of your target consumer segment(s) and non-consumers? How does this affect the purchasing of your product/service?

8) Is it possible to extend your product or service to consumers of different SES levels by tweaking the existing product/service efficiently?

9) What perceptions exist in the market regarding your product, service, or company and associations to SES levels or people of particular SES?

- **Subculture**

    1) To which subcultures do your core consumers belong based on:
    Race/Ethnicity – Age – Gender – Sexual Orientation – Religion – Consumption – Choice

    2) How does the importance of each subculture vary in the determination of a preference or choice depending on product category or service context?

    3) Which identity/identities is/are most salient and accessible when consumers are considering your product/service for purchase? How can this be used to your advantage or mitigated (if a disadvantage)?

- **Context, Environment, and Situation**

    1) How much thought has gone into the context in which a consumer collects information, purchases, and consumes your product? Do the features of the context align with the Self and (sub)cultural factors of the consumer?

    2) To what extent does the context stimulate each of the body's senses? How does this align with the sensory experiences, cognitions, and emotions from the consumers' Self profile?

    3) Are consumers aware the role the context is playing in their experience? In other words, is arousal being misattributed leading to a subtle influence or is the influence so obvious that consumers notice and are responding with assimilation, contrast/reactance, or no effect?

    4) Are there any constraints on consumers' time when engaging in information search, purchasing, or consumption? If so, how is this addressed or incorporated into the marketing strategy?

    5) Are there any noticeable time-of-day or seasonality effects in regards to the consumption of your product or service? If so, how are these incorporated into the marketing strategy to best provide value to the consumer and to you?

    6) To what extent is it possible to control how and where your consumers are gathering information, purchasing, and consuming your product so that you can exert some level of control over the contextual and situational influences? How is this incorporated into the marketing strategy?

SOLUTION

- **Value and Valuation**

    1) How do your consumers answer the questions, "How much do I prefer this product?", "Does the price seem fair for the product?", and, "Does my negative feeling toward acquiring the product outweigh my anticipated benefit of acquiring and using this product?"

    2) What opportunities exist for you to bolster the positive (gains) associated with your product or service and/or to mitigate the perceived costs (negatives) associated with your product or service?

3) Against whom (i.e., other products, services, companies) are your goods most often compared in the minds of consumers? How can you diminish the positive (gains) associated with those products and increase the perceptions of costs (negatives) for those products/services?

4) What insights does value laddering uncover about the positives and negatives associated with your products? How do these tie back to Self and Situational factors like core needs or (sub)cultural values?

5) Are quantitative measures of value you use understood by your target consumer segment(s) and/or producing any numeracy related biases?

7) Are there any context-dependent issues related to value such that your consumers value your product or service differently in different contexts?

8) How does the value for your product break down according to a utilitarian v. hedonic comparison? Which receives more focus from consumers?

9) What risk is associated with the positive and/or negative perceptions about purchasing and consuming your product? How can you allay those risks in the minds of consumers?

- **Decision Making**
    1) At what level of cognitive processing is your target consumer segment(s) operating when interacting with your product or service (by default)?

    2) Are consumers more/less receptive to your product or service when operating at a System 1 or System 2 level of processing? If so, does your marketing strategy include components that will likely shift consumers into mode of one processing more than the other?

    3) Which decision-making rule(s) does your target consumer segment(s) rely on when assessing your product or service?

    4) What features, if any, can you include in your marketing campaign to shift consumers to a particular decision-making strategy?

    5) When information searching, purchasing, and ultimately consuming your product or service, what biases are likely present for consumers throughout each of these phases?

    6) What features, if any, can you include in your marketing campaign to encourage (when helpful) or prevent (when unhelpful) your target consumer segment(s) to fall for a particular bias or biases?

RATE AND REPEAT

Execute: Using the traditional STP, 4Ps and 5Cs, integrate the insights uncovered using **The URG3S Model** into your overall marketing strategy. Make smart, practical decisions that will work well in the real world, but make sure those decisions are rooted in the consumer psychology presented in this model. What you want to create are marketing executions that certainly work at face value but, more importantly, are actually operating and influencing consumer psychology/behavior at a much *deeper* level.

Evaluate: To maximize the effectiveness of **The URG3S Model**, it is essential to include metrics designed to capture the effect of changes made to your marketing strategy. It is recommended that measures correspond to each specific change, as well as broader measures categorized by Self, Situation, and Solution to provide a broader level of analysis across these three key areas of Consumer Behavior. Keep what works, tweak what does not, and then repeat the process again. Dynamic worlds call for dynamic marketing campaigns, so keep up the good work.

My dear reader,

I sincerely hope you have enjoyed taking this enlightening journey with me. I hope it was at least somewhat entertaining while also being informative. If you *did* like it, be sure to tell your friends so that they, too, can read this book and be a part of our ultra-exclusive club. At the very least it will give them something to read while on a plane. Otherwise, they'll be stuck with SkyMall, and your resulting birthday gift this year might not be so great and you, friend, deserve greatness.

Until next time,

Jim

REFERENCES

Ackerman, Joshua M., Christopher C. Nocera, and John A. Bargh (2010). Incidental haptic sensations influence social judgments and decisions. *Science.* 328, 1712-1715.

Asch, Solomon E. (1951). Effects of group pressure on the modification and distortion of judgments. In H. Guetzkow (Ed.), *Groups, Leadership and Men* (pp. 177–190). Pittsburgh, PA:Carnegie Press.

Bandura, Albert, Dorothea Ross, and Sheila A. Ross (1961). Transmission of aggression through the imitation of aggressive models. *Journal of Abnormal and Social Psychology.* Vol. 63 (3), 575-582.

Bateson, Melissa, Daniel Nettle, and Gilbert Roberts (2006). Cues of being watched enhance cooperation in a real-world setting. *Biology Letters.* Vol. 2 (3), 412–414.

Berridge, Kent C. (1996). Food reward: Brain substrates of wanting and liking. *Neuroscience and Biobehavioral Reviews.* Vol. 20 (1), 1-25.

Dutton, Donald G. and Arthur P. Aron (1974). Some evidence for heightened sexual attraction under conditions of high anxiety. *Journal of Personality and Social Psychology.* Vol. 30 (4), 510-517.

Kahneman, Daniel, and Amos Tversky (1979). Prospect theory: An analysis of decision under risk. *Econometrica.* Vol. 47 (2), 263-292.

Knutson, Brian, Scott Rick, G. Elliott Wimmer, Drazen Prelec, and George Loewenstein (2007). Neural predictors of choice. *Neuron.* 147-156.

Madden, Mary. Teens Haven't Abandoned Facebook (Yet). Pew Internet & American Life Project, August 15, 2013, http://www.pewinternet.org/ Commentary/2013/August/Teens-Havent-Abandoned-Facebook-Yet.aspx, accessed on August 17, 2013

Mourey, James A., Ben C.P. Lam, and Daphna Oyserman (2014). *Consequences of Cultural Fluency.*

Norton, Michael I. and Dan Ariely (2011). Building a better America-One wealth quintile at a time. *Perspectives on Psychological Science.* Vol. 6 (1), 9-12.

Yoon, Carolyn, Angela H. Gutchess, Fred Feinberg, and Thad A. Polk (2006). A functional magnetic resonance imaging study of neural dissociations between brand and person judgments. *Journal of Consumer Research*, Vol. 33, 31-40.

INDEX

ABOUT THE AUTHOR

James (Jim) A. Mourey, Ph.D., has made it his life's mission to bridge the gap between marketing science and marketing practice…despite just turning 30. He began his marketing career as a toddler when, emulating his *Saturday Night Live* favorites by writing and performing comedy sketches for his parents in his family's living room, he realized the importance of 1) having an audience, 2) being aware of your audience's needs, and 3) the ability to adapt and update your product to continuously satisfy the needs of your audience. Afraid pursuing a career as an improv actor or the world's first exotic-dancing and fire-juggling singer would leave him on the streets of Nashville or badly burned in unfortunate places, Jim went to work as an account manager at a full-service marketing agency after graduating summa cum laude (4.0 GPA) from Washington University in St. Louis. Following this, Jim headed West to work as the director of a management and marketing consultancy's in-house research institute in sunny Los Angeles. With a nice tan and a more muscled physique, Jim returned to the Midwest to pursue his Ph.D. at the University of Michigan's Ross School of Business where he again nerded out (8.2/8 GPA) and won both university-wide and field-wide awards for his dissertation. His parents were pleased. Jim currently resides in Chicago, where he teaches the bright young minds at DePaul University's Driehaus College of Business and researches the big marketing ideas of tomorrow in his Modern Marketing Lab. Jim continues to fly around the country to consult and give keynote speeches to business executives and marketing managers when his schedule permits, a path that has taken him from Harvard to the University of Houston, Malibu to West Palm Beach in his quest to prove that academics can be entertaining, engaging, *and* sociable, as well as informative. Jim admits that he has come a *long* way from performing improv on a makeshift stage in his family's living room in southern Illinois, but he still tests his material out on his parents and siblings when he's home–it turns out they are all still each other's biggest fans. Some things never change.

11338976R00178

Made in the USA
San Bernardino, CA
13 May 2014